GCSE
SCIENCE
Di Barton

REVISE
GUIDES

Longman

LONGMAN REVISE GUIDES

SERIES EDITORS:
Geoff Black and Stuart Wall

TITLES AVAILABLE:
Art and Design
Biology
Business Studies
CDT: Design and Realisation
CDT: Technology
Chemistry
Computer Studies
Economics
English
English Literature
French
Geography
German
Home Economics
Mathematics
Mathematics: Higher Level and Extension
Music
Physics
Religious Studies
Science
World History

Longman Group UK Limited
Longman House, Burnt Mill, Harlow,
Essex CM20 2JE, England
and Associated Companies throughout the world.

© Longman Group Limited 1989

First published 1989
Sixth impression 1992

British Library Cataloguing in Publication Data

Barton, D.
    GCSE science. – (Longman GCSE revise
    guides)
    1. England. Secondary schools. Curriculum subjects: Science.
    GCSE Examinations.
    Techniques
    I. Title
    507′.6

ISBN 0-582-03856-1

Set in 10/12pt Century Old Style

Produced by Longman Singapore Publishers Pte Ltd
Printed in Singapore

CONTENTS

EDITORS' PREFACE

Longman Revise Guides are written by experienced examiners and teachers, and aim to give you the best possible foundation for success in examinations and other modes of assessment. Examiners are well aware that the performance of many candidates falls well short of their true potential, and this series of books aims to remedy this, by encouraging thorough study and a full understanding of the concepts involved. The Revise Guides should be seen as course companions and study aids to be used throughout the year, not just for last minute revision.

Examiners are in no doubt that a structured approach in preparing for examinations and in presenting coursework can, together with hard work and diligent application, substantially improve performance.

The largely self-contained nature of each chapter gives the book a useful degree of flexibility. After starting with the opening general chapters on the background to the GCSE, and the syllabus coverage, all other chapters can be read selectively, in any order appropriate to the stage you have reached in your course.

We believe that this book, and the series as a whole, will help you establish a solid platform of basic knowledge and examination technique on which to build.

Geoff Black and Stuart Wall

ACKNOWLEDGEMENTS

I am grateful to the following Examination Groups for permission to reproduce questions which have appeared in their examination papers. However the answers, or hints on any answers, are solely the responsibility of the author.

   London and East Anglian Group (LEAG)
   Midland Examining Group (MEG)
   Northern Examining Association (NEA), including:
     Associated Lancashire Schools Examining Board, Joint Matriculation Board,
     Northern Regional Examinations Board, North West Regional Examinations Board,
     Yorkshire and Humberside Regional Examinations Board
   Southern Examining Group (SEG)
   Welsh Joint Education Committee (WJEC)
   University of Cambridge Local Examinations Syndicate (UCLES)

I would like to acknowledge the major contribution made by Mike Evans to the following chapters: Matter and Particles, The Periodic Table, Chemical Reactions, Acidity, Metals and Polymers, and also the major contribution made by Stuart Farmer to the chapters on Variation, Evolution and Inheritance, and Feedback and Control.

   I would also like to thank Geoff Black and Stuart Wall for their help and guidance during the preparation of this book.

ASSESSMENT IN SCIENCE

AIMS

ASSESSMENT OBJECTIVES OR DOMAINS

CORE CONTENT

TECHNIQUES OF ASSESSMENT

WEIGHTINGS

GRADE DESCRIPTIONS

THE SYLLABUS

SUMMARY OF TOPICS

GETTING STARTED

More and more people in school are studying single or double award Science as part of their GCSE studies. Most single award Science courses give you a good all round understanding of many different topics in Science, such as the environment, energy and fuels, materials, and the human body. The double award Science courses usually involve you in twice the amount of time and lead to two GCSE qualifications. A double award in Science is usually a good foundation for studying separate Sciences at Advanced level.

The syllabuses from the different examination groups do vary, as do the single and double award syllabuses, so check before reading about a topic in this book that it is on the syllabus you are studying at school. The addresses of the examination groups are given on page 5, should you need further information.

At the end of each chapter there are some sample questions from the different exam papers, and outline answers. There are also some typical student answers, with comments from an examiner.

Remember, you need to be *actively involved* in your revision, and take responsibility for planning and organising your own time. Meeting deadlines for GCSE assignments has become part of your school life.

GCSE SCIENCE

The different Science syllabuses are based on agreed standards, so that a grade from one exam group is of a similar standard to that from another. Every syllabus is written to a common style, and contains a list of aims and of assessment objectives, a scheme of assessment and percentage weightings, grade descriptions and, of course, the subject content. Most Science syllabuses also contain a description of the criteria or standards used for assessing practical skills and examinations.

1 > AIMS

The aims are a description of the *purpose* of the syllabus, and are mostly concerned with long-term goals which cannot really be tested in an examination. For example: 'to stimulate interest in, and concern about, the environment'.

2 > ASSESSMENT OBJECTIVES OR DOMAINS

This is a list of the *abilities* which you should develop as a result of studying Science, and on which you will be assessed. There are three main groups of objectives, *knowledge and understanding*, *handling information*, and *practical skills*. The *scheme of assessment* should describe *how* each objective will be assessed by the different components of the examination.

3 > CORE CONTENT

All the Science syllabuses contain some basic *core content*, such as the environment, the human body, energy, and materials. The summary chart on page 5 shows how much the syllabuses overlap, but how some topics only appear on one syllabus. The order in which you have learnt about these different topics in school may not be the same as the order of the syllabus. However, you should be able to match up your own notes to the main headings of the syllabus that you are studying.

4 > TECHNIQUES OF ASSESSMENT

There are two types of assessment in GCSE Science, *written examinations* which are set by examiners, and the assessment of your *practical skills*, which is carried out by your teachers in school. Your final grade on the GCSE certificate will be a combination of the marks you have gained in the written exam together with the marks you have gained for your practical skills. The examiners will decide what mark will be awarded a grade A, a grade C and so on, by looking at *all* the marks and at the general standard of the papers.

Some syllabuses have exam papers which are taken by *all* candidates, with an *optional paper* for those who stand a good chance of gaining a higher grade. The optional paper will help the examiners to decide between the A and B grade candidates. It may be a good idea to discuss with your teachers which combination of exam papers is the best for you to take.

5 > WEIGHTINGS

In most Science courses the assessment of your *practical skills* counts for between 20% and 40% of your total marks. The other 80% or 60% will be obtained in the *written exam*. This will assess the various objectives grouped under *knowledge and understanding* and *handling information*, which may each carry half of the remaining marks (ie 40% or 30% each).

The papers themselves are also weighted. There is usually a *multiple-choice* paper, counting for as much as 25% of the total marks, with the other written papers carrying the remaining 55% or so of the total marks. The chart on page 3 summarises the various *schemes of assessment* for the main Science syllabuses. Try and identify the pattern of assessment which matches the syllabus you are following.

6 > GRADE DESCRIPTIONS

If you have a copy of the syllabus you may be interested to read the *description* of what you should be able to do to achieve a particular grade. For example, if you could suggest a *range* of solutions to a problem you would have reached a grade C, whereas if you could only suggest *one or two* solutions, you would have reached a grade F.

7 > THE SYLLABUS

The names and addresses of the main examination groups are listed on page 5 so that you can write and request an order form to purchase your own copy of the syllabus. You will then have to complete the order form and enclose the cost of the syllabus and postage. Find out from your teacher *exactly* which syllabus you are studying, as some exam groups have produced more than one syllabus for 'Science'. The syllabus *number* is also important, for example Midland Exam Group Science A is syllabus number 1760, while Science B is 1761. The copy of the syllabus will contain up-to-date information about the number and length of the various exam papers, and the type of practical assessment you will be faced with.

The chart below is an outline summary of the main syllabuses which are available, the number, length and type of papers, and their weightings.

Group	Papers	Length	Weighting	Description
LEAG				
Science (single)	Paper 1 (C–G)	1¼ hours	25%	Short answer compulsory
	Paper 2 (C–G)	2¼ hours	50%	Structured
	or 3 (A–D)	2¼ hours	50%	Essay style
	Practical		25%	Coursework
Science N (double)	Paper 1 (C–G)	2 hours	15%	Structured
	Paper 2 (A–B)	1 hour	10%	Structured
	Paper 3 (C–G)	2 hours	15%	Structured
	Paper 4 (A–B)	1 hour	10%	Structured
	Topic tests	6 (½ × 12) hours	20%	
	Practical		30%	Coursework
MEG				
Science – A	Paper 1 (C–G)	¾ hour	25%	Multiple choice
	Paper 2 (C–G)	1¼ hours	35%	Structured
	Paper 3 (A–B)	1¼ hours	–	Structured and free-response
	Practical		40%	Coursework
Science – B	Paper 5 (C–G)	¾ hour	25%	Multiple choice
	Paper 6 (C–G)	1¾ hours	50%	Structured
	Paper 7 (A–B)	1¼ hours	–	Structured and free-response
	Assignment		25%	Coursework
Combined Science (double)	Paper 1 (C–G)	2 hours	20%	Multiple choice
	Paper 2 (C–G)	2 hours	20%	Structured
	Paper 3 (C–G)	2 hours	40%	Structured and free-response
	Paper 4 (A–B)	2 hours	–	Structured and free-response
	Practical		20%	Coursework
Nuffield Co-ordinated (double)	Paper 1 (C–G)	2 hours	35%	Structured
	Paper 2 (C–G)	2 hours	35%	Structured
	Paper 3 (A–B)	2 hours	–	Structured and free-response
	Practical		30%	Coursework
NEA				
Dual award (double)				
Principles	Paper 1	1¼ hours		Multiple choice
	Paper 2	2 hours		Structured
	Paper 3 (level P) (C–G)	1½ hours	50%	Structured and free-response
	or Paper 3 (level Q) (A–E)	1½ hours		Structured and free-response
	Practical		50%	Coursework

Fig 1.1 Summary of examinations

Applications	Paper 1	1¼ hours		Multiple choice
	Paper 2	2 hours		Structured
	Paper 3	1½ hours		Structured and
	(level P) (C–G)			free-response
	or Paper 3	1½ hours		Structured and
	(level Q) (A–E)			free-response
	Practical		25%	Coursework
Modular (double)	Paper 1 (C–G)	1 hour	17%	Structured
	Paper 2 (A–C)	¾ hour	8%	Structured
	Module tests		45%	Structured
	(40 mins × 14)			
	Practical		30%	Coursework
NISEC				
Science (single)	Paper 1	1 hour	30%	Structured
	Paper 2	1½ hours	50%	Structured
	Paper 3	1½ hours		Structured
	Practical		20%	Coursework
SEG				
Science (single)	Paper 1	½ hour	14%	Structured
	Paper 2	¾ hour	11%	Multiple choice
	Paper 3	1½ hours	30%	Structured
	Paper 5 (A–B)	1¼ hours	25%	Structured and
				free-response
	Practical		20%	Coursework
Integrated Science (single)	Paper 1 (C–G)	2 hours	70%	Structured
	Paper 3 (A–B)	1½ hours		Structured
	Practical		30%	Coursework
Integrated Science (double)				
Applications	Paper 1 (C–G)	1½ hours	50%	Structured
	Paper 2 (C–G)	1½ hours	50%	Structured
	Paper 3 (A–B)	1 hour		Structured and
				free-response
Principles	Paper 1 (C–G)	1½ hours	50%	Structured and
				free-response
	Paper 3 (A–B)	1 hour		Structured and
				free-response
	Practical		50%	Coursework
WJEC				
Science (single)	Paper 1 (C–G)	2 hours	80%	Structured
	or 2 (A–E)	2 hours	80%	Structured
	Practical		20%	Coursework
Science (double)	Paper 1 (C–G)	2 hours	40%	Structured
	or 2 (A–E)	2 hours	40%	Structured
	Paper 3 (C–G)	2 hours	40%	Structured
	or 4 (A–E)	2 hours	40%	Structured
	Practical		20%	Coursework
UCLES/IGCSE				
Combined Science (single)	Paper 1	¾ hour	50%	Multiple choice
and	Paper 2	1 hour	50%	Structured
Additional Combined				
Science (double)	Paper 1	¾ hour	40%	Multiple choice
	Paper 2	1 hour	40%	Structured
	Practical		20%	Coursework
	or Practical test	2 hours	20%	Structured

8 > **SUMMARY OF TOPICS**

The chart below summarises in a general way the main *topics* which are covered by the different syllabuses. It is always a good idea to check with your teacher, or with your own copy of the syllabus, just to make sure.

Chapter and topic	LEAG	MEG	NEA	NISEC	SEG	WJEC	IGCSE
	N Double	A+B Double	Dual	Single	P+A	Double	CS + ACS
3 Energy and Fuels	x	x	x	x	x	x	x
4 Current Electricity	x	x	x	x	x	x	x
5 Electromagnetism	x	x	x	x	x	x	x
6 Waves	x	x	x	x	x	x	x
7 Force and Motion	x	x	x	x	x	x	x
8 Feedback and Control	x	x	x	x	x	x	x
9 The Human Body	x	x	x	x	x	x	x
10 Variation, Inheritance and Evolution	x	x	x		x	x	x
11 Ecology	x	x	x	x	x	x	x
12 The Solar System, Weather and Rocks	x	x	x		x	x	
13 Matter and Particles	x	x	x	x	x	x	x
14 The Periodic Table	x	x	x	x	x	x	x
15 Chemical Reactions	x	x	x	x	x	x	x
16 Acidity	x	x	x	x	x	x	x
17 Metals and Polymers	x	x	x	x	x	x	x

Fig 1.2 Syllabus Coverage Chart

EXAMINATION GROUP ADDRESSES

London and East Anglian Group
LEAG   'The Lindens', Lexden Road, Colchester CO3 3RL
                  Tel: 0206 549595

Midland Examining Group
MEG   1 Hills Road, Cambridge CB1 2EU
                  Tel: 0223 61111

Northern Examining Association
NEA   31–33 Springfield Avenue, Harrogate, North Yorkshire HG1 2HW
                  Tel: 0423 66991

Northern Ireland Schools Examinations Council
NISEC   42 Beechill Road, Belfast BT8 4RS
                  Tel: 0232 704666

Southern Examining Group
SEG   Stag Hill House, Guildford GU2 5XJ
                  Tel: 0483 503123

Welsh Joint Education Committee
WJEC   245 Western Avenue, Cardiff CF5 2YX
                  Tel: 0222 561231

International GCSE
IGCSE   University of Cambridge Local Examinations Syndicate
                  1 Hills Road, Cambridge CB1 2EU
                  Tel: 0223 61111

CHAPTER 1

EXAMINATION TECHNIQUE AND COURSEWORK

MULTIPLE CHOICE OR OBJECTIVE QUESTIONS

STRUCTURED QUESTIONS

FREE RESPONSE/ ESSAY STYLE QUESTIONS

TERMS USED IN EXAM QUESTIONS

MATHEMATICAL REQUIREMENTS

DIAGRAMS

COURSEWORK

SOME GENERAL HINTS

GETTING STARTED

Just as a tennis player learns new techniques and trains for a tournament, so there are a number of techniques which *you* can develop which will help you to improve your performance in the examination, and gain more marks. For example, you can practise answering questions to a set time limit, and without using books to help you, before the exam. You will then be better prepared to cope with the actual conditions you will meet in the exam.

Examination questions are written by examiners to find out how much you know and understand. They also test your ability to handle information and to apply what you know to new situations. You are often given information in a question to help you answer the question, so a lot depends on *reading the question fully*, and making use of all the available facts. You will only gain marks for answering the questions which are set by the examiner, not for answering your own version of the question!

You will need to develop confidence in answering different *types of question* in the exam. You may have already taken practice exams at school and be familiar with the three main types of questions:

■ multiple choice or objective questions;

■ structured questions;

■ free response questions.

ESSENTIAL PRINCIPLES

These questions test your knowledge and understanding of a wide range of topics from the syllabus. Each question has a 'stem', which is the main part of the question. The stem may include diagrams or tables of figures, and you need to read the stem carefully to obtain as much information as possible *before* you read the list of suggested answers, called 'options'. These options are usually labelled A to E, and only one of them is the correct answer, which is the 'key'. The incorrect answers are the 'distractors'.

One way of approaching this type of question is to look for the *correct answer* and to ignore the distractors. Alternatively, you can work through the list of options and *reject each distractor* until you are only left with the 'key'. Look at the following example.

❝❞ Example of multiple choice question ❝❞

Many types of different waves and rays bombard the Earth. Which one of the following makes us feel hot?

A gamma rays   **B** infra-red rays   **C** radio waves   **D** visible rays   **E** X-rays

You may know the correct answer to this (key = **B**), or you may be able to reject each of the distractors. For example, you may know that radio waves are involved in communication and so **C** can therefore be *rejected* as an answer to this question, and so on.

In the exam, you may be able to use rough paper or the question paper to work out your answer. You mark the answer which you have chosen on a special answer grid using a soft HB pencil. You can then rub out an answer if it is wrong and make a new mark. Remember, there is only *one* correct answer to each question, and every question carries one mark. If you get stuck on a question, leave it and go on to the next. You may have time to come back to that question later and at least have a guess at the answer before the exam ends. When you have completed as many questions as possible, you should *check* each of your answers carefully, making sure that you have put your answer against the number on the grid which corresponds to the question you have answered. Try to use all the time you have in the exam in this positive way instead of just doing nothing!

❝❞ Check your answers ❝❞

These questions are usually based on a particular topic or theme from the syllabus, such as 'acidity' or 'electricity'. There may be a diagram of some apparatus which you have used in a Science lesson, such as an electrical circuit, or a cathode ray oscilloscope. Above the diagram there may be a description about what the diagram shows, and below the diagram there is usually a series of short questions requiring one or two words for the answer, or asking for a sentence or two.

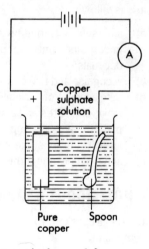

Fig 2.1 An example of part of a typical structured question.

i) Which part of the apparatus is the anode?

_____

ii) Name the electrolyte_____

❝❞ Example of a structured question ❝❞

iii) Explain how the process of plating takes place.

_____

_____

(4)
(LEAG)

At the end of the space for your answer you may see how many marks are being awarded for that part of the question. Your answer should aim to fill the space which is provided, but you can write more if you wish. Try and use as many scientific words as possible so that the examiner can see evidence of your knowledge and understanding in Science and can award you marks. Remember the general rule that one correct fact usually gains one mark.

If you are asked for the answer to a *calculation* always include the *units* for any number which you write: for example, the rate of doing work is 10 W or 10 watts, not just 10.

3 ▶ FREE RESPONSE/ ESSAY STYLE QUESTIONS

These questions usually require a longer answer in the form of a few sentences. The questions may ask you to 'explain how something happens', or to 'suggest reasons' for a particular observation. You may find it helpful to write the main points on rough paper before answering the question. Then check that you have matched up the number of facts to the number of marks allocated.

4 ▶ TERMS USED IN EXAM QUESTIONS

You can gain an idea as to what is required in an answer by looking at the word of 'instruction' in the question. Some examples are given below:

'**Describe**' means what actually happens, your observations, or what you would do.

'**Explain**' means that you must give reasons, and make some reference to a scientific principle or fact.

'**Suggest**' means apply your knowledge to a new situation or write about some reasonable scientific ideas.

'**Calculate**' is used when a numerical answer is required, with your working shown, together with the units used.

'**Define**' means that a fairly exact statement is required.

'**State**' means that a short, factual answer is required.

5 ▶ MATHEMATICAL REQUIREMENTS

You may be expected to have some skills in mathematics to answer some of the questions in a Science exam. You should find a list of these requirements at the back of your copy of the syllabus. The most common mathematical skills which seem to appear in the questions are as follows:

a) add, subtract, multiply and divide, using a calculator if necessary;

b) understand and use percentages, proportions or ratios, averages, fractions, and decimals;

c) recognise and use expressions in both decimal and standard form;

d) take account of variability and unreliability in experimental measurements;

e) make estimates and approximations;

f) plot graphs, selecting suitable scales and axes where appropriate;

g) interpret graphs, pie-charts and bar-charts;

h) solve simple equations.

A NOTE ABOUT GRAPHS

If you are asked to draw a graph in the exam there are some important points to remember:

a) use the axes and scale if they are given in the question;

b) if the axes and scale are *not* given in the question then decide on a scale which will fit the figures given in the data;

c) the x axis goes along the bottom or on the horizontal, the y axis goes upwards or on the vertical;

d) the factor which changes regularly, such as time, goes on the x axis;

e) label your axes, and indicate the scale used;

f) write a heading on your graph;

g) draw either a smooth curve through the points on the graph or the best-fitting straight line.

Marks are usually given for:

- use of appropriate scale and correct axes;
- correctly labelled axes and title;
- accurate plot of points;
- best straight line or best smooth curve.

6 ⟩ DIAGRAMS

You may be asked to draw diagrams to show apparatus, or possibly diagrams to show something like a magnetic field pattern or the arrangement of the planetary bodies in a solar eclipse.

- Use a *sharp HB pencil*.
- Try to make the diagram *fit* the space allowed on the exam paper, or use about a third to a half page of A4 if answering on lined paper.
- State the *magnification/scale* (if relevant).
- Write a *heading* above the diagram to state what it is showing.
- Use *labelling lines* to label the different parts of the diagram clearly. For example, Figure 2.2 below shows how you can use *radial labelling* lines around a diagram. Alternatively, as in Figure 3.1 (page 12), you can use a *list of labels* at the side of a diagram.
- Include as much *accurate detail* on the diagram as possible.
- When you draw apparatus, only draw the *relevant parts* of the apparatus and omit standard equipment such as retort stands, Bunsen burners, etc. The diagrams in this book may be useful to study for guidance.

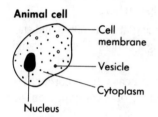

Fig 2.2 How to use radial labelling lines around a diagram.

Look at the *number of marks* allocated for the diagram. Five marks may mean that it's better to only spend about five minutes on a diagram. You can always come back to it later if you have extra time at the end.

7 ⟩ COURSEWORK

During your GCSE Science course you will probably have done some practical investigations in and out of the laboratory. Your teacher may have told you that you are being assessed on your practical skills on particular occasions, or you may have been assessed over a number of different practicals throughout the course. What you are being assessed on will vary according to the exact requirements of the syllabus which you are following, but there are basically four main areas:

a) using and organising apparatus;
b) observing, measuring and recording;
c) handling experimental observations and data;
d) planning and carrying out investigations.

There are normally two different methods by which you can be assessed on practical skills. One way is by your teacher watching you *carry out* a particular practical, perhaps involving you in the handling of apparatus or in following instructions. The second method is by your teacher assessing *what you have written* during a practical investigation.

The work you hand in for assessment may include your observations and a presentation of your results, perhaps as a chart or graph. Your teacher can then use your written work to assess your ability to make and record observations. You are usually assessed on more than one occasion for a particular skill, so don't worry if you haven't done too well on any one particular piece of work. You may be assessed on the same skill at a later date, or you may be able to arrange this with your teacher. The best person with whom to discuss the standards you have reached on your practical assessments is your teacher at school. He or she may not be able to tell you the actual mark for any particular skill, but may be able to give you some guidance about how you can improve your level of performance in a particular skill area.

Points to remember when *submitting coursework*:

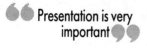
Presentation is very important

a) There should be a clear heading or title, and an introduction which describes the investigation, and shows that you understand what the investigation is about.
b) You should have your name, the date and your form or set, clearly written on the work.

c) Underline the headings and subheadings.

d) All diagrams, charts, graphs, photos, etc. should have a heading and labels.

e) List all relevant equipment and apparatus.

f) Describe any safety precautions which you have taken, for example wearing safety goggles, using small amounts of chemical substances, using a fume cupboard.

g) Present your results as a chart or graph.

h) Describe any problems you had during the investigation and suggest possible solutions.

i) Identify possible sources of error and suggest further investigations.

j) List any references which you may have used.

You will find it useful to keep all your coursework in a folder, as the exam boards usually look at the coursework from a random selection of about 10% of candidates from a centre. Your work may therefore go to an examiner, called a coursework moderator, who is responsible for ensuring that standards are similar between different schools.

8 SOME GENERAL HINTS

Use 'active' revision techniques

During your revision

■ Plan your revision time so that you study your notes in the weeks leading up to the exam. The Revision Planner at the end of the book will help you here.

■ Make your revision as active as possible, perhaps by looking at your notes and then writing a *summary* of key facts about a topic, or explaining a difficult idea to a friend, or even to your teddy bear!

■ Some students find it useful to *tape record information* using a cassette recorder. You can then listen to the tape as a change from reading notes, or swop tapes on key topics with a friend.

■ Practice answering questions without using any books, and working to the actual time allowed in the exam. Then check your answers and see where you are right and wrong.

On the day of the exam

■ Have some food – brains need energy to do work!

■ Have some fresh air so that you are clear headed.

■ Take into the exam:
  black or blue pens and biros (including spares); pencils; a rubber; a pencil sharpener; a ruler; a protractor; a compass; a calculator; and a watch.

ENERGY AND FUELS

FOSSIL FUELS

WHAT MAKES A GOOD FUEL?

USING FUELS TO GENERATE ELECTRICITY

ENERGY LOSSES AND INSULATION

ALTERNATIVE ENERGY SOURCES

GETTING STARTED

One of the most important topics in GCSE Science is the study of energy and fuels. In your home and at school you are using energy to heat and light the buildings you live and work in, to cook food and to make electrical appliances work. In industry, energy is being used to drive machinery to make many different types of consumer goods, such as cars and household items. Most of the energy which is used in this way is in the form of electricity which has been generated in a power station from a primary source of energy, such as the fossil fuels or nuclear fuel.

The *type* of fuel you use to heat your home may be affected by many different factors, such as how much a fuel costs, whether it is easy to store, and how cheap it is. Most people try to save money by reducing the amount of energy which is lost from their homes as heat, and you probably already know something about loft insulation and double glazing.

Fossil fuels, such as coal and oil, are finite and will eventually run out, so scientists and technologists are investigating *alternative* energy sources such as solar energy, tidal energy, wave energy and wind power.

E S S E N T I A L   P R I N C I P L E S

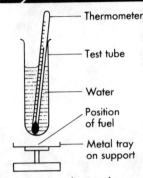

1 > FOSSIL FUELS

— Thermometer

— Test tube

— Water

— Position of fuel

— Metal tray on support

Fig 3.1 You may have used equipment like this to compare the amount of heat energy released by different fuels.

Fossil fuels are stores of chemical energy which is converted into thermal energy when the fuel burns. These fuels, such as coal and oil, were formed millions of years ago by the effect of heat and pressure on decaying plants and animals. Chemical energy is released as heat and light when the fuel is burned.

fuel + oxygen → carbon dioxide + water + heat

A *chemical equation* for this reaction would be:–

$$CH_4 + 2O_2 \rightarrow CO_2 + 2H_2O + heat$$

When fuels burn they may also produce oxides of sulphur, or oxides of nitrogen, as well as carbon monoxide. These waste products are one of the main causes of pollution. For example, sulphur dioxide dissolves in water vapour in the air to cause 'acid rain', which damages trees, and harms animal life in rivers and lakes.

You may have compared the amount of heat energy released by different fuels by measuring the rise in temperature of a known volume of water in a test tube.

2 > WHAT MAKES A GOOD FUEL?

" Which factor is most important to you as a consumer? "

You should be aware of some of the factors which affect *why* a certain fuel is used for a particular job.

Some of these factors are:

1 How much it costs to obtain, and consequently the cost to the consumer.
2 How easy it is to transport and to store, which depends on whether it is solid, liquid or gas.
3 How easily it catches alight and burns.
4 How much pollution is caused, poisonous gases and dust particles being released into the atmosphere.
5 How much energy is released when it burns.

For example the chart below shows how much *energy is released* when 1 kilogram of fuel is burned:

Gas	55 MJ per kg
Oil	44 MJ per kg
Coal	29 MJ per kg
Wood	14 MJ per kg

Although gas may be the 'best' fuel as it releases the most energy, 1 kilogram of gas takes up much more space than 1 kilogram of oil, and is more bulky to transport and to store. So you have to take account of *all* the factors mentioned above, and the main interests of the *user* of the fuel, before you can make a decision as to the 'best' fuel for a particular task.

3 > USING FUELS TO GENERATE ELECTRICITY

Fuels such as coal and oil are used in a power station to heat water and convert it into high-pressure steam. The steam is then used to turn huge turbines which spin around and in turn drive a generator, causing it to rotate very rapidly, at around 50 times per second. It is the *generator* which produces an alternating current at a frequency of 50 Hertz. The electricity is generated at a high voltage of about 25 000 volts, and it is usually increased using a transformer to 400 000 volts when it is passed through the overhead transmission lines of the National Grid. The high voltages mean that a *low current* is used and, as a result, very little power is lost during transmission to people's homes. The voltage is then decreased to the 240 volts required for the home.

Any fuel can be used to produce the steam in a power station. In nuclear power stations, nuclear fuel is used to heat carbon dioxide gas, which in turn converts water into steam.

In power stations the process of generating energy is inefficient and some energy is lost to the environment as heat. The *efficiency* of the power station can be calculated using the formula

$$efficiency = \frac{useful\ energy\ out \times 100}{total\ energy\ in}$$

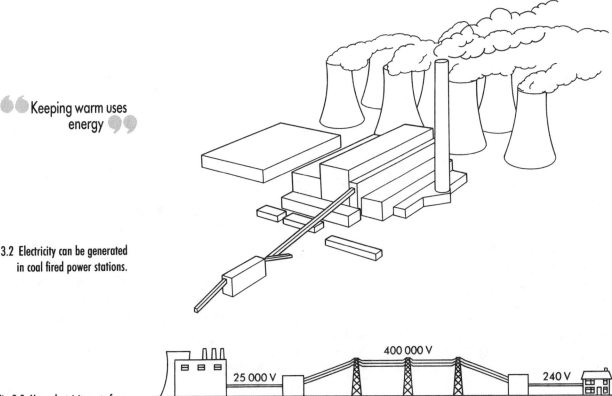

Fig 3.2 Electricity can be generated
in coal fired power stations.

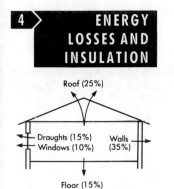

Fig 3.3 How electricity gets from
the power station to your home.

Power station   Step up   400 000 V   Step down   Home
25 000 V   transformer   240 V
                                                transformer

4 ENERGY LOSSES AND INSULATION

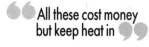

Roof (25%)

Draughts (15%)   Walls
Windows (10%)   (35%)

Floor (15%)

Fig 3.4 How heat is lost from a
house.

During cold weather, about a third of the energy produced in Britain is used to heat people's homes to a comfortable temperature of about 20°C. Some of this heat energy may come from using coal, oil or gas to heat up water in radiators in a central heating system, or from burning a fuel in a fireplace in the room. Some houses are warmed using heaters, which in turn use electricity that has been generated in a power station from burning fuels. Figure 3.4 shows the ways in which heat energy is lost from an ordinary house.

WAYS OF REDUCING HEAT LOSS

a) *Roof insulation*: laying an insulating fibre material which traps air in tiny spaces between the fibres. Air is a poor conductor of heat and reduces the heat escaping from the house.

Fig 3.5 How to reduce loss of heat
from a house.

a) Insulation in the roof.

Fibre fill material

b) *Double glazing of windows*: putting a second pane of glass in each window, so that a layer of air is trapped between the two panes, greatly reduces the amount of heat which can escape. In most new houses the windows are *installed* as sealed double-glazed units. These already consist of two panes of glass with a trapped layer of air to prevent heat escaping.

c) *Cavity wall insulation*: most recently built houses have walls which are made of two

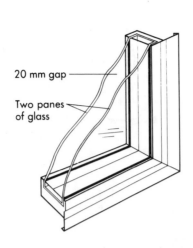

Fig 3.5b) Double glazing of windows.

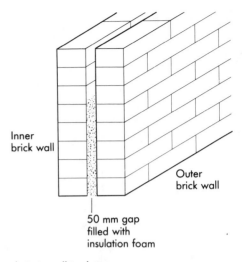

c) Cavity wall insulation.

layers of bricks with a gap in between. This gap can be filled with insulating foam, which again traps pockets of air and reduces heat escaping from the house.

d) *Draught excluders:* putting strips of draught-excluding material around doors and windows can prevent warm air escaping and stop cold air from coming into the room. However, people who burn fuel in a fireplace need to check that there is a good flow of air to keep the fire burning, and to prevent the build up of poisonous fumes within the room.

Heat escapes from buildings in **three** ways:
1 **Convection** – moving air carries heat away.
2 **Conduction** – walls and roofs transfer heat to the surroundings.
3 **Thermal radiation** – all hot objects lose heat to their surroundings.

5 > ALTERNATIVE ENERGY SOURCES

Energy can be obtained from natural resources. For instance, from the sun as solar energy; from water as hydro-electric power; from waves, tides and wind; and from the heat of the Earth itself.

SOLAR ENERGY

> These are renewable sources of energy

A common use of solar energy is to heat up water which is inside a solar panel. These panels are usually painted black so that they absorb as much heat as possible. The solar-heated water is then pumped to a normal hot water tank where it can be used to pre-heat the cold water. The warmed up water can then be further heated electrically. It is obviously much cheaper to heat water which has already been warmed up than to heat water from cold.

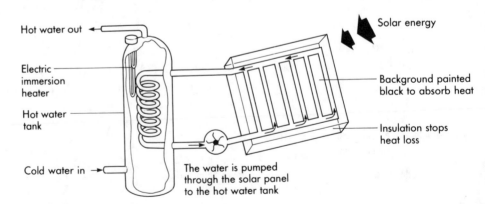

Fig 3.6 A hot water system which uses solar energy.

Solar cells

> Pollution free

These are devices which absorb the sun's energy and convert it into electricity. However, many thousands of cells are needed to produce useful amounts of electricity. One of their main uses is in satellites, where conventional batteries would be difficult to replace!

HYDRO-ELECTRIC POWER

Hydro-electric power (HEP) is the result of fast-flowing water driving turbines in a hydro-electric power station and thereby producing electricity. There is no pollution, and the source of energy is free. The only costs involved are in the building of the power station and in maintenance.

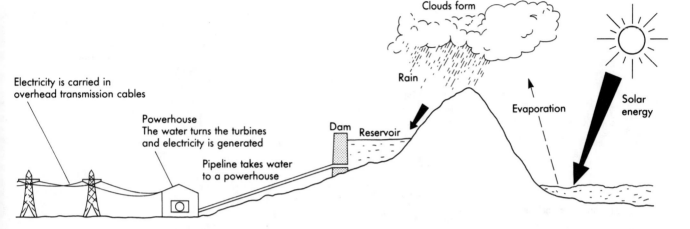

Fig 3.7 How electricity is generated from hydro-electric power.

WAVE POWER

Waves are produced as the wind blows across the surface of the sea. A wave power machine converts the up and down movement of the waves into electricity. The potential for generating electricity is very great but there are many technological problems to be overcome.

TIDAL POWER

The gravitational effect of the Sun and Moon on the Earth cause regular tidal movements of the oceans. These tidal movements can be used to push water into reservoirs, which can then be used to drive turbines and so produce electricity.

WIND ENERGY

Windmills which turn to generate electricity are called *aerogenerators*. A typical aero-generator, capable of generating enough electricity for a small village, would need to have blades 20–25 metres long.

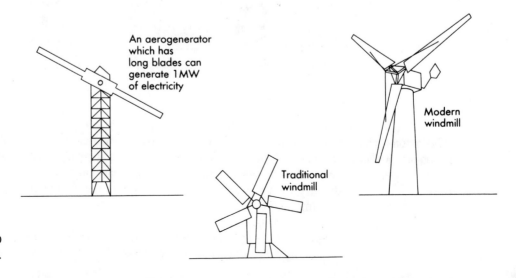

Fig 3.8 Using wind energy to generate electricity.

GEOTHERMAL POWER

Heat which is trapped in hot rocks deep in the Earth can be used to heat up water and convert it into steam. The steam can then be used via a heat exchanger to drive generators and produce electricity.

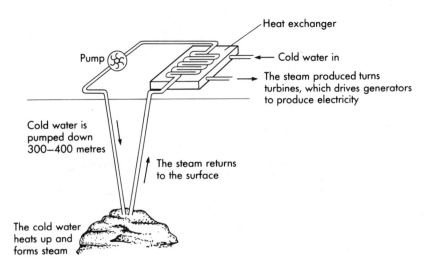

Fig 3.9 Using hot water from the Earth to generate electricity.

Why are alternative energy supplies being developed? There are three main reasons:
1   Fossil fuels are 'finite'. It has been predicted that in 600 years' time the known supplies of coal will have been used up.
2   Burning fossil fuels can cause pollution, especially acid rain.
3   There is an increasing *demand* for electricity from industry and from consumers. This may exceed the *supply* from existing power stations burning fossil fuels.

The chart below summarises the main alternative sources of energy, and their advantages and disadvantages:

ENERGY SOURCE	ADVANTAGES	DISADVANTAGES
Wind	■ will not run out ■ no fuel costs ■ no pollution ■ useful for isolated communities	■ windmills can spoil the environment ■ wind speeds may vary, so the generation of electricity is varied
Solar	■ will not run out ■ no fuel costs ■ no pollution	■ cloud cover blocks the sun ■ difficult to store energy produced ■ huge solar panels needed
Tidal	■ no fuel costs ■ no pollution	■ expensive to build power stations ■ may cause silting up of rivers
Geothermal	■ long-term supplies can provide hot water	■ not easily available ■ costly to obtain
Wave	■ will not run out ■ no pollution	■ many technological problems ■ hazard to shipping

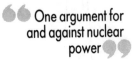
One argument for and against nuclear power

Nuclear power is another important source of energy. One of its main disadvantages is that the waste products are highly radioactive and are very difficult to dispose of safely. An advantage of nuclear power is that there are adequate supplies of uranium, and the nuclear power station does not release potentially harmful gases such as sulphur dioxide. Of course there is the disadvantage of the possible accidental release of radioactive substances into the atmosphere.

The tables and charts used in many of the questions which follow provide extra detail on a number of the *principles* we have considered. This is true throughout the book. So, as well as answering the questions, take note of the relevant information.

E X A M I N A T I O N   Q U E S T I O N S

MULTIPLE CHOICE

QUESTION 1

Which one of the following is a fossil fuel?

A coal   D uranium
B paper   E wood
C the Sun

QUESTION 2

What gas is released when coal is burned?

A carbon dioxide   D nitrogen
B hydrogen   E oxygen
C methane

QUESTION 3

Which one of the following is an advantage of using coal, instead of wind energy, to generate electricity?

A It is very cheap.
B It will not run out.
C It does not cause pollution.
D It is very easy to obtain.
E It can generate a lot of electricity.

QUESTION 4

The chart below shows some data on five different fuels. Which fuel, A, B, C, D, or E, costs the most to release 1000 units of energy?

Fuel	Price per 100g	Energy released per 100g
A	10p _5p_	2000
B	12p _4p_	3000
C	18p _3p_	6000
D	24p _6p_	4000
E	25p _5p_	5000

STRUCTURED QUESTIONS

QUESTION 5

a) Why is oil described as a fuel?

Because it is burned to make energy (produces light and heat when burned)   (2)

b) Suggest two reasons why gas is used to heat houses instead of solid fuel.

1 _It is easily compressed - can flow in pipes easily_

2 _easier to transport X less dust, soot etc_   (2)

c) Fossil fuels are non-renewable and will eventually run out. Name two sources of alternative energy which can be used to slow down the rate at which fossil fuels are being used.

1 _use non-renewable sources_

2 _Only use electricity when we really need it_   (2)

Wind

Tidal

QUESTION 6

The table below gives some information about reducing heat loss in the home.

Method of reducing heat loss	% of heat saved	Typical cost in £'s	Approx. time to recover cost (years)
Double glazing	15	1000	30
Carpet underlay	20	200	8
Draught proofing	25	50	1
Roof insulation	30	150	3
Cavity wall insulation	35	300	5

a) Which single method of reducing heat loss saves most energy?

Cavity wall insulation ✓

(1)

b) Which is the most effective method of reducing heat loss at the smallest relative cost? Explain your answer.

Method *Draught proofing* ✓

Explanation *Because it doesn't cost as much to put in, it is effective as it saves alot of energy and it only takes 1 year to recover cost* (3)

c) How much money do you save each year by using roof insulation?

£ 350.00

(2)

(NISEC; Specimen)

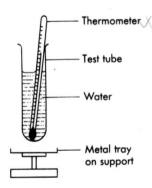

— Thermometer ✗

— Test tube

— Water

— Metal tray on support

Fig 3.10

QUESTION 7

a) Describe how you would use the apparatus shown opposite to compare the amount of heat released by three different samples of solid fuel. (7 lines available)   (5)

b) State **three** factors which should be considered when choosing the best fuel to heat a house.

1 *will it give off poisonous gases*

2 *How much it costs* ✓

3 *Is it easy to transport.* ✓

(3)

c) When fossil fuels burn they form sulphur dioxide gas. Describe and explain **one** effect that this gas has on the environment. (3 lines available)   (2)

Causes pollution which can form acid rain.

QUESTION 8

a) Name **two** fossil fuels. *Coal, oil*   (2)

b) Explain briefly how **one** of these fuels is formed and how it is extracted.   (2)
formed by pressure on earths crust forced up of

c) When fossil fuels are burned in power stations sulphur dioxide and carbon dioxide are produced. These gases appear to be having an effect on our environment especially with regard to the greenhouse effect and acid rain.
Explain how these gases affect our environment. *They pollute surrounding air and causes acid rain*   (4)

d) Some varieties of plants have begun to show remarkable tolerance to high levels of sulphur dioxide in the air. Describe the mechanism that could lead to the evolution of these plant varieties.   (3)

14

e) Nuclear power stations do not use fossil fuels.
  i) Name a fuel that they use. *Uranium* ✓ (1)
  ii) Give **three** different environmental arguments for or against the use of nuclear fuels. (3)

(MEG; 1988)

(F) *Lot of it*
easy to transport + use
produces a lot of electricity

(A) *causes radiation*
harm people
harm environment

QUESTION 9

The diagram below shows the main parts of a solar heating system designed to provide hot water for a house. Heat energy from the Sun warms the water in the solar panel. This water is then pumped through a spiral of copper tube inside the hot water tank so that it can transfer its heat to the water in the tank.

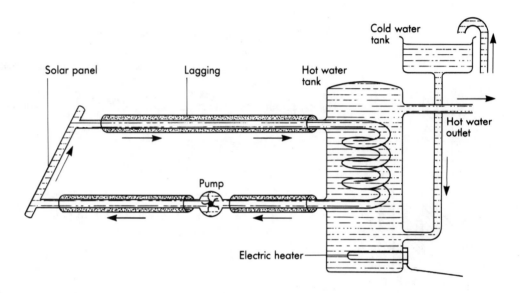

Fig 3.11

a) i) State one reason why copper is used to make the spiral.
  Good conductor of heat ✓

  ii) State one reason why a spiral tube is used and not a straight tube.
  Can hold more water
  Can conduct Surface area for more heat (2)

b) The pipes between the solar panel and the hot water tank are lagged.

  i) Name a suitable material for the lagging.
  foam

  ii) State one reason why this should be done.
  Good insulator ✓ (2)

c) Explain why the hot water outlet pipe is at the top of the hot water tank. (3 lines available) *Because cold water is at the bottom (2) the tp.*
  and the hot water rises and goes out the top. ✓

d) The electric heater in the hot water tank is rated at 240 V, 2 400 W. Electrical energy is sold in units called kilowatt hours (kWh). Each unit costs 5p.

  i) Calculate the electric current which will pass through the heater when it is switched on.
  240v X 10 amps

ii) How much energy is supplied by the heater if it is switched on for one hour?

2.4 kW per hour ✓

iii) What is the cost of using the heater for two hours?

_10p X 24p_

(6 marks)
(SEG; Specimen)

QUESTION 10

a) i) Explain the difference between renewable and non-renewable sources of energy.
    (4 lines available) _renewable can use again and again_ *(2)*
    non renewable will run out eventually.
    ii) Explain briefly why it is important to continue the development of renewable
    energy sources. (4 lines available) _Because when other sources_ *(2)*
    run out we will have those to fall back on

The bar graph shows the reserves of coal of several areas of the world.

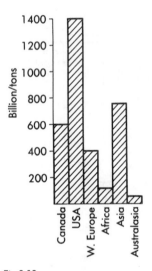

Fig 3.12

Fig 3.13

b) What are the reserves of coal in

    i) USA? _1400_ ✓ billion tons

    ii) Africa? _100_ ✓ billion tons

    iii) Western Europe is using coal at the rate of four billion tons per year. If this rate
    continues, for how long will its coal stocks last?

    3½ years   100 years ✓

    (3)

c) The dying bird below was photographed in a French bay following the wreck of the oil
    tanker 'Torrey Canyon' in 1967.

    i) Had the bird been rescued suggest one step which could have been carried out to
    remove oil from its feathers.

    heat and rub off   use detergant
    Uranium radiation

    (1)

    ii) What risk does your removal method carry for the bird?

    would harm the bird
    destroy feathers ✓

    (2)
    (NISEC; Specimen)

QUESTION 11

a) The following table shows five ways that are available for producing electricity, and
    their costs. 1 unit is 1 kilowatt-hour.

Oil	1.09p per unit
Coal	0.97p per unit
Nuclear	0.67p per unit
Hydro	0.18p per unit
Wind	1.4p–3.2p per unit

    i) Explain why oil and coal are known as fossil fuels.

    Because they were made up of dead plants
    and animals billions of years ago

    (1)

ii) What was the original source of the energy stored in fossil fuels?

Earths natural Sources y Sun ✓

(1)

iii) Which of the above methods of generating electricity is the cheapest?

Hydro power ✓

(1)

iv) Give **one** reason why the method given in iii) is cheap compared to other methods listed.

Because it is a renewable Source and it doesn't cost anything to make. water is free + continuous

(1)

v) Suggest **one** reason why it costs more to get electricity from wind power.

because its hard to heat up. ✓

(1)

b) Actual and estimated figures for the production of coal and oil for the past, present and future. (With acknowledgements to the *Nuffield-Chelsea Curriculum Trust*.)

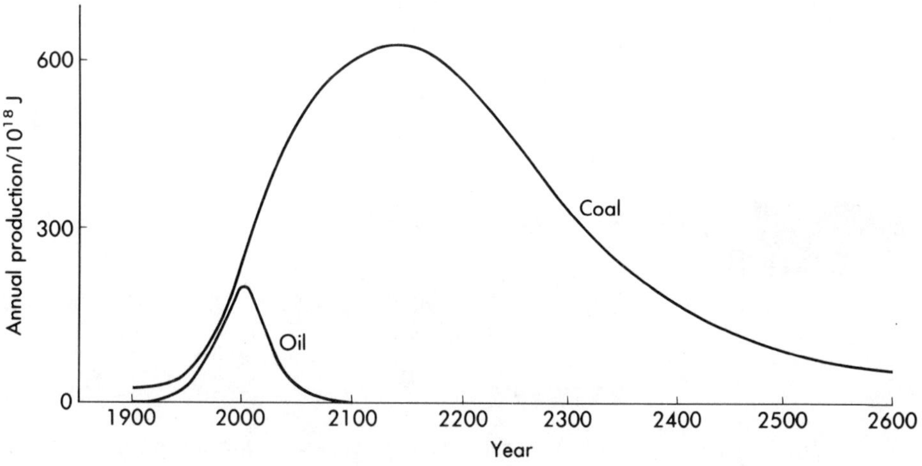

Fig 3.14

i) Using the graph:

1 Estimate the date for *maximum* oil production.

_2000_ ✓

(1)

2 Estimate the date for *maximum* coal production.

_2150_ ✓

(1)

ii) Why will the production of oil and coal reach a maximum and then decline?

Because their unlimited ess non renewable Sources they are runningout. less demand.

(3)

iii) Suggest **two** reasons why the estimated production of oil and coal for the future is almost certain to be inaccurate.

1 _Could find more_ ✓

(1)

2 _Wont know how much will be used._

(1)

c) It is expected that people's energy needs will soon be so great that energy production will have to be increased to meet demand. It has been suggested that one answer to this problem could be a greater use of nuclear energy.

i) State **one** advantage and **one** disadvantage of using nuclear energy.

Advantage: _Cheaper ✗ No pollution from fossil fuels._ ✓

(1)

Disadvantage: _Causes radiation_ ✓ _nuclear waste._

(1)

Another answer to the problem might be to develop alternative energy sources such as wind energy.

ii) State **two** alternative energy sources not already mentioned.

1 _Solar power (sun)   Geothermal_ ✓

(1)

2 _Tidal energy_ ✓

(1)

(Total marks 16)
(LEAG; Specimen)

O U T L I N E   A N S W E R S

ANSWER 1

Key A, coal, is the only fossil fuel. A common distractor is option E, wood, which is a fuel made from trees but not a fossil fuel. Option D 'uranium' is a nuclear fuel, and options B and C are other *distractors*.

ANSWER 2

Key A, carbon dioxide, is always formed when a fuel burns. Option C, methane, is the name for a fuel, natural gas, and option E, oxygen, is what all fuels need in order to burn.

ANSWER 3

Key E, coal, produces a lot of electricity. All the other options, A to D, are advantages of wind energy, and disadvantages of fossil fuels.

ANSWER 4

Key D is correct, as 1000 units of energy at this rate would cost a quarter of 24, which is 6p. Options A and E cost 5p, option B costs 4p, and option C costs 3p.

ANSWER 5

a)   Oil is a fuel because it releases heat and light when it burns.
b)   easy to transport through pipes to the house; less dust, soot or ash.
c)   i) wind power;   ii) tidal power.

ANSWER 6

a) cavity wall insulation;
b) Method – draught proofing.
   Explanation – cheapest method, recover cost in 1 year, and 25% of heat saved. The most efficient method which saves 35% costs 6 times as much and takes 5 years to recover costs.
c) about one third of the heating bill.

ANSWER 7

a)   These key points should appear in your answer:
   same mass of fuel used each time;
   same volume of water used at the same temperature;
   temperature of water measured before and after heating;
   method mentioned of preventing heat escaping;
   safety precautions such as wearing safety goggles;
   recording results in a chart;
   calculating and comparing temperature change.
b)   1 the cost of the fuel;
   2 whether it is a solid, liquid or gas;
   3 how easy it is to transport and store.
c)   Sulphur dioxide dissolves in the water vapour and forms acid rain. Acid rain can destroy trees and make water in lakes very acid, so killing the fish.

ANSWER 8

a)   coal, oil
b)   Coal was formed millions of years ago from trees and ferns which died and decayed, forming layers of peat. The peat layers were covered with mud and sand, and usually covered by the sea. This process was repeated many times over millions of years and the layers were pushed down. Owing to the pressure and the heat, the peat changed into coal seams.
c)   Sulphur dioxide forms acid rain when it dissolves in water vapour. The acid rain destroys trees and makes water in lakes very acid, so killing fish. Carbon dioxide in the atmosphere prevents heat escaping and produces the 'greenhouse effect', with a possible warming of the temperature of the Earth's surface.
d)   A few plants may be more resistant to sulphur dioxide, and these grow well and form seeds which in turn produce plants which are resistant. By a process of natural selection those plants best adapted survive and others die.
e)   i) uranium
   ii) nuclear fuels produce radioactive waste which is difficult to dispose of safely; nuclear fuels do not pollute the atmosphere with harmful gases like fossil fuels, which produce sulphur dioxide; there is always the danger of an explosion which would be difficult to control in a nuclear power station.

ANSWER 9

a)   i) copper metal is a good conductor of heat;
   ii) to increase the surface area for exchange of heat.
b)   i) any material which has lots of air trapped in it, such as insulating foam, woollen cloth, spongey tubing.
   ii) to reduce the amount of heat loss from the water on its way to the tank.
c)   Due to convection currents, hot water rises to the top of the tank and denser cold water sinks to the bottom of the tank, where it can be heated.
d)   i) Use the formula $W = V \times A$ (remember West VirginiA, i.e Watts = Volts × Amps)
   So, to find the current, use $\dfrac{W}{V} = A$

$$\frac{2400}{240} = 10 \text{ amps}$$

   ii) Energy supplied = power × time = 2.4 kW × 1hr = 2.4 kWh.
   iii) In 2 hours the energy used = 4.8 kWh. 1 kWh costs 5p. The cost of using the heater is 5p × 4.8 = 24p.

ANSWER 10

a)   i) Renewable resources are those which will always be available, such as the sun, the wind and the tides. Non-renewable resources are those which have taken a long time to form, such as fossil fuels, and are being used up. They cannot be replaced.
   ii) It is important to continue developing renewable energy resources as supplies of

coal and oil are being used up, and there is an increasing demand for energy in the form of electricity, especially for industry. Also fossil fuels cause pollution, whereas renewable energy resources such as wind power do not cause pollution.

b)   i) 1400
      ii) 100
      iii) 100 years
c)   i) Use detergent to remove the oil from the feathers.
      ii) This substance may be harmful to the bird, and destroy natural oils in the feathers.

ANSWER 11

a)   i) Coal and oil are fuels which have taken millions of years to form from remains of animals and plants.
      ii) the Sun
      iii) Hydro is the cheapest.
      iv) The water is free and continuous.
      v) The cost is greater because of the cost of developing and installing machinery. Also wind power is variable and does not give maximum output all the time.
b)   i) 1 year 2000
         2 year 2150
      ii) New reserves of coal and oil may be discovered and the easily accessible coal and oil will be used up so it will be harder to extract deeper reserves.
      iii) 1 We do not know how many new reserves of coal and oil will be found or what the extent of existing reserves are.
         2 The production of coal and oil depends on demand, and we cannot say what the demand will be in the future.
c)   i) *Advantage:* no pollution as from fossil fuels
         Disadvantage: difficult to dispose of nuclear waste
      ii) 1 tidal energy
         2 geothermal energy

A STUDENT'S ANSWER WITH EXAMINER'S COMMENTS

1 a)   George and Sybil live in adjoining semi-detached homes. George has an open coal fire and Sybil has an electric storage heater.

   i) In what way does most of the heat travel into George's room?

   by radiation

   (1)

   ii) Sybil tells George that his fire is a nuisance to the environment. State **two** reasons why this may be true.

   when coal burns it produces carbon
   dioxide.

   (2)

66 You were asked for *two* reasons. You could also mention the dust and soot which are formed. 99

   iii) Explain how **most** of the heat will travel around Sybil's room.

   by convection currents, hot air rises and
   cold air sinks.

66 Good 99

   (1)

b)   The word equations below show what happens when natural gas burns under different conditions:

   natural gas + plenty of air → heat + water + carbon dioxide.
   natural gas + limited air → heat + water + carbon monoxide.

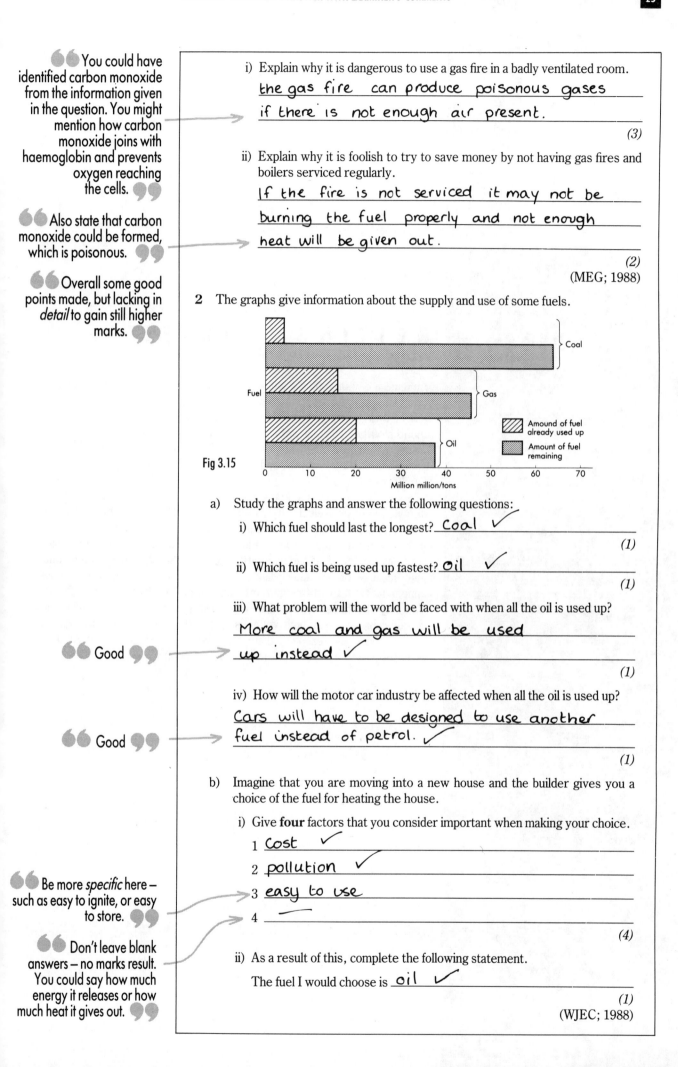

i) Explain why it is dangerous to use a gas fire in a badly ventilated room.

the gas fire can produce poisonous gases if there is not enough air present.

(3)

❝ You could have identified carbon monoxide from the information given in the question. You might mention how carbon monoxide joins with haemoglobin and prevents oxygen reaching the cells. ❞

ii) Explain why it is foolish to try to save money by not having gas fires and boilers serviced regularly.

If the fire is not serviced it may not be burning the fuel properly and not enough heat will be given out.

(2)

(MEG; 1988)

❝ Also state that carbon monoxide could be formed, which is poisonous. ❞

❝ Overall some good points made, but lacking in *detail* to gain still higher marks. ❞

2   The graphs give information about the supply and use of some fuels.

Fig 3.15

a)   Study the graphs and answer the following questions:

i) Which fuel should last the longest? Coal ✓

(1)

ii) Which fuel is being used up fastest? Oil ✓

(1)

iii) What problem will the world be faced with when all the oil is used up?

More coal and gas will be used up instead ✓

(1)

❝ Good ❞

iv) How will the motor car industry be affected when all the oil is used up?

Cars will have to be designed to use another fuel instead of petrol. ✓

(1)

❝ Good ❞

b)   Imagine that you are moving into a new house and the builder gives you a choice of the fuel for heating the house.

i) Give **four** factors that you consider important when making your choice.

1 Cost ✓
2 pollution ✓
3 easy to use
4

(4)

❝ Be more *specific* here – such as easy to ignite, or easy to store. ❞

❝ Don't leave blank answers – no marks result. You could say how much energy it releases or how much heat it gives out. ❞

ii) As a result of this, complete the following statement.

The fuel I would choose is oil ✓

(1)

(WJEC; 1988)

GETTING STARTED

Imagine a day in your life without electricity and you have some idea of how important electricity is to everyone, at home, at school and in offices and factories. Most people come home from school or work in the colder months of the year to a warm, well lit house, and sit in front of the fire to watch TV, with a cup of tea or coffee. At the same time dinner is being cooked in an electric oven, and an electric washing machine is doing the family wash!

So why do you need to know anything about electricity? Clearly a basic knowledge of how electricity can be used safely and how much it costs and an understanding of electrical circuits can be very important for you in your everyday life, as well as in a Science examination! For example, you may have seen all the decorative lights on the Christmas tree go out, just because of one faulty lamp, but other rows of decorative lights appear to work even though more than one of the lamps may be faulty. You may also have wondered why electricity is transmitted by overhead power cables at very high voltages, when the voltage used at home is only 240 V. Is the reason so that every house gets a share of the voltage, or is there a more correct, technical explanation?

ESSENTIAL PRINCIPLES

| 1 > | CURRENT ELECTRICITY |

Conductor	Insulator
Copper	Wood
Iron	Sulphur
Aluminium	Polythene
Carbon	Rubber
Sea-water	Paraffin
Sulphuric acid	Propanone

Fig 4.1

An electric current is a flow of charged particles around a circuit. Strictly speaking, it is the flow of negatively charged electrons around a circuit, from the negatively charged terminal to the positively charged terminal of the electrical supply. The conventional *direction* of conventional current flow is often shown by an arrow on a circuit diagram and is opposite to that of the electron flow. Current is *measured* in amps (A) by using an ammeter in the circuit. All circuits require an energy supply to push the particles around the circuit. All circuits should be made from good conductors, such as metals, as these allow the charged particles to pass through easily. Some substances are poor conductors or insulators, such as plastic and glass, and these do not allow significant amounts of current to pass through.

| 2 > | SERIES CIRCUITS AND PARALLEL CIRCUITS |

SERIES CIRCUITS

Figure 4.2 shows a simple *series circuit*, using the conventional symbols for circuit diagrams. (These symbols are shown at the end of the chapter to remind you.) As you can see, an ammeter is used to measure the amount of current flowing in the circuit. The *same* amount of current flows at any point in the series circuit, as no current is used up in the circuit. As the charged particles go through each lamp they lose some of their energy, owing to the resistance of the wire in the lamp filament.

We look at voltage in more detail below. However, we can say here that the energy given to the charged particles (electrons) by the battery to push them round the circuit is the *voltage* across the battery. The voltage is measured by a voltmeter. An ordinary battery or dry cell which you may have used in the lab has a voltage of 1.5 V. In a series circuit the battery voltage is split between each lamp. The total voltage across all the lamps is equal to the battery voltage.

Fig 4.2 Current in a series circuit.

PARALLEL CIRCUITS

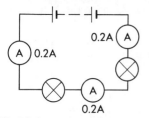

Fig 4.3 Currents in parallel circuits.

> 66 Parallel circuits are useful for Christmas tree lights 99

Figure 4.3 shows two lamps connected in *parallel*.

Each lamp glows brightly, as it has the total voltage of the battery across it. If the lamps each take 0.2 A (the readings on A2 and A3 will be 0.2 A), then the total current drawn from the battery will be 0.4 A (the readings on A1 and A4 will be 0.4 A). Most household power sockets are connected in parallel with the mains supply so that if one appliance is switched off the others remain working. Each appliance receives the mains voltage of 240 V.

Advantages of a parallel circuit

■ If one lamp is faulty, the others stay alight. This is especially useful in wiring decorative lights, for example on a Christmas tree, or along a street. In a series circuit, if one lamp is faulty, all the lamps go out.

Disadvantages of a parallel circuit

■ The circuit can be more difficult to set up and uses more wire, which can be expensive.

| 3 > | CURRENT AND CHARGE |

When an ammeter measures that 1 amp of current is flowing, this really means that in one second a coulomb of charge is passing that point. A *coulomb* is the unit of charge (about the same charge as 6.2×10^{18} electrons). The current through a household electric fire is about 4 amps which means that 4 coulombs are passing per second. The amount of current flowing is therefore charge divided by time. An easier way to remember this is:

charge = current × time

or $Q = I \times t$.

So if 10 amps (I) flow for 5 seconds (t) then 50 coulombs (Q) have passed through a point in the circuit.

4 ⟩ VOLTAGE

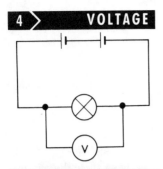

As we have seen, the voltage is the measurement of the energy of each coulomb of charge. A voltmeter is placed in a circuit in parallel with the place where energy is being converted. For example, in a lamp energy is being converted into heat and light. The voltmeter measures the change of electrical energy into another form of energy, and the voltage here is described as the 'potential difference' or PD between the two points of a circuit.

Fig 4.4 The voltmeter is in parallel with the lamp.

5 ⟩ CATHODE RAY OSCILLOSCOPE (CRO)

A CRO can be used as a *visual voltmeter* for measuring voltage. A bright spot is produced on the oscilloscope screen by a beam of electrons. The position of the spot can be altered by the voltage across the CRO. When the time base control is adjusted the dot moves across the screen and draws a visual graph of the voltage against time.

Figure 4.5 shows the waveform of a DC supply. The supply is positive + 4 V DC.

Figure 4.6 shows the waveform of an AC supply.

The gain control is set at 4 volts/cm, so the spot is deflected 1 cm upwards for every 4 volts across the input terminals. The amplitude of the waveform is 2 cm, so the *peak value*

$$= 2 \, \text{cm} \times 4 \, \text{V/cm} = 8 \, \text{V}.$$

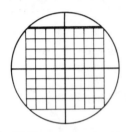

Fig 4.5 The pattern produced by a DC supply (+ 4V).

When a *diode* is placed in the circuit as shown in Figure 4.7, then the current only flows in one direction and halfwave rectification occurs.

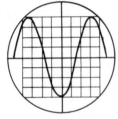

Fig 4.6 The pattern produced by an AC supply.

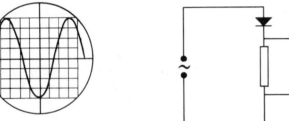

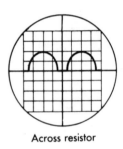

Across resistor

Fig 4.7 The pattern produced when a diode is placed in the circuit.

6 ⟩ RESISTANCE

Energy is required to push the charged particles around the circuit. The circuit itself can resist the flow of particles, particularly if the wires in the circuit are very thin and very long. For example, a filament in an electric light bulb is very thin and very long. Owing to this *resistance*, energy is given out as heat and light. Many household appliances, such as electric heaters, hair driers, toasters, ovens and electric fires, use a *high resistance wire* in their elements so that *heat* is given out.

Resistors can be used to *control* the current flowing in a circuit. For example, in a food mixer the control knob can increase or decrease the speed of the mixer. This knob is acting as a variable resistor and letting *different amounts* of current through. When the knob is turned to a high setting, the resistance is *decreased* and more current flows to the motor, so the speed increases.

Four factors affect the resistance of a wire:

1 *diameter*: thin wires have more resistance than thicker wires;
2 *length*: long wires have more resistance than shorter wires;
3 *the material used*: iron has more resistance than copper;
4 *temperature*: hotter wires have more resistance than cooler wires.

Resistance is measured in units called *ohms*, symbol Ω.

One ohm of resistance is given by a resistor if a voltage of one volt is required to push a current of one amp through the resistor. So a higher resistance means more voltage is required. To calculate the resistance you need to know the voltage and current.

❝❝ Everyday uses of resistance ❞❞

❝❝ High resistance means low current ❞❞

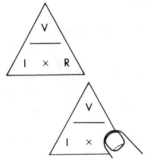

Fig 4.8 A useful way of learning the formula.

$$\text{RESISTANCE} = \frac{\text{VOLTAGE}}{\text{CURRENT}} \quad \text{or} \quad R = \frac{V}{I}$$

Figure 4.8 is a useful way of using this formula. You may, for example, have to calculate resistance, given the voltage and current.

OHM'S LAW

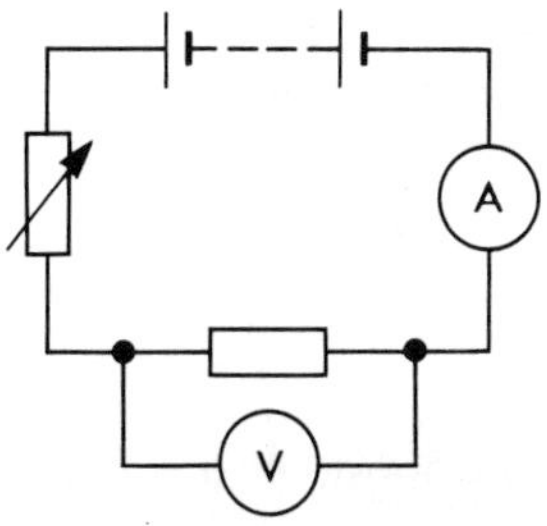

You may have carried out a practical investigation to compare the relationship between the voltage and amount of current flowing in a resistor. Figure 4.9 shows the circuit you may have used.

The current flowing is *proportional* to the voltage (at constant temperature). This relationship is called Ohm's Law and is shown in Figure 4.10.

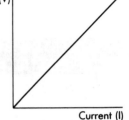

- Ohm's Law can be written as:

$$I \propto V$$

Fig 4.10 This graph shows the relationship between current and voltage using a resistor in the circuit.

Fig 4.9 You may have used a circuit like this to investigate Ohm's Law.

7 ▷   MAINS ELECTRICITY

Three key points to remember:

1 The voltage of the mains electricity in your home is 240 volts.
2 The direction of flow changes 50 times per second so its frequency is 50 Hertz.
3 Live and neutral wires carry the mains electricity, and the insulation around the wires is colour coded so you know which is which.

WIRING A THREE PIN PLUG

❝ An important safety point here ❞

1 The live wire is coloured brown, and is connected to the live pin.
2 The neutral wire is coloured blue, and is connected to the neutral pin.
3 The earth wire is coloured green and yellow, and is connected to the earth pin at the top of the plug, as shown in Figure 4.11.

The purpose of the earth wire is to make sure that current flows to earth if, for any reason, the appliance becomes faulty. This may happen if the live wire touches part of the metal casing of the appliance. If the earth wire was *not* connected, then a current would flow to a person who touched the metal casing of the appliance.

FUSES

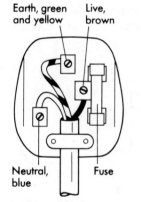

Earth, green and yellow   Live, brown

Neutral, blue   Fuse

Fig 4.11 Learn the colour code for the three-pin plug.

Each plug needs a *fuse* of the correct rating. The fuse is simply a thin piece of wire which melts and breaks the circuit if too much current is flowing. To find out the size of fuses use the following formula:

$$\text{current} = \frac{\text{watts}}{\text{volts}}$$

This is the same as:

power = current × voltage   ie $P = I \times V$

For example, a 60 W table lamp uses 60/240 or (60 ÷ 240) = 0.25 A, so a 3 amp fuse would be the correct one to use. However, an electric kettle using 2000 W would take a current of $\frac{2000}{240}$ = 8.3 amps, so a 13 amp fuse is needed.

Magnetic circuit breakers

These are sometimes used instead of fuses. They have the advantage that they are very easy to reset after they have broken the circuit.

Double insulation .

Some electrical appliances have a plastic casing, so that there is no chance of someone getting an electric shock when they touch the appliance if it is faulty.

BUYING ELECTRICITY

How much you have to pay for electricity depends on:

1 how many electrical appliances are in use;
2 how long they are used for;

3   what the power rating is of each appliance.

The basic unit of energy used to calculate cost is the kilowatt-hour (kWh). This means 1 kW (1000 watts) being used for 1 hour, which costs approximately 6p.

■ An electric fire, rated at 2 kW, which is used for 2 hours will use up 4 units or 4 kilowatt hours of electricity. The cost of using the fire for 2 hours is 4 × 6p = 24p.

■ A table lamp, rated at 40 W switched on for five hours, uses 0.04 × 5 units = 0.2 kWh. The cost of using the table lamp is 0.2 × 6p = 1.2p.

8 ▷ TRANSMISSION OF ELECTRICITY

Electricity from a power station is *transmitted* across the country by the National Grid system. The commonest method is by overhead power cables, carried on pylons. Sometimes, underground transmission lines are used. The chart below summarises some of the main advantages (A) and disadvantages (D) of each method:

Overhead cables

■ cheaper to install (A)

■ easier to repair (A)

■ unsightly (D)

■ dangerous to people, especially those using kites, moving boats with high masts or carrying fishing rods (D)

Underground cables

■ more expensive to install (D)

■ more difficult to repair (D)

■ hidden underground (A)

■ no danger to people (A)

Electricity is transmitted from power stations at voltages of 400 000 V. The reason for using such high voltages is that there is a very low current, and the energy loss is very small. If electricity was transmitted at a lower voltage there would be a greater current, and more energy would be lost as heat. A simple model of this situation can be set up in the laboratory, using 12 V to represent a low voltage line, and 240 V to represent a high voltage line. A short piece of high resistance wire is used to represent the actual power lines which are used in the transmission of electricity. Two circuits are set up as shown below.

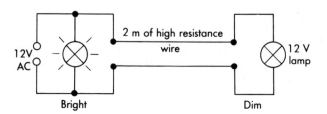

Fig 4.12 A low-voltage power line.

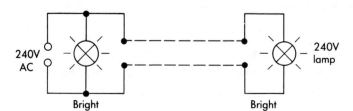

Fig 4.13 A high-voltage power line.

Energy is lost from the low voltage line as the second lamp glows only dimly. In the high voltage model the second lamp glows very brightly.

The *output power* equals the *input power minus the power loss.*

$$P_{OUT} = P_{IN} - P_{LOSS}$$

Power loss is I^2R, so low currents therefore reduce power loss. Step-down transformers (see chapter 5) are used to reduce the high voltages used in the transmission of electricity to the 240 V which is used in domestic electricity. The reason why alternating current (a.c.) is used in the transmission of electricity is that transformers only work on alternating current.

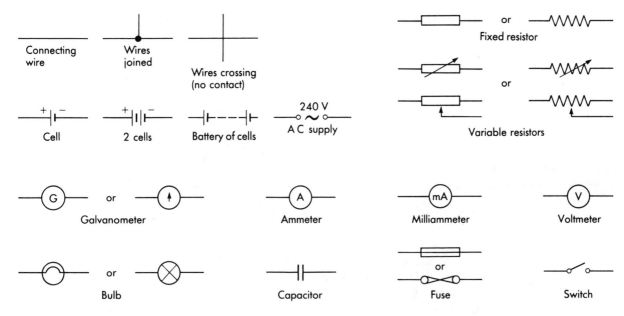

Fig 4.14 Some of the conventional symbols for circuit diagrams

9 SOME USEFUL DEFINITIONS

- **current** is a flow of charge, measured in amps
- **1 amp** = 1 coulomb of charge per second
- **voltage** is the measurement of the energy of each charge
- **1 volt** = 1 joule of energy per coulomb
- **power** is the rate of energy transfer, measured in watts
- **1 watt** = 1 joule of energy per second
- **power** = current × voltage
  P   = I × V
- **resistance** = $\dfrac{\text{voltage}}{\text{current}}$

  $$R = \dfrac{V}{I}$$
- **power loss** = I^2R
- **charge** = current × time
  Q   = I × t
- **Ohm's Law:** current flowing is proportional to the voltage
  $I \propto V$

EXAMINATION QUESTIONS

MULTIPLE CHOICE

QUESTION 1

Which one of the following is the symbol for a switch in a circuit?

A —o o—

B —[   ]—

C —| |—

D —⊖—

E —| |—

QUESTION 2

The diagram below shows a three core cable connected to a three-pin plug.

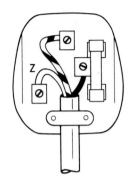

What should be the colour of the cable labelled Z?
A blue   D green and yellow
B brown   E red
C green

QUESTION 3

Which of the circuits below would be suitable for measuring the resistance of a lamp?

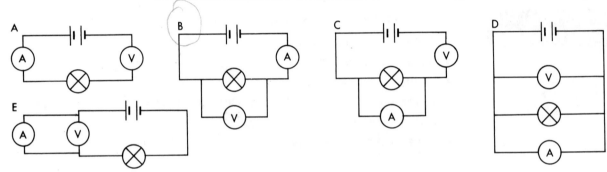

(LEAG; 1988)

QUESTION 4

Which one of the following is a unit of power?
A Ampere   D Watt
B Joule   E Volt
C Newton

QUESTION 5

When wiring a house, the switches and fuses should be connected in only one arrange-ment. This arrangement has:
A switches in the live side and fuses in the neutral
B switches in the neutral side and fuses in the live
C switches and fuses both in the live wire
D switches and fuses both in the neutral wire
E switches and fuses both in the earth wire

(LEAG; 1988)

QUESTION 6

The diagram below shows a circuit in which one of the lamps is faulty. None of the other lamps in the circuit can work because of the faulty lamp. Which of the lamps is faulty?

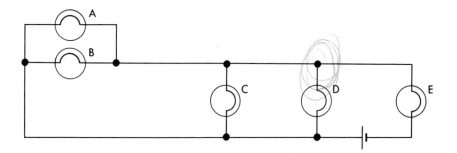

QUESTION 7

The diagram below shows a circuit. The resistor has a value of 2.5 Ω and the reading on the voltmeter is 5 V.

What is the reading on the ammeter?
A 0.5 A   D 7.5 A
B 2.0 A   E 12.5 A
C 5.0 A

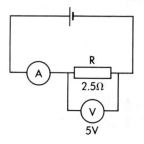

QUESTION 8

What is the frequency in Hertz of the mains electricity supplied to your home?
A 13; B 50; C 100; D 240; E 2500

QUESTION 9

What is the cost of using a 2 kW fire for 3 hours if a unit of electricity costs 6p per unit?
A 6p; B 12p; C 18p; D 24p; E 36p

STRUCTURED QUESTIONS

QUESTION 10

a) Decorative tree lights can be arranged in two ways, as shown in the diagrams below.

Circuit A: bulbs in series

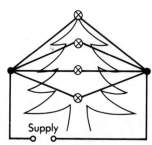

Circuit B: bulbs in parallel

i) If one bulb blows in each of the circuits, in which circuit will the remaining bulbs stay alight?

B

_____

(1)

ii) A set of lights has 20 bulbs in series, as in circuit A. Each is a 12 V bulb. What is the total voltage required for the set?

_____

_____

(1)

iii) Another set of lights has 20 bulbs in parallel, as in circuit B. The voltage supplied to the set is 240 V. What is the voltage across each bulb?

_____

_____

_____

(1)

b) A diagram of a typical light bulb is shown opposite.

    i) In the light bulb, electrical energy is converted to _____

    and _____

(2)

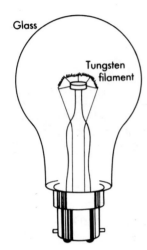

Glass

Tungsten filament

    ii) Suggest **one** property which makes tungsten a suitable metal to use for the filament.

_____

(1)

c) The diagram below shows a three-pin plug.

    i) What important safety feature, other than the top, is missing?

_____

(1)

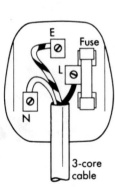

E

Fuse

L

N

3-core cable

    ii) The fuse used in a plug should be suitable for the appliance connected to it. Using the following relationship,

      Power measured in watts = Current in amps × Voltage in volts,

    complete the table. Choose the most suitable fuse from 3 A, 5 A and 13 A.

(2)

Appliance	Power rating in watts	Voltage supplied in volts	Current rating of the most suitable fuse in amps
Kettle	3000	250	12
Video recorder	50	250	0.2

(1)

(1)

(MEG; Specimen)

QUESTION 11

The kilowatt-hour is known as 1 unit of electricity. This is the amount of electricity used by a 1 kW appliance in 1 hour. One unit costs 5p.

a) What is the cost of using

    i) a 1 kW heater for 2 hours?

_____

(1)

    ii) a 3 kW fire for 10 hours?

_____

(1)

iii) a 1500 W iron for 2 hours?

_____

(1)

b)   A student set up the circuit shown in the diagram below and then moved the contact to points **K, L, M, N** in turn.

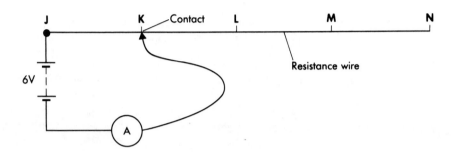

The current was measured by reading the ammeter, and the results are given below.

Contact made at	**K**	**L**	**M**	**N**
Ammeter reading	2	1	0.6	0.5

i)   What units are missing from the results table?

_____

(1)

ii)   As the wire under test becomes longer what happens to the electric current flowing in the circuit?

_____

(1)

iii)   If resistance $= \dfrac{\text{voltage}}{\text{current}}$

what is the resistance of the wire between **J** and **K**?

_____

(1)

(MEG; 1988)

QUESTION 12

Study the diagram of the hot glue gun then answer the questions below.

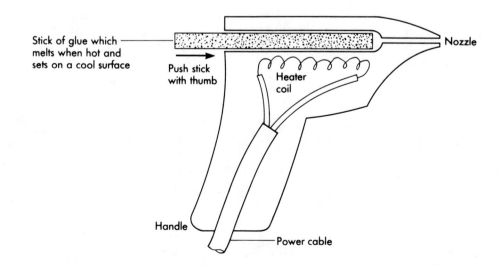

a) What happens to the solid stick of glue when the heater coil is switched on?

_____

(1)

b) What should come out of the nozzle when the glue gun is working?

_____

(1)

c) For the **wire** in the heater coil and the **wires** inside the power cable compare the following features and properties. Use words from the following list to complete the table below. You can use the words once, more than once, or not at all.

high   copper   quite thick   none   plastic   low   thin

Feature/property	Power cable wires	Heater coil wire
i) thickness		
ii) electrical resistance		
iii) covering insulation		

(3)

d) The label on the handle of the glue gun includes the following information:

> **V 240 ~**
> **W 100**
> **AC only 50 HZ**

i) State what the following letters from the label stand for:

V _____   W _____

ii) A battery will not operate this glue gun. Give **one** reason for this, *using information from the label.*

_____

_____

iii) Name a very common electrical household object which is also rated at 100 W.

_____

(3)

(WJEC; 1988)

QUESTION 13

a) The diagram shows a hydro-electric power station.

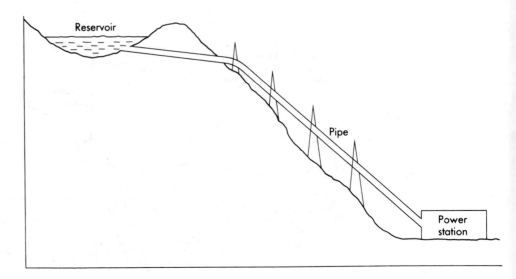

What kind of energy does the water have

i) in the reservoir? (1)

ii) just before it enters the power station? (1)

b) Electricity from power stations travels to your home, where it can be used for lighting. The diagram below shows part of a house lighting circuit. Each of the lamps carries a current of 0·25 A.

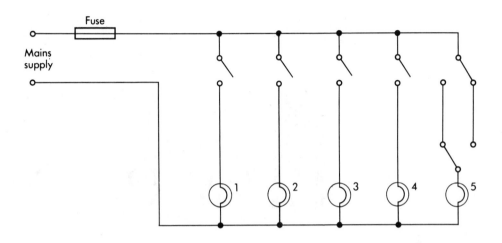

i) Explain why a fuse of 1 amp is not large enough for this circuit. (1)

Lamp 5 is controlled by two-way switches.

ii) Draw diagrams to explain how the switching system works. (2)

iii) What is the benefit of a two-way switching system? (1)

c) Electricity is also used to power appliances such as an electric kettle. Such an appliance is usually rated at 240 V 3 kW.
Calculate:

i) the current through the kettle, using the formula
Power (W) = Voltage (V) × Current (A) (2)

ii) the resistance of the kettle. (2)

iii) the cost of using the kettle for 5 minutes if electricity costs 6p per kWh. (3)

d) Explain why in some parts of the country water is hard and the insides of electric kettles become coated with mineral salt deposits. (2)

(MEG; 1988)

QUESTION 14

a) Maria's father has read a leaflet which tells him that his electric heating system should cost £400 per year to run. His annual bill totals £650.
Describe **four** ways by which he might save money on heating and still keep his house at a comfortable temperature. (4)

b) Maria was able to investigate the heating effect of an electric current at school. She used the circuit diagram opposite to connect her apparatus.

Using this apparatus, Maria took the following readings:

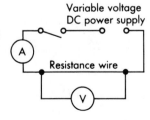

Variable voltage
DC power supply

Resistance wire

potential difference V (V)	0	1.0	2.0	3.0	4.0	5.0	6.0	7.0	8.0	9.0
current I (A)	0	0.30	0.68	1.00	1.30	1.55	1.64	1.72	1.78	1.82

    i) Use the graph paper provided to plot a graph of potential difference V(V) (y axis) against current I(A) (x axis). *(4)*

    ii) Use your graph to find the potential difference when the current is 1.7 A. *(1)*

    iii) Calculate the resistance R of the wire at this value. *(2)*

    iv) Explain what is happening to the resistance of the wire as the current increases. *(2)*

c) People often burn themselves on hot electric appliances like fires. Briefly describe how you would treat someone who had burned themselves badly on a hot electric fire. *(2)*

(MEG; 1988)

A N S W E R S   T O   E X A M I N A T I O N   Q U E S T I O N S

MULTIPLE CHOICE

ANSWER 1

Symbol A is the switch, B is a resistor, C is a capacitor, D is a lamp, and E is a cell.

ANSWER 2

Key A. The colour should be blue to the neutral pin.

ANSWER 3

Key B is the correct circuit. In option A the voltmeter is wrongly connected in series. In option C the ammeter is wrongly connected across the lamp. Remember a voltmeter should always be connected across the circuit component.

ANSWER 4

Key D.

ANSWER 5

Key C. The switches and fuses should both be in the live wire.

ANSWER 6

Key E. If any of the other lamps went out the electricity could 'bypass' the fault.

ANSWER 7

Key B. Use the formula current = voltage ÷ resistance.

ANSWER 8

Key B. Option D is the mains voltage, not the frequency. Option A is the maximum current of a three pin plug.

ANSWER 9

Key E. Remember a kilowatt hour is 1 kW for 1 hour. The fire uses 6 kW, so the cost is 6p × 6 = 36p.

ANSWER 10

a) i) circuit B (this is the parallel circuit)
    ii) 240 V   (20 bulbs × 12 V = 240 V)
    iii) 240 V
b) i) light and heat
    ii) it has a high resistance and glows when hot
c) i) the cable grip
    ii) kettle 13 A (current = watts ÷ volts, 3000 ÷ 250 = 12)
        video 3 A (current = watts ÷ volts, 50 ÷ 250 = 0.2).

ANSWER 11

a) i) 10p (1 kW × 2 × 5p)
    ii) £1.50 (3 kW × 10 × 5p)
    iii) 15p (1.5 kW × 2 × 5p)
b) i) amps or A
    ii) it decreases
    iii) 3 ohms (6 volts ÷ 2 amps).

ANSWER 12

a) The glue melts and is able to flow.
b) liquid glue
c) i) quite thick; thin
    ii) low; high
    iii) plastic; none
d) i) V is Volts   W is Watts
    ii) The symbol on the label V 240 ~ means that an alternating current is needed.
        Batteries only supply direct current, at a much lower voltage.
    iii) a light bulb.

ANSWER 13

a) i) gravitational potential energy
    ii) kinetic energy
b) i) each lamp takes 0.25 A. There are 5 lamps, so the total current is 1.25 A.
       A 1 amp fuse would blow.
    ii)

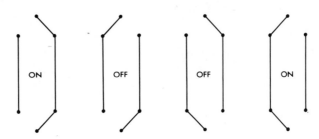

    iii) so that the lights can be switched on or off from either switch.
c) i) current = power ÷ voltage
              = 3000 ÷ 240
              = 12.5 A
    ii) resistance = voltage ÷ current
                  = 240 ÷ 12.5
                  = 19.2 Ω
    iii) cost for one hour is 6p × 3 kWh = 18p
         cost for 5 minutes is 18 ÷ 12 = 1.5p
d) Hard water is caused by calcium salts which have dissolved out of limestone rocks.
    When hard water is boiled in a kettle the dissolved salts change back into limestone
    which is deposited inside kettles as 'scale'.

ANSWER 14

a) 1 By insulating the roof with insulating fibre material to trap air. Air is a poor conductor of heat.
    2 By double glazing the windows, using a secondary pane of glass to trap air in between the two panes.
    3 By having foam insulation put in the cavity walls.
    4 By draught proofing around doors to prevent cold air coming in and warm air escaping.

b) i)

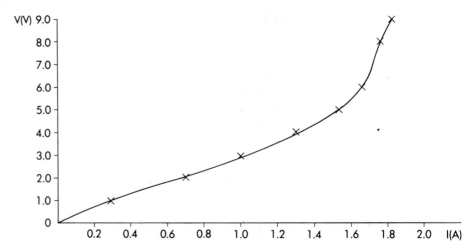

Graph to show heating effect of an electric current.

    ii) 6.4 V
    iii) The resistance is 3.75 Ω.
    iv) As the current increases the resistance increases.

c) 1 Place burned area under cold water.
    2 Phone for doctor or take person to doctor or hospital.

A STUDENT'S ANSWER WITH EXAMINER'S COMMENTS

The following article recently appeared in a local newspaper:

OVERHEAD VERSUS UNDERGROUND

'Protestors at yesterday's meeting voted against the proposal that electricity pylons should be built to carry power to remote farms on the island. They wanted the power cables to be buried underground. Some local residents, however, were not in favour of underground cables as some trees would have to be destroyed, and it takes longer to repair underground cables than overhead cables. The Central Electricity Generating Board pointed out that overhead cables capable of carrying 400 kV through the National Grid cost £506 000 per km, whereas underground cable costs £6 506 000 per km.'

a)   From this article and your own knowledge, suggest **two** disadvantages of overhead cables, and **two** disadvantages of underground cables.

Disadvantages of **overhead** cables:

1   they are dangerous to people who may climb on them.

2   they spoil the appearance of the enviroment.

Good, but a pity about the spelling of 'environment'

(2)

Disadvantages of **underground** cables:

1   they cost a lot of money.

2   they are difficult to repair as they are underground.

Good

(2)

b)   Most domestic appliances in Britain are rated at 220–240 V. Why is it necessary to carry electricity through the National Grid at 400 kV (400 000 V)?

so that all the appliances in the house have the correct voltage.

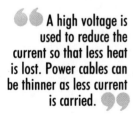
A high voltage is used to reduce the current so that less heat is lost. Power cables can be thinner as less current is carried.

(2)
(MEG; 1988)

CHAPTER 5

ELECTRO-MAGNETISM

GETTING STARTED

When a coil of wire is placed between two magnets, the coil turns when a current is passed through it. This effect was observed by Michael Faraday, who first realised that electric currents also have magnetic fields, just like ordinary magnets. When two magnetic fields interact, then movement can take place. This is the basis of the electric motor which is used in many household appliances, such as a record turntable, a hair drier, a food mixer, a vacuum cleaner and an electric oven fan. These motors have the ability to turn, owing to the *combined* effects of electricity and magnetism.

An electric current, flowing through a coil of wire, has the effect of making the coil act as a magnet, but when an iron bar is put inside the coil an *electromagnet* is made. The iron bar becomes a magnet *only* when the current is flowing, and so the magnetic effect can be switched on and off. Electromagnets are used in many machines, such as microphones, loudspeakers, radios, televisions and telephones.

ESSENTIAL PRINCIPLES

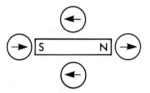

1 ▷ MAGNETS AND MAGNETIC FIELDS

The effect of a magnetic field around a magnet can be shown by using a plotting compass to find out which is the north-seeking or N pole of a magnet. If you place the plotting compass near the end of the magnet, the needle of the compass is repelled from the N pole, as shown in Figure 5.1.

You can also show the magnetic field by shaking iron filings around a magnet. The iron filings line up along the lines of force. Figure 5.2 shows the pattern produced.

These patterns show the lines of magnetic force. The magnetic field patterns produced between two attracting (unlike) poles and two repelling (like) poles are shown in Figures 5.3 and 5.4 respectively.

When two magnetic fields come together there is either a force of *attraction* or a force of *repulsion*, and as a result there is a possibility of movement. Magnets are usually made from magnetic alloys, and attract other magnetic metals such as iron and steel. Magnets do *not* attract non-magnetic metals such as copper, tin, and zinc.

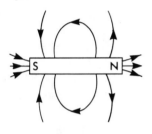

Fig 5.1 The compass needle is repelled from the N pole of the magnet.

Fig 5.2 The magnetic field pattern around a magnet.

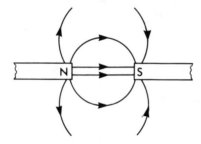

Fig 5.3 Attraction between unlike poles of two magnets.

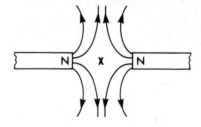

Fig 5.4 Repulsion between like poles of two magnets.

2 ▷ ELECTRO-MAGNETISM

A magnetic field is produced around a straight wire whenever an electric current flows through the wire. Plotting compasses or iron filings can be used to show this magnetic effect.

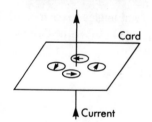

Fig 5.5 Plotting compasses can be used to show the magnetic field around a current flowing through a wire.

Fig 5.6 The pattern produced for a single wire carrying current. The current is flowing upwards out of the page.

Fig 5.7 The pattern produced for a single wire carrying current. The current is flowing downwards into the page.

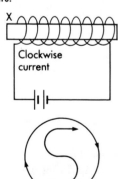

Fig 5.8 The current flows in a clockwise direction around the X end of the core.

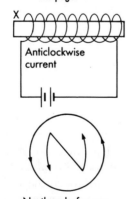

Fig 5.9 The current flows in an anti-clockwise direction around the X end of the core.

These magnetic fields are fairly weak, and the effect can be increased by using a coil of wire called a *solenoid*. The magnetic effect depends on the size of the current and the number of turns on the coil.

A soft iron bar placed inside the coil creates an even more powerful magnetic field, and becomes an *electromagnet*. Figure 5.8 shows the current flowing in a *clockwise* direction around the X end of the core. This end becomes the *south* pole.

When the current flow is *anti-clockwise* then X becomes a *north* pole as shown in Fig 5.9. So the *polarity is changed* by *reversing* the current direction.

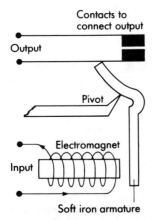

Fig 5.10 An electromagnetic relay.

ELECTROMAGNETIC RELAY

A simple application of this principle is in the *electromagnetic relay*. The relay is a simple switch, operated by an electromagnet, in which a small input current controls a larger output current. Stages 1 to 4 below describe how it works:

1   The input current causes the electromagnet to become magnetised.
2   The electromagnet attracts a soft iron armature, which closes the contacts and causes a greater current to flow through the output circuit.
3   The output circuit controls a device such as a motor.
4   When the input current stops then the output current is switched off and the motor stops.

3 ▷ **FORCES ON CURRENTS IN MAGNETIC FIELDS**

When an electric current is passed through a length of copper wire which is placed in the field of a strong magnet, the wire moves at 90° to the direction of the magnetic field. If the *current direction* is reversed, then the *force on the current* is reversed and the wire moves in the opposite direction. The direction of force is always at right angles to the current direction and the field direction.

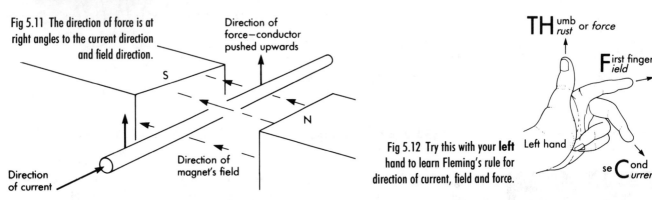

Fig 5.11 The direction of force is at right angles to the current direction and field direction.

Fig 5.12 Try this with your **left** hand to learn Fleming's rule for direction of current, field and force.

Some people learn this rule by using *Fleming's left-hand rule*:
If the thumb and first two fingers of the left hand are held at right angles to each other, then the *thumb* gives the direction of the force, the *first finger* points in the same direction as the field, and the *second finger* points in the direction of the current.

One important application of this effect is in the moving coil loudspeaker.

MOVING COIL LOUDSPEAKER

Figure 5.13 shows the three main sections of the loudspeaker. When an alternating current is passed through the coil, the coil is pushed backwards and forwards, causing the paper cone to vibrate and give out sound waves. The frequency and amplitude of the alternating current which flows through the coil affect the type of sound produced.

Fig 5.13 A moving coil loudspeaker.

4 ▷ **ELECTRIC MOTORS**

A simple motor contains several coils of wire, wound on a core which is pivoted on an axle between two permanent magnets, as shown in Figure 5.14.

The coil is connected to a power supply by two carbon contacts called *brushes*. These are held in position against two halves of the *commutator*, which is a split ring made of copper. When a DC current is passed through the coil, the magnetic field created is attracted to the opposite poles of the permanent magnets and this causes the coil to spin in a clockwise direction. When the N and S poles of the coil lie opposite the S and N poles of the permanent magnets, the coil should stop *turning*, but it carries on *spinning* because the two brushes now press against the opposite half rings of the commutator. The current now flows in the *opposite direction* and this results in the N and S poles of the coil being

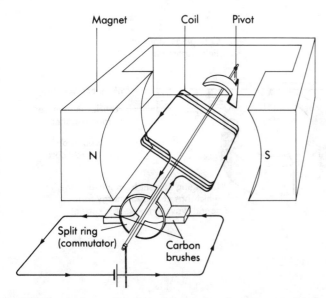

Fig 5.14 The construction of a simple electric motor.

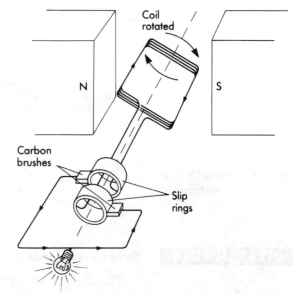

Fig 5.15 The construction of a simple AC generator or alternator.

reversed. The coil then spins round to the S and N poles of the permanent magnets, and once again the current direction is reversed as the coil is about to stop.

MORE COMPLEX MOTORS

Real motors which are used in everday appliances such as electric drills, washing machines and food mixers usually have several coils, each of which may have its own commutator. The purpose of these is to produce a smoother and more powerful turning effect, and thereby allow the motor to run more evenly without stopping. The coils are usually wound on a soft iron core, called an *armature*. The effect of this is to increase the strength of the magnetic field.

5 > GENERATORS AND ALTERNATORS

Generators produce electricity

GENERATORS

You may have used a simple *generator* in the form of a dynamo to light the lamps on a bicycle. Generators transfer kinetic energy to electrical energy.

On an industrial scale, generators are used in power stations to supply mains electricity. Most generators work on the same principle that a current can be induced in a coil by turning it in a magnetic field.

There are basically two types of generators:

1 DC generators, which produce one-way direct current.
2 AC generators or *alternators*, which produce alternating current, such as those found in power stations and in cars.

ALTERNATORS

Alternators are generators which produce alternating current

The alternating current is induced as the coil rotates between the permanent magnets. The coil is linked to the outside circuit by two carbon brushes which press against two carbon slip rings which are fixed to the end of the coil, as shown in Figure 5.15.

The current can be increased by four factors:

1 having more turns on the coil;   3 winding the coil on a soft iron armature;
2 using stronger magnets;   4 rotating the coil at a higher speed.

6 > TAPE RECORDING

Know how your tape-recorder works

An everday application of electromagnetism is tape recording. Inside the recording head of a tape recorder is a small electromagnet, consisting of a coil wound on a circular iron core. There is a small slit at the front of the core, as shown in Figure 5.16.

The strength of the electromagnet changes as the current from the microphone changes. As a result there is a changing magnetic field across the slit, which magnetises the particles on the tape. The pattern of particles on the tape therefore reflects the pattern of the changing strength and frequency of the sound waves.

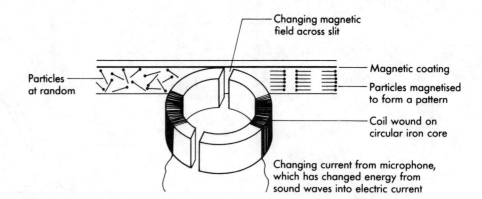

Fig 5.16 The recording head is an electromagnet.

Changing magnetic field across slit

Particles at random

Magnetic coating

Particles magnetised to form a pattern

Coil wound on circular iron core

Changing current from microphone, which has changed energy from sound waves into electric current

7 ⟩TRANSFORMERS

Three important facts to remember:

1 Transformers change voltage.
2 Transformers only work on alternating current.
3 Transformers contain an iron core and two coils of wire, a primary coil and a secondary coil.

Figure 5.17 shows a step-up and a step-down transformer.

Fig 5.17

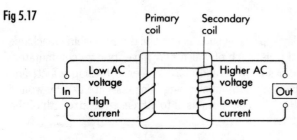

Primary coil   Secondary coil

In   Low AC voltage   Higher AC voltage   Out
High current   Lower current

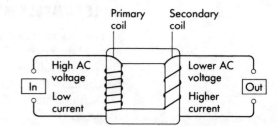

Primary coil   Secondary coil

In   High AC voltage   Lower AC voltage   Out
Low current   Higher current

a) A step-up transformer gives out a higher voltage than the input voltage.

b) A step-down transformer gives out a lower voltage than the input voltage.

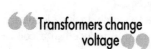

Transformers change voltage

A *step-up* transformer gives out a higher voltage than the input voltage and has more turns on the secondary coil than the primary coil. A *step-down* transformer gives out a lower voltage than the input voltage, so there are more turns on the primary coil than the secondary coil.

When the primary coil is connected to an alternating current, it acts like an electromagnet which is switched on and off very quickly. This sets up a changing magnetic field in the iron core, which induces alternating current in the secondary coil. You can calculate the voltage induced in the secondary coil using the following formula:

$$\frac{\text{voltage across secondary coil}}{\text{voltage across primary coil}} = \frac{\text{number of turns in secondary coil}}{\text{number of turns in primary coil}}$$

In symbols $\frac{V_2}{V_1} = \frac{N_2}{N_1}$

For example, if a step-down transformer has 100 turns on the primary coil and 10 turns on the secondary coil, you can calculate the output voltage given that the input voltage is 240 V.

$$V_2 = \frac{10}{100} \times 240 = 24 \text{ V}$$

The output voltage is 24 volts.

One of the main uses of transformers is in the National Grid system, where *step-up* transformers increase the voltage and lower the current so that less electricity is wasted as heat. *Step-down* transformers are used in many household appliances, such as televisions, computers, radios and washing machines, in order to reduce the mains voltage to a lower voltage.

E X A M I N A T I O N   Q U E S T I O N S

MULTIPLE CHOICE

QUESTION 1

Which one of the following substances is used to make the core of a transformer?
A aluminium; B carbon; C copper; D iron; E steel

QUESTION 2

A step-down transformer has 300 turns on the primary coil and an input voltage of 240 volts. The secondary coil has an output voltage of 40 volts. How many turns must there be on the secondary coil?
A 40; B 50; C 100; D 250; E 400

QUESTION 3

What is the advantage of using an electromagnetic relay switch in a transistor circuit?
A   A large input current controls a small output current.
B   A large output current controls a small input current.
C   A small output current controls a large input current.
D   A small input current controls a small output current.
E   A small input current controls a large output current.

QUESTION 4

Two bar magnets are placed so that their north poles are 2 cm apart. Which of the following diagrams best represents the resulting magnetic field?

(LEAG; 1988)

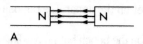  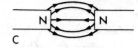

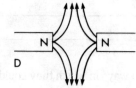 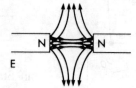

QUESTION 5

In the National Grid system, the transmission of electrical energy is by means of overhead conductors. These conducting wires carry
A   alternating current at high voltage
B   alternating current at high frequency
C   alternating current at low voltage
D   direct current at low voltage
E   direct current at low frequency.

QUESTION 6

The circuit opposite was set up as shown and connected to an oscilloscope.
Which one of the following traces was produced on the oscilloscope screen?

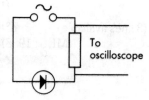

To oscilloscope

  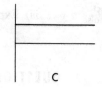

(SEG; 1988)

QUESTION 7

The diagram opposite shows a horizontal wire carrying a current, placed between the poles of two magnets.

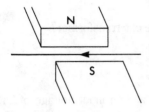

In which direction is the force on the wire?
A   vertically downwards between the two magnets
B   vertically upwards between the two magnets
C   the same direction as the current flows in the wire
D   from the north pole to the south pole of the two magnets
E   from the south pole to the north pole of the two magnets.

STRUCTURED QUESTIONS

QUESTION 8

a)   Some students set up the apparatus shown in the diagram opposite to show that a current flowing through a wire produces a magnetic field.

   i) State **two** methods of detecting the magnetic field around the wire that they could have used.

       1 _____
                                                                                        (1)

       2 _____
                                                                                        (1)

   ii) Sketch the magnetic field obtained.   *(1)*

b)   The teacher then challenged the students to see if they could obtain electricity from magnetism. The students set up the apparatus opposite.

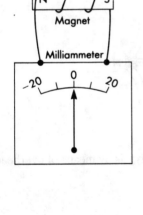

     The apparatus was left lying on the bench but no reading was seen on the milliammeter.

   i) What should the students do to get a reading on the milliammeter?

       _____

       _____
                                                                                        (1)

   ii) State **two** ways in which they could increase the milliammeter reading.

       1 _____
                                                                                        (1)

       2 _____
                                                                                        (1)

c)   A useful application of electromagnetism is the electromagnetic relay which is shown opposite.

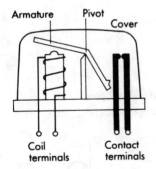

   i)   What is the armature made of?

       _____
                                                                                        (1)

   ii) Describe how the relay works when a current flows in the coil. (3 lines available)
                                                                                        (3)

   iii) Explain why relays are used in some electrical circuits. (3 lines available)   *(2)*
                                                                                 (MEG; 1988)

QUESTION 9

The diagram at the top of page 49 shows a simple motor which has been made by a student in a laboratory.

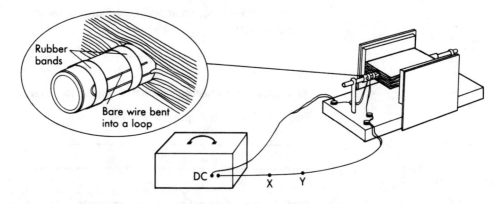

a) Describe what happens when the motor is connected to a DC supply.

_____

_____

(1)

b) What would happen to the speed of the motor if a resistor was added to the circuit between points X and Y?

_____

_____

(1)

Adjustable knob

c) Many modern electrical appliances, such as the food mixer shown opposite, have variable speeds.

Explain how turning the knob on the mixer causes the speed of the motor to increase. (4 lines available) *(3)*

d) Explain the purpose of a commutator in an electric motor. (6 lines available) *(3)*

e) Why do motors used in electrical appliances usually have at least three commutators and complex coils? (3 lines available) *(2)*

f) When a tape recording is made, the microphone converts the energy in sound waves into changing electrical currents. Name the electrical device which receives these electrical currents and magnetises the particles on the tape.

_____

(1)
(MEG; 1988)

QUESTION 10

The figure shows the main parts of a meter designed to measure electric current. There are two iron bars inside a coil. One bar is fixed and the other is on the end of a pivoted pointer.

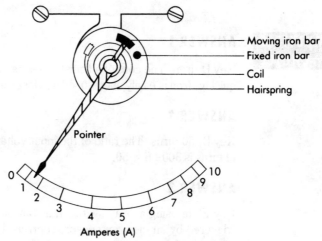

a)   i) Apart from heat, what will be produced inside the coil when electricity passes
        through it?

        _____

                                                                                    (1)

    ii) Explain what effects this will have on the two iron bars. (6 lines available)   *(4)*

b)   Suggest what the hairspring does.

     _____

     _____

                                                                                    (1)

c)   Another way of detecting electric currents is to use an oscilloscope. The diagrams
     below show two possible traces on the oscilloscope screen. Explain what **each** trace
     represents.

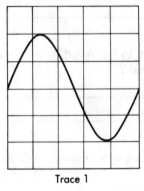

Trace 1

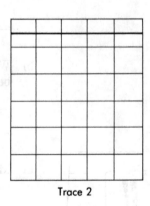

Trace 2

Trace 1 _____

     _____

     _____

                                                                                    (2)

Trace 2 _____

     _____

     _____

                                                                                    (2)
                                                                              (SEG; 1988)

ANSWERS TO EXAMINATION QUESTIONS

ANSWER 1

Key D, iron. The core of a transformer has to become magnetised and demagnetised very
quickly. Iron is easily magnetised and loses its magnetism easily.

ANSWER 2

Key B, 50 turns. The ratio of the input voltage to the output voltage is 6:1. So the number
of turns is $300 \div 6 = 50$.

ANSWER 3

Key E. In using a relay switch in a transistor circuit, a small input current, such as that
triggered by an electron sensor, controls a large output current, such as that used by a
motor.

ANSWER 4

Key D. The poles are both N poles so they repel each other. Option C shows the pattern of attraction which would be produced by two *unlike* poles.

ANSWER 5

Key A. The National Grid carries AC, and high voltages are needed to produce a low current and prevent loss of heat.

ANSWER 6

Key D. The diode has the effect of halfwave rectification.

ANSWER 7

Key B. The force on the wire is upwards. Remember Fleming's left hand rule. Hold the thumb and first and second finger of the left hand at right angles to each other. The second finger points in the direction of the current, the first finger points in the field direction, and the thumb gives you the direction of movement.

STRUCTURED QUESTIONS

ANSWER 8

a) i) 1 iron filings sprinkled on the card   2 a plotting compass placed on the card
    ii)

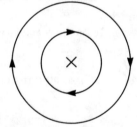

b) i) move the magnet in and out of the coil
    ii) 1 put more turns on the coil   2 use a stronger magnet

c) i) soft iron
    ii) a magnetic field is produced when the current flows in the coil which attracts the armature. As the armature moves, it closes the contacts and completes the circuit.
    iii) a relay is used because a small current controls a larger current.

ANSWER 9

a) the motor spins
b) the speed would slow down
c) the knob is linked to a variable resistor. As the knob is turned, the resistance is decreased and more current flows, so the motor gets faster.
d) the commutator changes the direction of the current flowing through the coil, so that the coil keeps on spinning.
e) so that the motor is more efficient and runs smoothly
f) an electromagnet

ANSWER 10

a) i) a magnetic field

    ii) The iron bars become magnetised temporarily and repel each other. The moving iron bar is fixed to a pointer, which moves along the scale. The higher the current the further the iron bars repel each other.

b) The hairspring resists the rotation of the coil and prevents the pointer moving off the scale.
c) Trace 1 shows an alternating current. The top of the wave shows the maximum forward current. The bottom of the wave shows the maximum reverse current.
    Trace 2 shows a direct positive current. The height of the line above the zero can indicate the voltage if the scale is known.

A STUDENT'S ANSWER WITH EXAMINER'S COMMENTS

A student was working in a laboratory and needed to produce a 3 V AC electrical supply to light a lamp. The only power pack available was set at a fixed output of 12 V AC.
The student drew a sketch of a transformer which could be made from two iron C-cores and some insulated wire.

a)   i) How many coils of wire should there be on each C-core?   (2)
     ii) Explain how you calculated the number of coils on each C-core.   (2)

b)   Draw a diagram to show how the student could use the 12 V AC supply, together with two iron C-cores, two lengths of insulated wire and the 3 V lamp to produce a 3 V supply and light the lamp.   (4)

c)   Explain how an output is produced from the secondary coil of the transformer.   (3)

d)   Why is it necessary to use an AC supply for a transformer instead of a DC supply?
                                                             (2)

                                                   (MEG; 1988)

Here are **two** student answers, one scoring very high marks and the other rather low marks.

Version 1: maximum marks

a)   i) 40 on the primary coil, 10 on the secondary coil   Good, over 10 coils used.

 Correct formula.

    ii) using the formula $\dfrac{V_2}{V_1} = \dfrac{N_2}{N_1}$; $\dfrac{12}{3} = \dfrac{4}{1}$

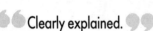 Clearly explained.

The ratio of turns is therefore 4:1, so 40 turns on the primary and 10 turns on the secondary.

b)

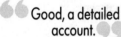

You understand the circuit and the principle of a transformer. Also correct ratio of turns.

Good, a detailed account.

c)   Current flows backwards and forwards through the primary coil, and sets up an alternating magnetic field in the core, which induces a current of the same frequency in the secondary coil.

Yes, you have established the main points.

d)   An alternating current is needed which changes direction to induce an EMF in the secondary coil.

Version 2: low marks

a)   i) 4 on the primary, and 1 on the secondary   At least 10 turns are needed.

    ii) $\dfrac{12}{3} = 4$

Show how you used the formula $\dfrac{V_2}{V_1} = \dfrac{N_2}{N_1}$

b)

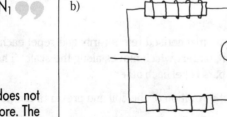

This is a series circuit and does not show that you understand transformers.

The current does not flow through the core. The changing magnetic field in the core induces a current in the secondary core.

c)   The current flows through the core from the secondary to the primary coil.

d)   AC means alternating current   Yes, but what does it do?

WAVES

GETTING STARTED

When you listen to the radio, watch TV, read a magazine, or sit by a fire, you are making use of the different effects of a group of waves known as electromagnetic waves. These waves, together with sound waves, seismic waves and water waves all transfer energy *without* the transfer of matter.

An earthquake is the result of a very large amount of energy travelling through the Earth. This energy can cause great destruction of buildings, roads and bridges, and great loss of life. Waves at sea also carry very large amounts of energy, and research is being carried out into ways in which this energy can be used to generate electricity.

ESSENTIAL PRINCIPLES

1 > OSCILLATIONS

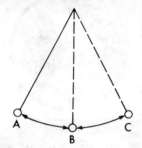

Fig 6.1.

If you hang an object on a piece of string and let it swing backwards and forwards, then you are allowing it to 'oscillate'. Eventually the oscillations slow down and the object comes to a stop. When you start it moving the size of the oscillations is large and then become gradually smaller. So one complete oscillation is from A to B to C and back to A, as shown in Figure 6.1.

A child on a swing is oscillating backwards and forwards. If the child makes 10 complete swings in 60 seconds then the frequency of the oscillation is 0.16 cycles per second or 0.16 Hertz.

OSCILLATIONS AND THE BODY

The oscillations produced by a ship which is rolling from side to side at sea can cause people to feel seasick. A drum beat which produces very low frequency oscillations can make people feel giddy and cause blurred vision. Sometimes people who work in factories are affected by the oscillations of the machinery which they operate. Musical instruments, such as a piano, produce sounds because of the oscillations of the piano strings.

2 > WAVE MOTION

There are two types of waves, longitudinal and transverse. Electromagnetic waves and waves in water are examples of *transverse* waves. These are like the waves produced in a piece of rope when it moves up and down as shown in Figure 6.2.

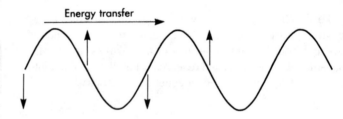

Fig 6.2 Energy is being transferred along this transverse wave, but the particles only move up and down.

Each part of the rope is oscillating up and down, as the energy is being transferred along the rope.

Sound waves are the only waves which are *longitudinal* waves. These waves are like the waves produced by a long spring, as shown in Figure 6.3. The energy is being transferred along the spring, but the particles are oscillating from left to right.

❝Longitudinal waves are examples of mechanical waves❞

Fig 6.3 Energy is being transferred along this longitudinal wave, but the particles are oscillating from left to right.

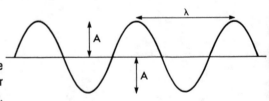

Fig 6.4 The letter 'A' shows the amplitude of the wave. The letter 'λ' shows the wavelength.

AMPLITUDE AND WAVELENGTH

The length of each *complete* oscillation of the wave is the *wavelength*. The *size of the wave* is the *amplitude*. As shown in Fig 6.4.

The distance marked λ (lambda) is the *wavelength*, and is the distance between two troughs or two crests. The distance marked A is the *amplitude*, and is the amount by which a particle is displaced up or down.

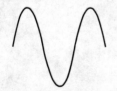

Fig 6.5a) A low frequency wave.

Fig 6.5b) A high frequency wave.

FREQUENCY

The *frequency* of the wave is the number of complete cycles per second, measured in *Hertz* (Hz). (Imagine standing on a beach and counting the waves as they come towards you. This would give you the frequency of the waves.) Figure 6.5a) shows a wave with a low frequency and large amplitude, and Figure 6.5b) shows a wave with a high frequency and small amplitude.

SPEED, FREQUENCY AND WAVELENGTH

$$\underset{\text{(in metres per second)}}{\textbf{Speed}} = \underset{\text{(in Hertz)}}{\textbf{frequency}} \times \underset{\text{(in metres)}}{\textbf{wavelength}}$$

For example, if a wave is travelling with a frequency of 30 Hz and has a wavelength of 3 m, its speed or velocity is 90 m/s. The waves in the *electromagnetic spectrum* all travel at the same velocity of 300 000 000 metres per second, or 3×10^8 m/s. *Sound waves*, however, travel much more slowly, at approximately 330 metres per second. For example, if a sound wave has a wavelength of 0.6 m, and travels at 330 m/s, its frequency is 550 Hz.

$$\text{frequency} = \frac{330}{0.6} = 550 \text{ Hz}$$

3 > ELECTRO-MAGNETIC AND MECHANICAL WAVES

The chart below summarises the main points of difference between electromagnetic waves, such as radio waves, and mechanical waves, such as sound waves.

Electromagnetic
- transverse waves
- travel through a vacuum, do not need a material medium
- travel very fast (3×10^8 m/s)

Mechanical
- longitudinal waves
- need a material such as air to travel
- much slower speed (e.g. speed of sound in air is 300 m/s approx.)

ELECTROMAGNETIC WAVES

These are a group of *transverse* waves which have electric and magnetic properties. They are all produced by changing magnetic fields and changing electric fields, and travel at the very high speed of 300 000 000 metres per second. Figure 6.6 shows the position, relative wavelength and frequency of the different electromagnetic waves.

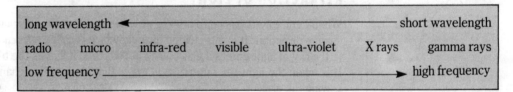

Fig 6.6

The chart below summarises the different waves and their uses:

Type of wave	Uses	Source
radio wave: long wave medium wave short wave	radio communication	radio transmitters
VHF UHF	stereo radio television	electronic circuits
micro waves	satellite communication, radar, microwave ovens	
infra-red	electric fires, ovens	any hot object
visible light	electric lights	very hot objects
ultra-violet	suntanning	extremely hot objects glowing gases
X-rays	used in hospitals to photograph bones	X-ray tubes
gamma rays	used to irradiate food to kill germs; can penetrate very dense metal	radioactive materials

4 > REFLECTION

When a wave hits a barrier it is *reflected* away from the barrier. If a plane wave hits the barrier at *right angles*, it 'bounces back' along its original path, at the same wavelength, frequency and velocity. If the wave hits the barrier at an *angle*, it is reflected at the same angle away from the barrier, as shown in Figure 6.7.

The angle of incidence equals the angle of reflection, and the wavelength, frequency and velocity stay the same.

REFLECTION OF LIGHT

> Light rays are reflected into your eyes

You see the world around you because *light rays* are reflected from different objects into your eyes. When you look at yourself in the mirror you see an image of yourself reflected in the mirror. Your image appears as far behind the mirror as you are in front of the mirror. The image is described as a *virtual* or *imaginary* image. It is the same way up as you are but the left and right sides are reversed. Figure 6.8 shows how an image is formed by a plane mirror.

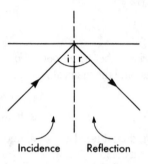

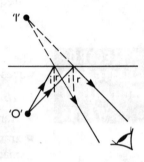

Fig 6.7 The angle of incidence equals the angle of reflection.

Fig 6.8 The image 'I' of the object 'O' appears to be behind the mirror.

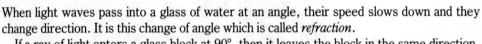

5 > REFRACTION

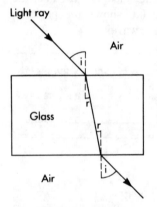

Fig 6.9 The light ray is bent or 'refracted' as it enters and leaves the glass.

Waves travel at a certain speed in air, but when they pass into a different medium, such as water, the speed slows down. The velocity of waves will also decrease as they pass from deeper to shallower water, ie their speed slows down.

REFRACTION OF LIGHT

When light waves pass into a glass of water at an angle, their speed slows down and they change direction. It is this change of angle which is called *refraction*.

If a ray of light enters a glass block at 90°, then it leaves the block in the same direction. It is when the light ray enters *at an angle* that its direction changes, both on entering and leaving the glass.

Light refracts or bends towards the normal (an imaginary line at 90° to the glass surface) as it enters the glass, which is more dense than the air. The light ray then refracts or bends away from the normal as it leaves the glass and passes into the air, a less dense medium.

6 > THE SPECTRUM

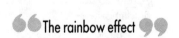

> The rainbow effect

White light is made up of seven different colours, each of which has a different wavelength. When a ray of white light enters a prism, each of the different wavelengths is refracted or bent by different amounts, because they travel through the prism at different speeds. This effect produces a *spectrum* of all the different colours which make up white light.

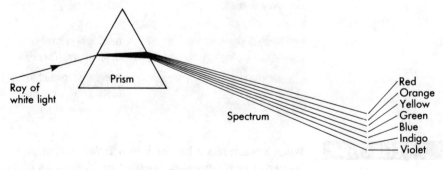

Fig 6.10 White light is split into a spectrum of colours as it passes through the prism.

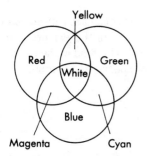

Fig 6.11 The three primary colours make all the other colours.

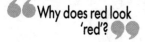
Why does red look 'red'?

COLOURED LIGHT

Red, green and blue are the three *primary colours* which *cannot* be made by mixing any other colours. All the other colours *can* be made from two or three of these primary colours, as shown in Figure 6.11.

When you *mix* two primary colours on a white screen, a new colour, called a *secondary colour* is produced. For example, mixing red and green light produces yellow light. If the third primary colour, blue, is now mixed with the yellow, white light is produced.

COLOUR MIXING OF PAINTS

Coloured dyes in paints and clothes *absorb* part of the spectrum of colours and *reflect* the other colours into our eyes so that we see a particular colour. For example, a red dress absorbs green and blue and reflects red, the colour we see. Green plants look green because the pigment in the leaves absorbs red and blue light and reflects the green.

When two coloured paints are *mixed together*, for example red and yellow, the paint appears to be orange, the colour that is *not absorbed* by either red or yellow. The red paint absorbs green and blue and reflects red and orange. The yellow paint absorbs red and blue and reflects orange, yellow and green. So *both* paints reflect orange.

HOW COLOURED PICTURES ARE PRODUCED ON A TV SCREEN

1 When a TV scene is filmed, light enters the camera, and is split into red, blue and green light.
2 These different signals then go to three different 'tubes', which then send out the corresponding signal on ultra-high frequency waves, to the three electron guns at the back of the TV screen.
3 The electrons hit millions of tiny red, green and blue dots covering the TV screen, which glow when the electrons hit them.
4 Depending on which coloured dots glow, the different colours are produced on the screen.

7 > THE EYE

The retina of the human eye detects coloured light. On the retina are cells which are sensitive to red, green and blue light. When these cells are stimulated by light, an impulse is sent to the brain via the optic nerve. The brain then forms images as a result of the impulses it receives. Figure 6.12 shows the structure of the main parts of the eye.

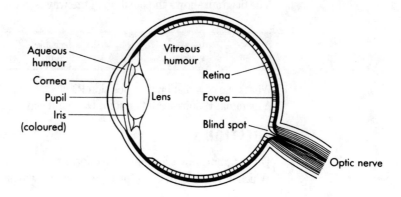

Fig 6.12 The structure of the eye.

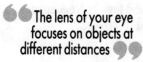
The lens of your eye focuses on objects at different distances

Light is refracted or bent as it enters the eye through the transparent cornea. It is then refracted even more by the convex lens of the eye, and focused on the retina at the back of the eye. The lens is able to adjust to looking at objects which are close to or far away. This is known as *accommodation*.

8 > THE EAR

The ear drum detects the compressions and rarefactions of the air which are caused when sound waves are produced from a vibrating source. The vibrations of the ear drum are passed through the three small bones or *ossicles* in the middle ear. The fluid in the cochlea or inner ear then vibrates and impulses are passed via the auditory nerve to the brain.

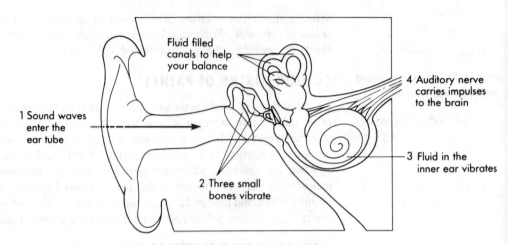

Fig 6.13 The structure of the ear.

EXAMINATION QUESTIONS

MULTIPLE
CHOICE

QUESTION 1

Which one of the following is an example of a longitudinal wave?
A infra-red radiation   D sound waves
B micro waves   E X-rays
C radio waves

QUESTION 2

The diagram shows the position of the waves in the electromagnetic spectrum.

	micro-waves		visible light		X-rays	P

What type of radiation is at position P?
A gamma; B infra-red; C radio; D sound waves; E ultra-violet

QUESTION 3

The diagram shows a simple wave form.
Which letter – A, B, C, D, or E – shows the wavelength?

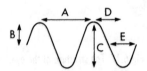

QUESTION 4

Which one of the following waves has the longest wavelength and lowest frequency?
A gamma; B infra-red; C radio; D ultra-violet; E visible light

QUESTION 5

A swinging pendulum makes 80 complete swings in 20 seconds. What is the frequency of the oscillation?
A 2 Hertz; B 4 Hertz; C 8 Hertz; D 20 Hertz; E 80 Hertz

QUESTION 6

A sound wave travels at 300 metres per second and has a frequency of 60 Hertz. What is its wavelength?
A 0.2 m; B 5 m; C 60 m; D 360 m; E 18 000 m

QUESTION 7

Which one of the following types of radiation is used to irradiate food and kill germs?
A micro-waves   D X-rays
B infra-red   E gamma rays
C ultra-violet

QUESTION 8

Which one of the following diagrams correctly shows the path of a ray of light as it passes through a glass block?

A   B   C   D   E

QUESTION 9

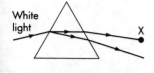

White light   X

A narrow beam of white light is passed through a glass prism and forms a spectrum on a screen. The lines drawn show the limits of the visible spectrum.
What colour of light appears at X?
A blue; B green; C red; D violet; E white

STRUCTURED QUESTIONS

QUESTION 10

Waves were produced in a ripple tank as shown in the diagram below. A ruler was placed along the edge of the tank.

The wave motion was frozen by a stroboscope set at 7 flashes per second.

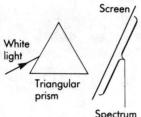

0   10   20   30 cm

Wave   Ripple   Wave
generator tank   crests

a)   i) What is the wavelength of the water waves in cm?

_____

(1)

ii) Suggest **two** possible frequencies of the wave motion.

1 _____

(1)

2 _____

(1)

iii) What would be the effect on the wavelength if the wave generator produced more waves per second?

_____

(1)

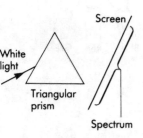

Screen

White
light

Triangular
prism

Spectrum

b)   Light is also a wave motion and forms part of the electromagnetic spectrum. The following experiment was set up using white light and a prism.

i) Complete the diagram, showing the dispersion and refraction of white light by the prism to form a spectrum.   *(3)*

ii) Show clearly where you would expect to find red light on the screen.   *(1)*

c)   i) Name the types of radiation that would occur at **A** and **B** in the electromagnetic
         spectrum shown below.

         radiowaves

            microwaves

               A＿＿＿＿＿＿＿＿＿＿＿＿＿＿＿＿＿＿＿＿＿＿＿＿＿＿＿＿＿＿＿＿＿＿＿＿＿＿＿
                                                                                                    (1)

                   visible light

                      ultra-violet light

                         B＿＿＿＿＿＿＿＿＿＿＿＿＿＿＿＿＿＿＿＿＿＿＿＿＿＿＿＿＿＿＿＿＿＿＿
                            γ-radiation
                                                                                                    (1)

      ii) Which radiation shown in the spectrum has the shortest wavelength?

         ＿＿＿
                                                                                                    (1)

d)   Give a practical use for:

      i) microwaves:

         ＿＿＿

         ＿＿＿
                                                                                                    (1)

      ii) γ-radiation:

         ＿＿＿

         ＿＿＿
                                                                                                    (1)
                                                                                          (MEG; 1988)

QUESTION 11

a)   Why are red light, blue light and green light described as primary colours? (3 lines
      available)   *(1)*

b)   Name the part of the eye which detects coloured light.

      ＿＿＿
                                                                                                    (1)

The diagram below shows spotlights focused on a white screen.

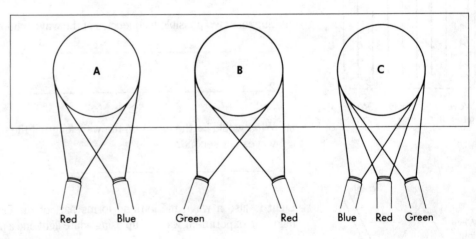

c)   In each case state which colour will be produced on the screen at:

A _____

B _____

C _____

(3)

d)   Explain how coloured pictures are produced on a television screen. (4 lines available)

(3)

(MEG; 1988)

O U T L I N E   A N S W E R S

ANSWER 1

Key D. Sound waves are the only longitudinal wave on the list, all the others are electromagnetic waves and are transverse.

ANSWER 2

Key A. Gamma radiation has a shorter wavelength than X-rays. The position of visible light and microwaves gives you a clue.

ANSWER 3

Key A. The wavelength is the distance from one crest to another. Option B marks the amplitude.

ANSWER 4

Key C, radio waves. Option A gamma rays have the shortest wavelength and the highest frequency.

ANSWER 5

Key B, 4 complete cycles per second. Divide the number of complete swings by the time. $80 \div 20 = 4$.

ANSWER 6

Key B, 5. Remember speed = frequency × wavelength, so divide speed by the frequency to find the wavelength. $300 \div 60 = 5$.

ANSWER 7

Key E, gamma rays, are involved in irradiation of food. Option A micro-waves just heat up food so it can be eaten hot!

ANSWER 8

Key A. The light ray bends away from the normal as it leaves the denser glass block. Option D is the closest, but light doesn't follow the 'normal' path straight through the block.

ANSWER 9

Key C. Red light is refracted the least by the glass block.

STRUCTURED QUESTIONS

ANSWER 10

a)   i) 5 cm (measure the distance using the ruler above the diagram)
     ii) 7 Hz, 14 Hz
     iii) The wavelength would decrease.

b)   i) ii)

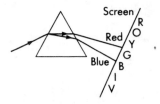

c)   i) A infra-red
        B X-rays
     ii) gamma rays

d)   i) cooking food
     ii) sterilising equipment.

ANSWER 11

a)   They cannot be made from mixing other colours.

b)   the retina

c)   A: magenta
     B: yellow
     C: white

d)   The TV screen is covered in thousands of tiny red, green and blue dots which glow when hit by electrons.

A STUDENT'S ANSWER WITH EXAMINER'S COMMENTS

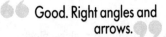

Good. Right angles and arrows.

a)   The diagram below shows an observer in an underground shelter.

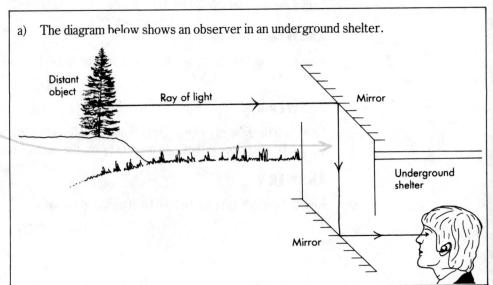

i) Complete the ray of light from the object to the observer's eye.

ii) Suggest another use for such an arrangement of mirrors.

66 Yes, but state 'periscope' and 'to see the surface of the sea'. **99**

in a submarine.

(2)

b) i) Complete the path of the ray in the diagram below.

66 No, the light ray bends towards the 'normal'. **99**

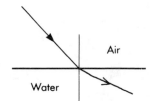

Air

Water

66 No, incorrect. As the light is entering a denser medium, it bends *towards* the normal. **99**

ii) Explain what is happening.

the light ray bends away from the normal.

iii) What is the name given to this effect?

66 *Refraction* is the word required. **99**

Bending of light.

(3)

c) i) Complete the diagram below to show dispersion of white light as it passes through a prism.

66 Oh dear! See Figure 6.10. The ray is split as it *enters* the prism. **99**

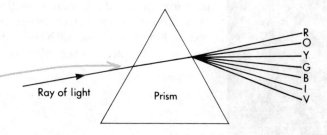

Ray of light

Prism

R
O
Y
G
B
I
V

ii) Visible light is part of the electromagnetic spectrum. Place the following in order of *increasing* wavelength:

radiowaves, infra-red, visible light, X-rays

Shortest wavelength:

66 Wrong order here. **99**

X-rays ✓
visible ✓
{ radio waves ✗
  infra-red   ✗

iii) Explain how selective absorption of light produces the following effects.

66 Yes, but state it does not 'absorb' light, as the question asks. **99**

1 White paper: it reflects all the light.

66 Yes, but it *absorbs* all the light. **99**

2 Black ink: does not reflect any light.

66 Good, well done. **99**

3 A red apple: absorbs green and blue, and reflects red.

(9)

(LEAG; 1988)

CHAPTER

FORCE AND MOTION

SPEED

ACCELERATION

FORCE AND
ACCELERATION

WEIGHT, MASS
AND GRAVITY

GRAVITATIONAL
POTENTIAL ENERGY

KINETIC ENERGY

GETTING STARTED

Walking, running, swimming, cycling and flying are all ways in which you may have moved at different *speeds*. The speed at which you travel depends on two factors: *how far* you have moved and *how long* it has taken. Light waves and sound waves also travel at *different* speeds, with both waves moving a large distance in a short time.

You have probably experienced *acceleration* when sitting in a car or bus which has started moving and then got faster and faster. You may also have experienced *deceleration* as friction from the brakes caused the car or bus to slow down. *Forces* are needed to change the *motion* of moving bodies. For instance you will have worn a seat belt when travelling in the front seat of a car, or when taking off and landing in an aeroplane.

ESSENTIAL PRINCIPLES

1 > **SPEED**

Speed is the distance travelled in a unit of time, such as metres per second, or kilometres per hour. In the laboratory you may have made measurements of speed using a *ticker-timer*. This instrument is a type of clock which produces 50 ticks every second, equal to 5 ticks every 0.1 second. These ticks appear as dots on a strip of ticker tape paper, which shows how far the tape has moved between each dot. The time interval between each dot is 0.02 seconds. When the dots are close together the tape has been moved slowly. When the dots are far apart the tape has been moved quickly.

$$\text{Speed} = \frac{\text{distance}}{\text{time}}$$

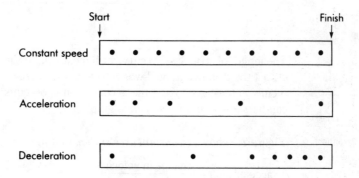

Fig 7.1 Each piece of ticker tape shows a different type of movement.

The ticker tape is usually attached to a moving trolley to study how the trolley moved. The tape shown in Figure 7.2 was produced by a trolley moving down a runway.

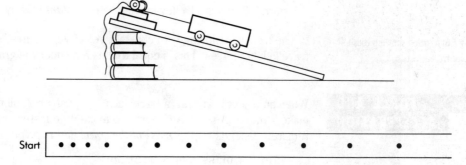

Fig 7.2 The ticket tape shows how the trolley accelerated.

The trolley started slowly and then accelerated.

2 > **ACCELERATION**

When a long piece of tape is pulled through the ticker-timer, the tape can be cut up into 5-dot lengths, each representing a time interval of 0.1 s and fixed on to paper as shown in Figure 7.3.

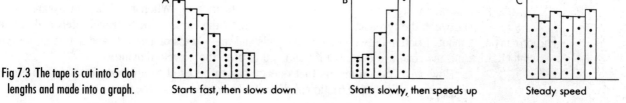

Fig 7.3 The tape is cut into 5 dot lengths and made into a graph.

A Starts fast, then slows down   B Starts slowly, then speeds up   C Steady speed

The velocity for each piece of tape can be found by measuring the distance travelled in 0.1 seconds.

Fig 7.4 Each length of tape is the distance travelled in 0.1 seconds.

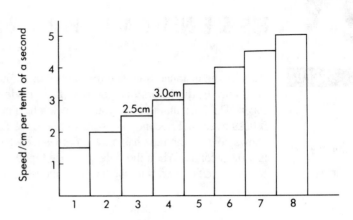

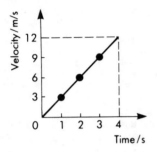

Fig 7.5 A graph showing constant acceleration.

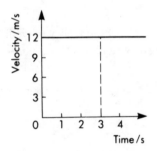

Fig 7.6 A graph showing constant velocity.

The length of strip 3 is 2.5 cm, which means the trolley moved 2.5 cm in 0.1 s (25 cm/s). In strip 4 the distance moved was 3.0 cm in 0.1 second (30 cm/s), so the *change* in velocity is 5 cm/s in 0.1 second and the acceleration is 50 cm/s². The information from ticker tapes can be shown on a *velocity-time* graph.

Figure 7.5 shows a *constant acceleration* of 3 m/s²

$$\text{acceleration} = \frac{\text{change in velocity}}{\text{time taken}}$$

$$a = \frac{(12 - 0)}{4} = 3 \, \text{m/s}^2$$

The *distance travelled* is the *area under the graph*, which equals the area of the triangle, ½ × base × height.
  In this example it is ½ × 4 × 12 = 24 m.

Figure 7.6 shows a trolley moving with *constant velocity*.

The trolley is moving with constant velocity of 12 m/s, so in 3 seconds the car will have travelled 36 metres. This is equal to the area under the graph.

3 ▶ FORCE AND ACCELERATION

When an object is at rest, a force such as a push or a pull must be exerted on the object to make it move. A force is required to make it go faster or accelerate. The *amount of force* required depends on the *mass of the object* and is given by the formula below:

force = mass × acceleration
$$F = m \, a$$
or $\quad a = F/m$.

The amount of acceleration produced depends on two factors – the size of the force, measured in Newtons, and the mass of the object, measured in kilograms. If the force doubles, or the mass is halved, then the acceleration is doubled. For example, if a force of 15 N acts on a mass of 3 kg, then its acceleration is 5 m/s². If the force doubles to 30 N, then the acceleration is 10 m/s².

FRICTION

When you push an object to start it moving, the object will eventually slow down and stop, owing to the force of *friction* which resists motion. When travelling in a car, friction between the tyres and the roads is essential if the car is going to travel safely and not skid about. Friction between the brake pads and the wheels of a bicycle and between the tyres and the road are essential if you need to stop the bicycle moving.

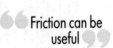
Friction can be useful

However, friction means that energy has to be used to *overcome* it, and so there are many ways of reducing friction as described below:

1 Oil is used in car engines to reduce the friction of the parts rubbing against each other.
2 Air is used in hovercraft to reduce the friction between the boat and the water.
3 Ball bearings are used to reduce the friction between the wheel and the axle of a skateboard.

PAIRS OF FORCES

When an object is acted on by a force, then the object exerts an equal force in the opposite direction. For example, if you kick a ball, then your foot exerts a force on the ball, and the ball exerts an equal and opposite force on your foot; a rocket moves forward when the rocket engine pushes out a large mass of waste gases behind the rocket.

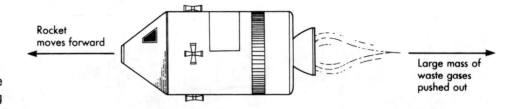

Rocket moves forward

Large mass of waste gases pushed out

Fig 7.7 The rocket accelerates due to the force of the gases being pushed out.

FREE-FALL

An object which is allowed to fall freely near the Earth's surface has a *constant acceleration* of 10 m/s^2. For example, if two objects one of 5 kg and one of 20 kg were dropped from a weather balloon, they would both have the same acceleration. The larger object would need *more force* to accelerate its greater mass.

| 4 | WEIGHT, MASS AND GRAVITY |

The force which is acting on free-falling objects is the force of *gravity* caused by the Earth's gravitational field. This is described as the *weight* of the object.

weight = mass × gravitational field strength

The weight of an object depends on how far it is from the Earth's centre. The gravitational pull of the Earth is decreased the further away an object is, so the weight is reduced. At the Earth's surface, the force acting on 1 kilogram is 10 Newtons. Therefore:

the weight of the 5 kg mass is 5 × 10 = 50 N
the weight of the 20 kg mass is 20 × 10 = 200 N

$$acceleration = \frac{force}{mass}$$

for the smaller object $a = \frac{50}{5} = 10$ m/s^2

for the larger object $a = \frac{200}{20} = 10$ m/s^2

5 kg   20 kg

Fig 7.8 Both the 5kg object and 20kg object would have the same acceleration.

(assuming negligible air resistance).

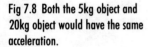

g is acceleration due to gravity

ACCELERATION DUE TO GRAVITY (*g*)

One way of measuring *g* by free fall is to time how long it takes for a ball to drop through a known height. The acceleration of the ball can be calculated. The apparatus used is shown in Figure 7.9.

When the power supply to the electromagnet is switched off, the ball starts to drop and an electronic timer is automatically switched on. When the ball hits the gate and opens it, the timer is switched off. It is usual to repeat this timing several times and obtain an average time: t seconds, over s metres.

$g = 2$ s/t^2

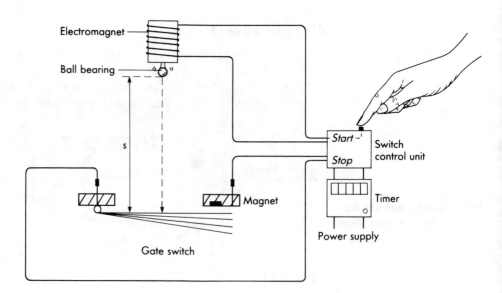

Fig 7.9 Apparatus for measuring
the acceleration due to gravity.

WEIGHT ON THE MOON

The mass of the Moon is smaller than that of Earth, so the gravitational pull of the Moon is about one sixth that of Earth. An object of mass of 10 kg would weigh 16 N on the Moon, whereas on Earth it would weigh 100 N.

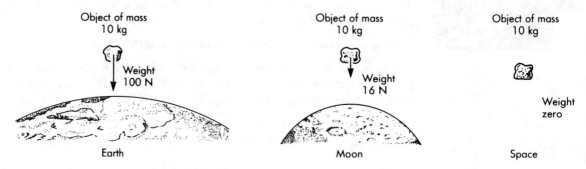

Fig 7.10 The mass of the object
stays the same but the weight
changes.

SATELLITES IN ORBIT

The gravitational pull of the Earth provides the pull required to make a satellite follow a circular path around the Earth. For a satellite to orbit just above the atmosphere it needs to orbit at about 8000 m/s. The Moon, a natural satellite of Earth, orbits much further away from Earth at a speed of about 1000 m/s.

When an object is at a point above the ground it has *gravitational potential energy*. If you hold a book above your desk, the book has gravitational potential energy, equal to the amount of work which you did to lift it to that height, which is given by force × distance moved.

The **gravitational potential energy** of an object is mgh

where mg is the upward force needed to lift the object, and h is the vertical height above the ground.

For example, if the book has a mass of 2 kg, and is held 3 m high, then:

$$\text{gravitional potential energy} = 2 \text{ kg} \times 10 \text{ m/s}^2 \times 3 \text{ m}$$
$$= 60 \text{ J}$$

The *kinetic energy* (E) of a moving object depends on the mass (m) of the object and its velocity (v), as stated in the formula

$$E = \tfrac{1}{2} \, m \, v^2$$

If a person of mass 60 kg is travelling with a velocity of 2 m/s, the kinetic energy =
  ½ × 60 × (2 m/s)² = 120 J
If the same person is travelling twice as fast, at 4 m/s, the kinetic energy =
  ½ × 60 × (4 m/s)² = 480 J
The kinetic energy has increased four times, as the speed has doubled.
If the *mass* of the person doubled to 120 kg, and the speed stayed at 2 m/s, the kinetic energy would be doubled:

$$E = ½ × 120 × (2 \text{ m/s})^2 = 240J$$

CARS ON THE MOVE

These ideas about kinetic energy are very important when applied to real life situations such as the braking distances of cars. When a car brakes to a stop, the kinetic energy is transferred to the brakes and to the road. The amount of energy transferred is equal to the braking force times the distance taken to stop.

"Travelling *twice* as fast needs *four* times the stopping distance"

If a car has twice the mass of another car, but is travelling at the same speed, it will have twice the amount of energy and need twice the braking distance for the same braking force. If two cars have the same mass but one is travelling twice the speed of the other car, it will have four times the amount of energy and need four times the braking distance. Wet road surfaces and smooth tyres will also increase the braking distance, as will the time it takes for the driver to react to a situation and to think about applying the brakes of the car.

EXAMINATION QUESTIONS

MULTIPLE CHOICE

QUESTION 1

During an investigation into how objects move, the ticker tape sample shown below was produced by a moving model vehicle.

Direction

Which one of the following correctly describes how the vehicle moved?
A got faster and then slowed down
B steady, constant speed all the time
C steady, constant speed and then slowed down
D steady, constant speed and then got faster
E started slowly and then got faster.

QUESTION 2

The graph opposite represents the journey of a car

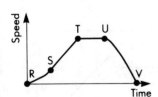

During what part of the journey is the car braking?
A R–S; B S–T; C T–U; D U–V   (SEG: Specimen)

QUESTION 3

What is the average speed of a vehicle which travels 30 kilometres in 15 minutes?
A 2 km/h; B 45 km/h; C 120 km/h; D 250 km/h; E 450 km/h

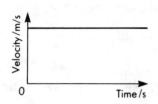

QUESTION 4

The graph opposite shows how the speed of an object varies with time.

The object is
A falling freely
B moving with constant speed
C moving with constant acceleration
D moving with constant deceleration.

(SEG; 1988)

QUESTION 5

The force on a 10 kg mass is 25 N. The acceleration is
A $0.4\,\mathrm{m\,s^{-2}}$ C $25\,\mathrm{m\,s^{-2}}$
B $2.5\,\mathrm{m\,s^{-2}}$ D $250\,\mathrm{m\,s^{-2}}$

(SEG; 1988)

QUESTION 6

Using the pattern

Energy = ½ × mass × speed²

what is the energy of a car of mass 6000 kg moving at a speed of 10 m/s?
A 6000 J   D 300 000 J
B 30 000 J   E 600 000 J
C 60 000 J

QUESTION 7

The Moon's gravitational field strength is one sixth that of Earth. An object on Earth has a mass of 60 kg and a weight of 600 N. What is the mass and weight of the object on the Moon?

	Mass	Weight
A	10	100
B	10	600
C	60	100
D	60	600

QUESTION 8

Using the formula

gravitational potential energy = m g h,

what is the gravitational potential energy of an object which has a mass of 5 kg and is 6 m above the ground?
A 30 J; B 50 J; C 60 J; D 300 J; E 600 J

STRUCTURED QUESTIONS

QUESTION 9

The graph below represents the movement of a car during a short journey.

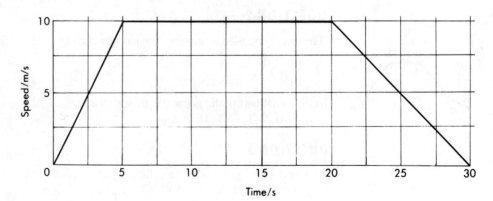

a) What is happening to the car

  i) in the first 5 seconds?

  _____

  (1)

  ii) between 5 seconds and 20 seconds?

  _____

  (1)

b) How far does the car travel between 5 seconds and 20 seconds?

  _____

  (1)

c) Between 20 seconds and 30 seconds the car comes to rest without the use of brakes. Explain how this could happen.

  _____

  _____

  (1)
  (MEG; 1988)

QUESTION 10

The astronaut shown in the diagram below has a weight of 690 N on Earth.

a) If the force of gravity on the Moon is ⅙ (one sixth) that on Earth, what would be his weight on the Moon? Show how you arrive at your answer. *(2)*

  Weight on Moon = _____ N

b) By reference to part a) explain briefly why an astronaut who walks on the Moon wears heavy boots.

  _____

  _____

  _____

  (2)
  (NISEC; Specimen)

Moon

Weight ?N

Earth

690N

QUESTION 11

On 17th May, 1974, the first geostationary weather satellite was launched from Cape Canaveral. The satellite was capable of detecting visible light and infra-red radiation on a continuous 24-hour basis. It was placed in a position 36 000 km above the Equator at 45° W. The satellite recorded the development of a frontal wave over the Atlantic Ocean between 2100 hours on 12th June and 0900 GMT on 13th June, and transmitted this information to Earth.

a) What was the main advantage in this case of having the infra-red detectors on the satellite? *(2)*

Geostationary satellites appear to be stationary in the sky.

b) What does this tell you about the orbiting speed of the satellite compared to the rotation of Earth? *(1)*

c) What force keeps the satellite in orbit around the Earth? *(1)*

d) Explain how and why the weight of the satellite would change when it is in orbit compared to its weight on Earth. *(2)*

e) Suggest how a satellite could be constructed to meet its own energy needs over a long period of time. *(2)*

  (MEG; 1988)

QUESTION 12

A car of mass 1000 kg starts off from rest at traffic lights, and accelerates away uniformly, as shown in the graph below.

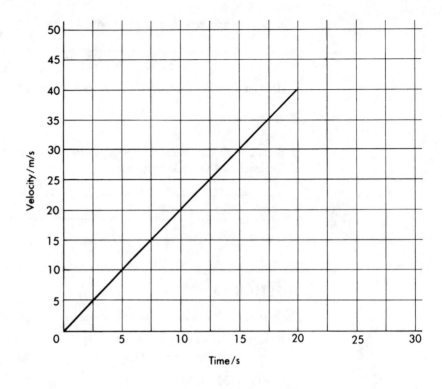

a) i) What is meant by 'accelerates'?

_____

_____

(1)

   ii) Calculate the acceleration of the car and state the units. (4 lines available)   *(3)*

b) The kinetic energy of a moving body can be found from the pattern

   Energy = ½ mass × (velocity)^2

   Find the kinetic energy of the car at 10 seconds after the start, stating the units.
   (4 lines available)   *(3)*

c) The input energy is produced by petrol burning in the engine. Car engines waste some of this input energy, because not all of it can be converted to kinetic energy.
   i) What is the other main form of energy produced?

_____

(1)

   ii) What use can be made of this energy? (3 lines available)   *(1)*

   The car has an input energy of 400 kJ 10 seconds after the start.
   The efficiency of the engine is found from the pattern:

   Efficiency = $\dfrac{\text{kinetic energy}}{\text{input energy}}$ × 100

   Calculate the efficiency of the engine after 10 seconds. (3 lines available)   *(3)*

d) 20 seconds after the start, the driver of the car puts on the brakes and comes to a stop in 5 seconds.

   Force = mass × acceleration

   Calculate the braking force, stating the units. (3 lines available)   *(3)*

   (15)

   (LEAG; 1988)

A N S W E R S   T O
E X A M I N A T I O N   Q U E S T I O N S

MULTIPLE CHOICE

ANSWER 1

Key C, constant speed then slowed down. As the dots are not evenly spaced, option B is wrong. The direction the tape is moved indicates that it is slowing down instead of getting faster, so options A, D and E are incorrect.

ANSWER 2

Key D, U–V. Options A and B show the speed increasing, and option C, region T–U, shows constant speed.

ANSWER 3

Key C, 120 km/h. The catch here is km/h. The distance travelled is for 15 minutes, so multiply by 4 to find the speed in one hour. Option A is for people who divide the 30 by 15.

ANSWER 4

Key B. The straight horizontal line shown on the graph represents moving with constant speed.

ANSWER 5

Key B. Acceleration is force divided by mass, $25 \div 10 = 2.5$.

ANSWER 6

Key D, 300 000 J. Multiply 6000 by ½, then multiply the answer by 10×10.

ANSWER 7

Key C. Remember the mass on the Moon stays the same, so it is 60 kg. The weight is one sixth, so 600 divided by 6.

ANSWER 8

Key D, 300 J. Multiply $5 \times 10 \times 6$.

STRUCTURED QUESTIONS

ANSWER 9

a) i) It is accelerating constantly.
    ii) It is moving at constant speed.
b) 150 metres (at 10 m/s for 15 seconds, $10 \times 15 = 150$)
c) The car could be moving uphill, or the person could take their foot off the accelerator pedal.

ANSWER 10

a) The weight is $690 \div 6 = 115$ N.
b) Heavy boots are needed to keep the astronaut on the surface, as there is very little gravity on the Moon.

ANSWER 11

a) The frontal system developed during the night from 9 pm to 9 am. The satellite was able to detect infra-red radiation instead of visible light.
b) The speed is the same.
c) The gravitational pull of the Earth.
d) The weight would become less, as the effect of the Earth's gravitational pull is less.
e) Solar panels could be used to convert solar energy into electricity.

ANSWER 12

a) i) The velocity of the car increases.

ii) acceleration $= \dfrac{\text{change in velocity}}{\text{time taken}}$

$= \dfrac{20-0}{10}$

$= 2\,\text{m/s}^2$

$= 2$ metres per second per second

b) (The mass of the car is stated above the graph, the velocity can be read from the graph.)

kinetic energy $= \frac{1}{2} \times 1000\,\text{kg} \times 20^2$

$= 500 \times 400$

$= 200\,000$ Joules

$= 200\,\text{kJ}$

c) i) heat energy

ii) to heat the inside of the car

iii) efficiency $= \dfrac{200\,\text{kJ}}{400\,\text{kJ}} \times 100$

The efficiency is 50%.

d) force $= 1000\,\text{kg} \times 8\,\text{m/s}^2$

$= 8,000$ Newtons

A STUDENT'S ANSWER WITH EXAMINER'S COMMENTS

a) The table below is taken from the Highway Code.
It is for a medium sized family car.

SPEED (miles per hour)	SHORTEST STOPPING DISTANCES (feet)		
	Thinking distance	*Braking distance*	*Overall stopping distance*
20	20	20	40
30	30	54	75
40	40	80	120
50	50	125	175
60	60	180	240
70	70	245	315

i) Explain carefully what is meant by:

1 thinking distance ✓ (1)

How long it takes to react

2 braking distance ✓ (1)

how long it takes to stop

Before applying brake

After braking

ii) Use the table above to explain how speed is related to:
1 thinking distance *(1)*

> its the same

2 braking distance *(1)*

> at 40mph its four times as far as 20mph ✓

iii) On the graph paper below, plot the **car's speed** against the **overall stopping distance**. *(4)*

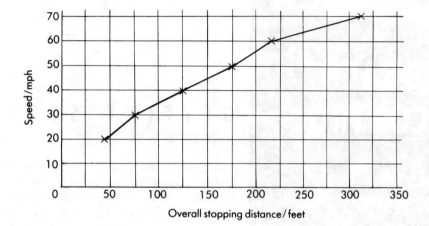

iv) What is the stopping distance at a speed of 45 miles an hour? *(1)*

> about 150 feet ✓

v) If fog reduces the visibility on a motorway to 100 feet, what should the maximum vehicle speed be? *(1)*

> less than 36 mph ✓

b) Explain clearly, with reasons, what effect the following factors would have on thinking and braking distances:
i) wet, slippery roads *(1)*

> it will take longer to brake as there is less friction ✓

ii) a tired driver. *(1)*

> it takes longer to think as reactions are slower. ✓

c) What effect will there be on the **overall stopping distance** if a car is fully loaded with passengers and luggage? Explain your answer clearly. *(2)*

> the energy doubles as the mass doubles so the car would take longer to stop. ✓

(Total marks 14)
(LEAG; 1988)

Examiner's comments (margin):

- Add 'in feet' as the speed is in miles
- Very good. You have identified the pattern
- Take care! Some points are not correct. At 40 mph the distance is 120, not 125. At 60 mph it should be 240, not 215.
- Line drawn
- Good
- Due to wet road
- Good
- Kinetic

FEEDBACK AND CONTROL

PRINCIPLES OF FEEDBACK SYSTEMS

BIOLOGICAL SYSTEMS

MECHANICAL SYSTEMS

ELECTRONIC SYSTEMS

DIGITAL SYSTEMS

LOGIC GATES

GETTING STARTED

Biological, physical and chemical systems usually need to be in a state of *homeostasis*, that is stable and controlled. If our biological systems become unstable, we become ill and may die unless control is regained and stability restored. Electronic, mechanical and chemical systems will break down and cease to function if control is lacking.

Stability is important in all sorts of situations. For example, if you are riding a bicycle you use information from your sense organs to calculate your stability on two wheels; as you become off balance, your brain sends messages to muscles which contract or relax to return you to a balanced position. Such minute adjustments occur at a rate of many times per second so that you can ride safely.

Your deep freeze, your goldfish pond and many other systems may need to remain stable. Each consists of a large number of factors that vary as time passes and which need to be controlled if the system is to remain stable. At least three components are necessary to keep a system stable:

1 A *receptor* or *sensor* which detects any change from the normal or set value.
2 A *control mechanism* or *comparator* which initiates the corrective measures.
3 An *effector* or *actuator* to bring about the corrective measures.

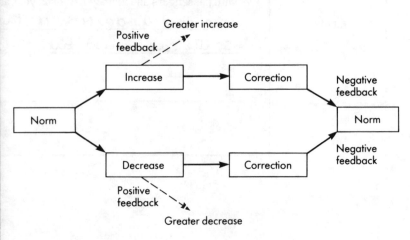

Fig 8.1 Feedback mechanisms.

ESSENTIAL PRINCIPLES

Feedback in the kitchen!

This idea is easier to understand if we look at an example. Whenever we use energy we need to control it. If we don't, then the results are often disastrous. Heat energy, released from the elements in an electric oven, needs to be very carefully controlled if a burnt cake is to be avoided. All systems that we want to control will consist of inputs and outputs. In this system the *input* is the amount of electricity and the *output* is a constant oven temperature. To *control* this system we can use information about the output – the temperature of the oven – in order to control the input of electrical energy. By reading a thermometer and adjusting the amount of electricity being used, we could control the system ourselves by turning up the electrical supply when the temperature dropped, and turning it down when the temperature rose too high. To save us time and trouble, modern ovens are fitted with simple control devices called *thermostats* which can be set at the desired temperature and left to do the adjustment automatically.

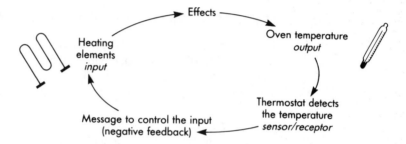

Fig 8.2 How negative feedback controls an oven.

In the oven the thermostat acts as both sensor *and* comparator; the actuator is the heating element that can bring the level of the output back to the set point. The actuator needs to be linked to the sensor so that appropriate action is taken. Information about the temperature of the oven is linked to the amount of current flowing to the heating element. This information is known as **feedback**.

Feedback can be either **positive** or **negative**. Positive feedback can lead to systems going out of control, so it is not useful in maintaining homeostasis. The example above illustrates how negative feedback can be used to maintain a steady state.

Feedback carries simple messages that are often in code. The messages being transmitted in the oven example were of two types, each reversing the direction of the temperature change taking place. This is why we use the term 'negative' feedback. The two messages were:

1 'The oven is too hot, *reduce* the current to the heating elements.'
2 'The oven is too cold, *increase* the flow of current.'

If the message had been 'The oven is too hot, *increase* the flow of current to the heating elements', this 'positive' feedback would have resulted in a very burnt cake! A good example of positive feedback is the chain reaction which occurs in a nuclear reactor out of control.

Body temperature and *water content* need to be automatically controlled and monitored in mammals, and provide two good examples to remember.

CONTROL OF BODY TEMPERATURE

An example of negative feedback

In mammals, a part of the brain, the *hypothalamus*, responds to temperature changes both inside and outside the body. The temperature of the blood flowing through the brain is monitored by the hypothalamus. Information about external temperature comes from special *thermoreceptors* in the skin which are connected by nerves to the hypothalamus. The brain initiates responses appropriate to the information received. If the temperature is *too high*:

1 the body is cooled by sweating;
2 the hair lies flat against the skin;
3 blood is pumped to capillaries just below the skin surface;
4 there is a general lowering of the body's metabolic rate.

A *fall* in temperature would cause the *opposite* responses plus shivering to raise the temperature by producing heat in the muscles. Mammals are very sensitive to temperature change and humans soon die if the body core temperature is too high or too low.

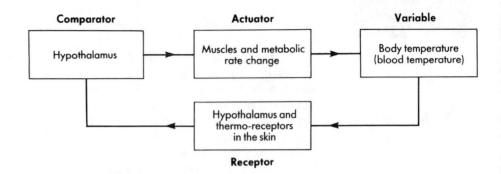

Fig 8.3 Temperature control in a mammal.

CONTROL OF WATER CONTENT – OSMOREGULATION

The average adult human body is some 58% water, and it is vital that the amount remains constant. If we drink too much our body fluids become dilute; if we lose too much water they become too concentrated. Either way, cells would cease to function properly. *Osmoregulation* is the term we use to describe the process of maintaining the correct fluid balance in our bodies.

The organ which controls the amount of water leaving the body is the kidney, which works with the hypothalamus and anti-diuretic hormone (ADH) to achieve homeostasis, as shown in Figure 8.4.

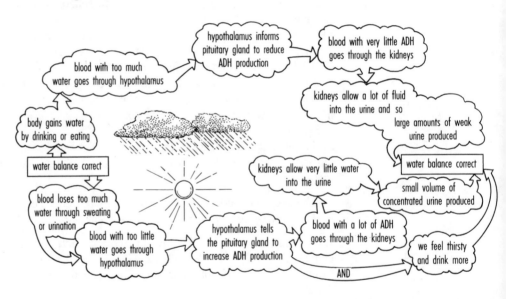

Fig 8.4 How fluid level is controlled in mammals

THE REFLEX ARC

The *reflex arc* is the functional unit of the nervous system and demonstrates how homeostasis may be achieved automatically. The reflex arc shown in Figure 8.5 is the direct pathway from a receptor to an effector, via the central nervous system (CNS). Sensory and motor nerve cells (neurones) may connect directly, although more often they do so through an intermediate neurone. There are **two** main sorts of reflex pathway:

1 the simple reflex;
2 the conditioned reflex.

Simple reflexes consist only of a reflex arc, and result in a very fast and automatic response to a stimulus. They are instinctive and usually increase an animal's chance of survival. Examples are coughing, blinking and eye-focusing, withdrawing a limb from a source of pain, and the well known knee jerk reflex, as shown in Figure 8.6. The sequence of events is labelled 1–7.

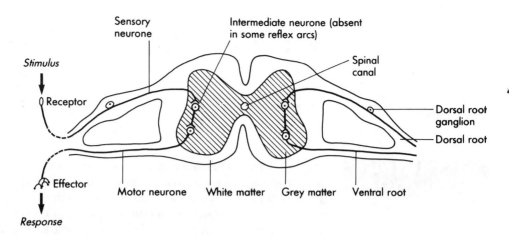

Fig 8.5 The reflex arc.

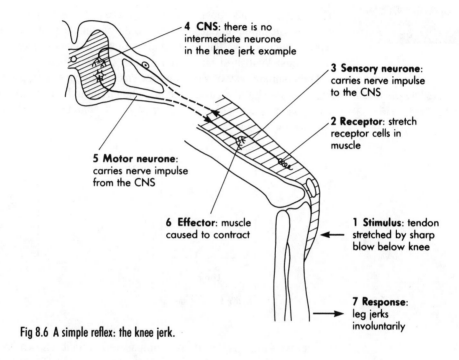

Fig 8.6 A simple reflex: the knee jerk.

Conditioned reflexes involve learning and memory, and they allow us to ride bicycles and drive cars without too much conscious thought.

3 MECHANICAL SYSTEMS

Automatic *mechanical* systems are very common. For example, a household central heating system contains many automatic control devices, such as ballcocks (Figure 8.7), radiator thermostats, flame-out protectors on the gas boiler, etc. *Bimetallic strips* are often used in thermostats. These are made up from two *dissimilar* metals joined together. When heated, the metals expand at different rates and cause the strip to bend. This bending movement can be used to switch various devices on or off; this device is found in domestic irons (Figure 8.8).

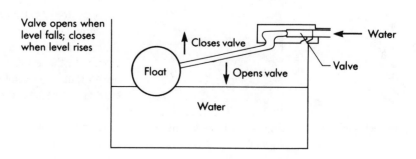

Fig 8.7 Automatic water control – a ballcock.

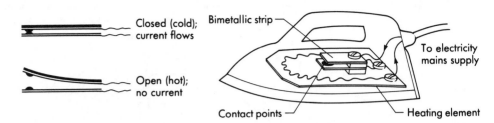

Fig 8.8 Bimetallic strip thermostat in an iron.

4 ELECTRONIC SYSTEMS

Many *electronic* circuits employ feedback mechanisms in their control applications. Both positive and negative feedback systems are used; the former for *latching*, and the latter to maintain *stable* situations, as in temperature control. Professional electronics engineers apply a *systems approach* to solving problems and do not usually deal with single components, as you did when you studied current electricity. Integrated circuits contain *many* components in a single microchip.

5 DIGITAL SYSTEMS

> Digital systems can be either **on** or **off**

The voltage signals applied to a system are either analogue or digital; the former can have any voltage input or output value, but the digital systems respond only to one of two signals, high or low. These are usually described as *logic level 1* and *logic level 0*. This idea can be best illustrated using a normal switch, as in Figure 8.9.

The common way of showing how circuits behave is to produce a *truth table*, which is a summary of what the circuit can do. The circuit in Figure 8.9 has its switch either on or off, and its lamp is also either on or off. If 1 = ON and 0 = OFF, Figure 8.10 will be the truth table for the circuit.

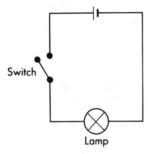

Fig 8.9 On/Off logic.

Switch	Lamp
0	0
1	1

Fig 8.10 Truth table for circuit in Fig 8.9

The working of the more complicated circuit shown in Figure 8.11 can also be summarised in a truth table. Look at the truth table in Figure 8.12 and check it through.

L = Lamp   S = Switch

Fig 8.11 A more complicated circuit.

Switch			Lamp	
S_1	S_2	S_3	L_1	L_2
0	0	0	0	0
1	0	0	0	0
1	1	0	1	0
1	0	1	0	1
1	1	1	1	1

Fig 8.12 Truth table for a more complicated circuit.

+9V   +9V

A

B

0V   0V

Fig 8.13 Series logic with two switches.

Switch		Lamp
A	B	
0	0	0
1	0	0
0	1	0
1	1	1

Fig 8.14 Truth table for circuit in Fig 8.13.

As systems get more complicated they can be simplified by removal of the supply, with just two lines drawn to represent the positive (+) and negative (−) sides of the circuit. In these logic circuits the switch can be left on or off so that all possible connections can be made; Figure 8.13 is such a circuit.

A truth table can be produced, as before, to summarise possibilities for the circuit, as in Figure 8.14.

6 〉 LOGIC GATES

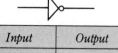

Input	Output
0	1
1	0

Fig 8.15 NOT-gate symbol and truth table.

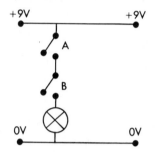

Fig 8.16 A simple AND-gate.

These are electronic 'gates' in a circuit which only allow an output signal in response to particular input situations. They are termed *gates* because they are either open (logic 1) or closed (logic 0). A gate is a piece of electronic circuitry which is described by the way its output will become logic HIGH = 1 when its input is changed. Three common gates are the 'NOT', the 'AND' and the 'OR'.

1 The NOT-gate is sometimes called an *inverter* because it does just that: a high = 1 input causes a low = 0 output and vice versa. Its symbol and truth table are shown in Figure 8.15.

2 The AND-gate has an output that goes high if both inputs are also high. A simple circuit, as in Figure 8.16, shows this: the lamp will only light when both switches are on.

  The symbol of the AND-gate and its truth tables are shown in Figure 8.17. Any system that gives this output is called AND. Remember, the output is high if both one input AND the other are high.

3 The OR-gate is called an 'OR' because the output goes high if either of the inputs goes high, as shown in Figure 8.18.

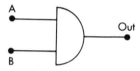

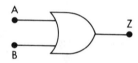

Input		Output
A	B	Z
0	0	0
1	0	0
0	1	0
1	1	1

Fig 8.17 AND-gate symbol and truth table.

Input		Output
A	B	Z
0	0	0
1	0	1
0	1	1
1	1	1

Fig 8.18 OR-gate symbol and truth table.

Two other gates often used are the NAND and the NOR (Figure 8.19).

Name of gate	Symbol	Truth table			Description
NAND		0	0	1	Opposite of *AND* gate
		0	1	1	
		1	0	1	
		1	1	0	
NOR		0	0	1	Opposite of *OR* gate. Output high if neither A *NOR* B is high
		0	1	0	
		1	0	0	
		1	1	0	

Fig 8.19 NAND and NOR-gates.

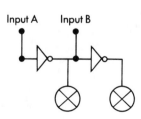

Fig 8.20 Two NOT-gates.

Once the function of a logic gate is known, it can be built into a circuit with others and be of practical use in electronics.

BISTABLE CIRCUITS

These may be built in a number of ways and their main feature is that whatever happens to the input, the output has only one of two stable states, which are achieved by feedback. In Figure 8.20, if input A is logic high and input B not connected, then indicator A is off and the B input is at logic 0. Similarly if input A is not connected and B is at logic 1, the output of B is at logic 0 and the input A is at logic 0.

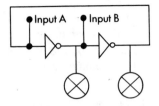

Fig 8.21 A bistable system.

In these circuits a connection between output and input *reinforces* information. If the output of B is fed back to the input of A, a *bistable* system is created (Figure 8.21).

Input A goes high, input B is not yet connected: output A goes low, output B goes high and reinforces (feedback) the high input to A. If the original connection to A is removed, the message is retained: the system has a memory.

Two NOR-gates can be used to produce a bistable latch (circuit inside the dashed box, Figure 8.22), which could be used as a burglar alarm activated by the burglar's flashlight beam. In this example only one of the two outputs is in use. If the switch is in the position shown, there is no output, whether the light dependent resistor (LDR) is illuminated or not. When the switch is up, the bell is activated when the light shines on the LDR and remains sounding until the switch is moved again. This is a 'latch' system, keeping one steady desired state.

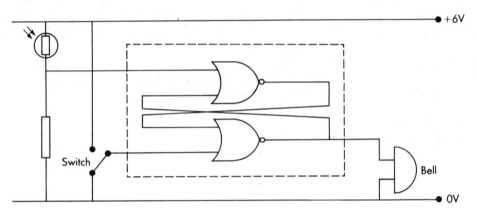

Fig 8.22 A bistable latch burglar alarm.

EXAMINATION QUESTIONS

MULTIPLE CHOICE

QUESTION 1

Which part of the control system in an electric oven is the actuator?

A the control knobs   C the thermostat
B the on/off switch   D the heating element

QUESTION 2

Which part of the body detects the temperature of the blood?

A the brain   C the kidneys
B the heart   D the skin

QUESTION 3

The diagram below shows a circuit activated by low light intensity.

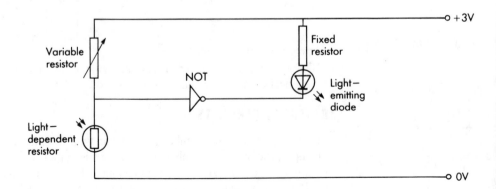

Which component detects a change in light intensity?
A light dependent resistor   C NOT-gate
B light emitting diode   D variable resistor

QUESTION 4

The diagram below shows a thermistor in a circuit.

Which of the following describes the purpose of this circuit?
A   to switch on the buzzer if the temperature falls
B   to switch on the buzzer if the light intensity increases
C   to switch on the buzzer if the temperature rises
D   to make the buzzer go on and off

STRUCTURED QUESTIONS

QUESTION 5

An alarm system, installed near a nuclear reactor, is set off if the light intensity or temperature increases above a certain level. The system used is shown below.

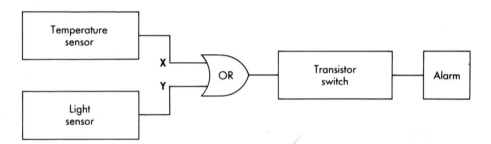

a) Name **one** electronic device which may be used in this system to sense a change in

   i) temperature ___Thermistor___

   ii) light intensity ___high Dependent Resistor___   (1)
                                                                                            (1)

b) Complete the truth table
    for the OR-gate.

Inputs		Output
X	**Y**	
0	0	0
0	1	1
1	0	1
1	1	1

(3)
(MEG; 1988)

QUESTION 6

a) A thermostat can be used to control a system. Figure 1 shows how a bimetallic strip can be used in a simple fire alarm.

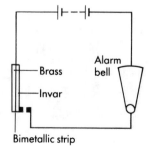

Fig 1

   i) Explain fully how a fire would cause the alarm to sound. (5 lines available)   (4)
   ___heat strip and send current to buzzer___

   ii) State **two** ways in which the thermostat could be altered to sound the alarm at a lower temperature.

   1 _____
                                                                                            (1)

   2 _____
                                                                                            (1)

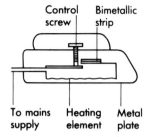

Control   Bimetallic
screw   strip

To mains   Heating   Metal
supply   element   plate

b) In an electric iron it is important to be able to set the temperature of the iron, which should then remain constant.

Describe how the working temperature of the iron is:

i) set _By altering Bimetallic strip_
Mains Supply

(2)

ii) kept constant _Control Screw:_

(2)

c) The graph shows the temperature of an iron varied with time after the iron is switched on.

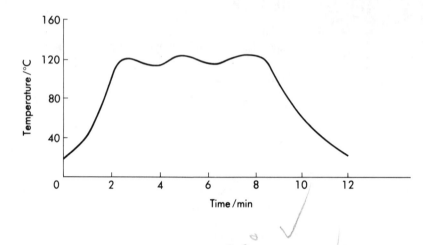

i) What was the room temperature? _20°_ ✓

(1)

ii) To what temperature was the iron set? _120°_ ✓

(1)

iii) Explain why the temperature of the iron does not remain exactly constant.
because more heat is created when
pressure is put on.

(2)

(Total marks 14)
(LEAG; Specimen)

QUESTION 7

a) The circuit in Figure (a) contains two switches, A and B, which can be either open or closed. Figure (b) is a truth table for the circuit. It shows what will happen to the lamp when the switches are in different positions.
  i) Complete the truth table for the circuit.
  ii) State in words the condition for the lamp to be lit. (1 line)

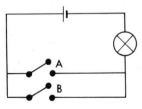

Switch A	Switch B	Lamp ON or OFF
Open	Open	OFF
Closed	Open	ON
Open	Closed	ON
Closed	Closed	ON

Figure (a)   Figure (b)

b) The truth table in Figure (c) refers to a certain two-input logic gate.

Input		Output
A	B	
0	0	0
0	1	1
1	0	1
1	1	1

Figure (c)

i) What logic gate is indicated by this table?
ii) Draw a symbol representing this logic gate.

c) A circuit is to be designed so that a bell will ring if a push switch is operated, but only if there is also an input from a light sensor, a heat sensor, or both. These requirements can be summarised in the table in Figure (d).

Push switch	Light sensor	Heat sensor	Output
0	0	0	0
0			0
0			0
0			0
1	0	0	0
1			
1			
1			

Figure (d)

i) Complete the table.
ii) This result can be achieved by using two two-input logic gates between the switch and sensors and the bell. Show how this can be done completing the lines below.

From push switch _____

From light sensor _____ to bell.

From heat sensor _____

(NISEC; 1988)

ANSWERS TO EXAMINATION QUESTIONS

ANSWER 1

Key D. The actuator is the part of the control system which brings about the correction; in this example it is the heating element.

ANSWER 2

Key A, the brain, detects the temperature of the blood. The skin detects the external temperature.

ANSWER 3

Key A, the LDR. The resistance of the LDR falls as more light falls on it.

ANSWER 4

Key C. The resistance of the thermistor falls as the temperature rises and so switches on the buzzer.

STRUCTURED QUESTIONS

ANSWER 5

a) i) a thermistor
   ii) a light dependent resistor
b) the output should be 0
                                1
                                1
                                1

ANSWER 6

a) i) When the bimetal strip becomes hot the brass expands about twenty times as much as the invar, so the strip bends and pushes the strip towards the two contacts. When the contacts close the current flows to the alarm bell, which rings.
   ii) 1 Make the contacts closer together
      2 Use thinner metal in the bimetallic strip
b) i) The control screw closes the circuit and adjusts the position of the contacts so that when the iron reaches the required temperature the bimetallic strip bends away from the contact and breaks the circuit.
   ii) The strip now cools and straightens and so the circuit is closed again.
c) i) 20°C
   ii) 120°C
   iii) When the iron reaches just above its required temperature, the bimetal strip bends and breaks the circuit. The iron cools down to just below the set temperature before the strip makes contact again.

ANSWER 7

a) i) See Figure (i).

Switch A	Switch B	Lamp
Open	Open	Off
Closed	Open	On
Open	Closed	On
Closed	Closed	On

Figure (i)

   ii) The lamp is ON if either A or B or both are closed (an OR-gate).
b) i) The table represents an OR-gate.
   ii) See Figure (ii).

Figure (ii)

c) i) See Figure (iii).
   ii) See Figure (iv). The system needs to link the heat and light sensors with an OR-gate. The output combines with the push through an AND-gate.

Push switch	Light sensor	Heat sensor	Output
0	0	0	0
0	1	0	0
0	0	1	0
0	1	1	0
1	0	0	0
1	1	0	1
1	0	1	1
1	1	1	1

Figure (iii)

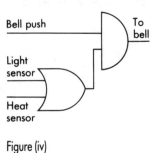

Figure (iv)

A STUDENT'S ANSWER WITH EXAMINER'S COMMENTS

Figure 1 is a diagram of a kidney tubule (nephron) and surrounding blood vessels.

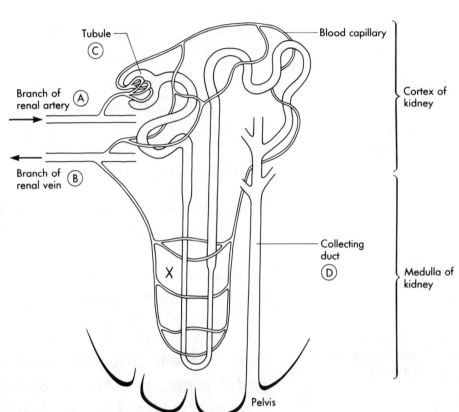

> 66 Anti-diurectic hormone (ADH) affects the kidney tubule. 99

Figure 1

Adapted from *Biology – A course to 16+* by G. Jones and M.Jones (1984), by kind permission of Cambridge University Press.

a) Samples of fluids were taken from **A**, **B**, **C** and **D** shown in the diagram above. Table 1 shows the relative amounts of protein, glucose, salt, water, oxygen and carbon found in each sample.

Table 1

Sample No.	Water	Protein	Glucose	Salt	Oxygen	Carbon dioxide
1	70%	High	High	High	High	Low
2	95%	None	None	Medium	Very low	Very low
3	70%	High	High	High	Low	High
4	98%	None	High	High	Very low	Very low

i) Identify which sample came from each of the points **A**, **B**, **C** and **D**.

Sample 1 came from point __A__ ✓

Sample 2 came from point __D__ ✓

Sample 3 came from point __B__ ✓

Sample 4 came from point __C__ ✓   *(4)*

> 66 Good. High oxygen in artery. No glucose in urine. 99

ii) On the diagram, label a point X where the hormone ADH acts to control water balance.   *(1)*

b) Sara's kidneys do not work. She has to go on a 'kidney dialysis' machine twice a week. This machine does a job similar to normal kidneys.

i) Explain why it is important in between dialysis sessions that she:

1 does not drink a lot of water

the kidneys filter a lot of water normally so if they don't work she shouldn't drink.

2 eats no added salt

the kidneys normally reabsorb salt into the blood.

3 does not eat a lot of protein

the kidneys remove protein from the blood as urea.

(6)

ii) Why is she able to eat as many salty things as she likes while she is on the machine?

because the machine does the work of the kidney.

(1)

c) The kidney is an example of a control system.

i) Explain how **feedback** is used in the control of water balance in the human body. (You may draw diagrams.)

The brain detects the water in the blood and sends a message to a gland to realease ADH. If the blood does not have much water in it then a lot of ADH is produced so the kidneys remove only a little water from the blood. If there is a lot of water in the blood then less ADH is produced and more water is removed.

BRAIN ⟶ GLAND ADH ⟶ KIDNEY ⟶ VARIABLE WATER IN BLOOD

FEEDBACK

(5)

ii) Explain how feedback mechanisms are used to control the petrol level in the carburettor of a car. (You may draw diagrams.)

The level of petrol goes down and the petrol goes into the tank.

The petrol fills up the tank then no more gets in. The information is being fed back to the valve about the level of petrol.

(5)

(22 marks)
(LEAG; 1988)

Good. This is quite a difficult point.

Yes. They remove urea not protein.

Good. The brain is the sensor. The pituitary gland is the actuator.

Good.

Yes. A valve is opened here as a float goes down.

Good. Again state 'The valve is closed by a float in the tank.'

Good point.

More marks could be gained here by using the language of control systems. The *petrol level* is the *controlled variable*. The *float* is the *sensor*. The *petrol pump* is the *actuator*. The *valve* is the *comparator* which registers a difference.

THE HUMAN BODY

GETTING STARTED

Taking responsibility for your own body, for what you eat, and for how fit you are, is an important part of your everyday living. If you have a basic understanding about how your body works, you will be more able to understand the importance of a balanced diet, regular exercise and relaxation, and the need to avoid cigarette smoking, excessive alcohol and dangerous drugs. In this chapter we look at the basic structure of your body, and then consider nutrition, circulation and respiration in more detail.

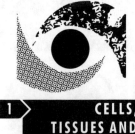

ESSENTIAL PRINCIPLES

1 CELLS, TISSUES AND ORGANS

Your body is made of about 50 million million tiny *cells*, which can be thought of as the building blocks of your body. The cells carry out a variety of different functions: for example, red blood cells carry oxygen around your body to the muscle cells; nerve cells transmit impulses from sense organs to the brain.

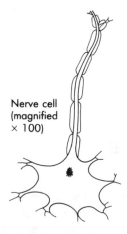
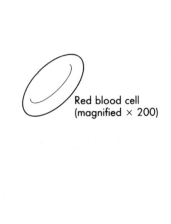

Nerve cell (magnified × 100)

Red blood cell (magnified × 200)

Fig 9.1 Two different cells in your body.

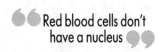

Red blood cells don't have a nucleus

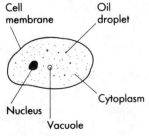

Fig 9.2 A typical cell showing cell structure.

Every cell, except the red blood cells, has a *nucleus* which controls the cell's activities and contains the chromosomes, the site of the genetic information of the cell. The nucleus is surrounded by *cytoplasm* which is surrounded by a *cell membrane*.

Most of the cells in your body are grouped together to form *tissues*, so that they work more effectively. For example, the large muscle in your upper arm, the biceps muscle, is a group of millions of tiny muscle cells which contract and relax so that you can raise and lower your arm.

When different tissues join together, they form *organs*, which make up the seven main systems in your body. The hierarchy of structures in your body is as follows:

cells → tissues → organs → organ systems

The seven main *systems* in your body are:

1 The *circulatory system*, which carries oxygen, glucose and amino acids to every cell, and carries waste products such as urea and carbon dioxide away from the cells.
2 The *respiratory system*, which takes in oxygen and removes carbon dioxide.
3 The *digestive system*, which breaks down and absorbs the food taken into your body.
4 The *excretory system*, which removes unwanted, harmful waste produced by your body, such as urea produced by the liver and removed by your kidneys.
5 The *skeletal system*, which protects and supports your organs and muscles, and enables your muscles to move your body.
6 The *nervous system*, which controls all the organs in your body and enables you to respond to the information received by sensory cells in your body.
7 The *reproductive system*, which enables you to make eggs or sperm so that you can pass on genetic information to create the next generation.

2 NUTRITION

The cells in your body are made from many different elements, such as carbon, hydrogen, oxygen, nitrogen, sulphur and phosphorous. Plants and animals obtain these elements from their environment in different ways: by photosynthesis and by absorbing minerals from the soil in the case of plants; by eating plants or other animals in the case of animals.

A BALANCED DIET

Human beings require a *balanced diet*, which should include some of each of the seven main types of food shown in the chart below:

Type of food	Reason		Source
Carbohydrate	glucose, sucrose } for energy starch		jams, sweets, bread, potato
Protein	amino acids – for growth and repair of cells		meat, cheese
Fats	fatty acids – storage and energy		butter, oils
Vitamins	A, B, C, D – good health		fresh vegetables and fruit
Minerals	eg iron, calcium – good health		fruit, green vegetables
Roughage	to help bowel movement		vegetables
Water	for all the reactions in the body		fruit and vegetables

Your daily dietary requirements will vary according to age, pregnancy, illness, and how active a person you are. For example, if you do a lot of exercise you will use up a lot of energy and will need more carbohydrate and fats which can be broken down to supply energy to your muscle cells. A young person who is still growing will need more protein than an adult who has stopped growing, to supply amino acids for the growth of extra body cells to make more tissues and muscles.

Deficiencies

Many people in under-developed countries suffer from a *lack* of one or more of the different types of food from their daily diet. For example, a *lack of protein* causes a disease called *kwashiorkor* and children are unable to grow and develop properly. A lack of *vitamin A* causes 250 000 children to go *blind* every year, and many more children suffer severe eye problems. A lack of *iodine* in the diet causes many children in less developed countries to suffer *mental retardation*.

DIGESTION

> Some students find digestion confusing, but it's going on inside you most of the time! Remember, digestion is just breaking down food molecules

The food which you eat contains large molecules which have to be *broken down* into smaller molecules so that they can pass through the wall of your gut into your bloodstream. The process of breaking down the large molecules is described as 'digestion'. In your body you make chemical catalysts, called *enzymes*, which speed up the rate of breakdown of your food.

1. The process of digestion starts in your *mouth* when your teeth crush and chew the food, which is mixed with *saliva*. The saliva contains an enzyme called *amylase* which starts to break down or digest the large molecules of starch.

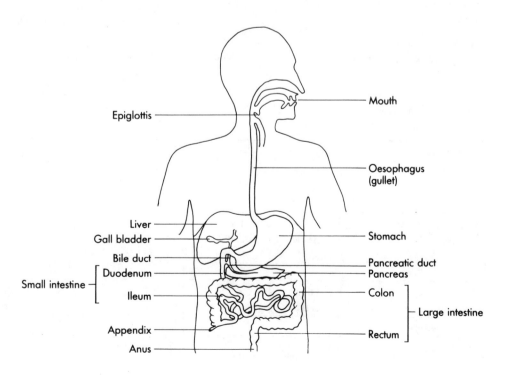

Fig 9.3 The human digestive system.

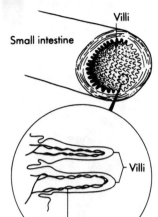

Fig 9.4 The villi in the small intestine increase the area for absorption.

2. The food is then swallowed and goes to your *stomach* for about 3 or 4 hours. The stomach lining secretes a dilute acid to create an acidic environment so that the enzyme *pepsin* can break down the large protein molecules into smaller molecules.

3. The partly digested food is then passed into the next part of the gut, the *small intestine*, where enzymes from the *pancreas* continue the process of digestion. The starch is eventually converted into the small molecules of glucose, the protein is broken down into amino acids, and the fats are broken down into fatty acids.

4. The small molecules are then absorbed through the *lining of the gut* into the bloodstream.

5. The undigested food and other waste products then pass into the *large intestine*, where water is absorbed and faeces are formed.

6. The faeces then pass out of the body through the *rectum* and *anus*.

Eating a good amount of fibre or roughage in your diet each day helps you to pass faeces out of your body at regular intervals. If you do not eat sufficient fibre in your diet, then you become constipated and it is difficult to pass the faeces out of your body.

3 ❯ ENERGY FROM FOOD

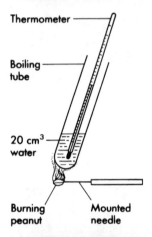

The blood system carries the small molecules of glucose and amino acids, together with oxygen, to every cell in your body. A chemical process called *respiration* takes place in the cells to release the energy from the food.

food + oxygen → carbon dioxide + water + energy

The carbon dioxide and water are carried by the blood to your lungs and breathed out. The energy is used by your cells for the various functions of the cells. Muscle cells need energy for contraction, gut cells need energy for secretion and absorption.

You may have investigated the energy released from different foods by letting them burn under a measured volume of water, and measuring the change in temperature, as shown in Figure 9.5.

Fig 9.5 Finding out how much energy is released when a peanut is burned.

4 ❯ THE BLOOD SYSTEM, ARTERIES AND VEINS

The blood is like a transport system which carries many substances such as glucose, oxygen, carbon dioxide, hormones, and urea to and from every cell of your body. The blood flows in a series of tubes or blood vessels called *arteries* and *veins*, which divide into very small blood vessels called *capillaries*.

Fig 9.6a) The arteries have much thicker walls than the veins.

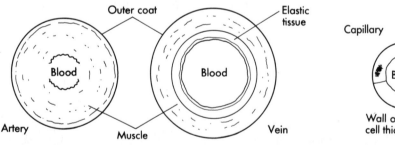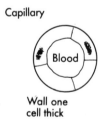

Fig 9.6b) This chart compares arteries, veins and capillaries.

Comparison	Artery	Vein	Capillary
Internal (lumen) diameter	Fairly narrow; can expand (= pulse)	Fairly wide.	Very narrow; red blood cells squeeze through.
Wall structure	The wall is relatively thick and also elastic, to withstand pressure.	The wall is relatively thin; there are valves to keep blood moving in one direction.	Wall is composed of a single cell layer; gaps between cells allow exchange of materials with surrounding tissues.
Blood direction	Blood flows away from the heart.	Blood flows towards the heart.	Blood flows from arteries to veins.
Blood pressure	High.	Low.	Very low.
Blood flow rate	Rapid, irregular.	Slow, regular.	Very slow.

Arteries have thick muscular walls, as they carry blood *away* from the heart under pressure. *Veins* have much thinner walls, and possess valves to help the blood to flow one way *towards* the heart. The blood in the veins is at a lower pressure than blood in the arteries, and the muscles of your arms and legs help to squeeze the blood back to the heart.

HOW OXYGEN AND FOOD REACH THE CELLS

1 Oxygen and food molecules diffuse out of the blood into the tissue fluid which surrounds every cell.
2 These substances then diffuse into the cell.
3 Waste products diffuse out of the cell into the tissue fluid and into the blood, to be carried away from the cells to the excretory organs.

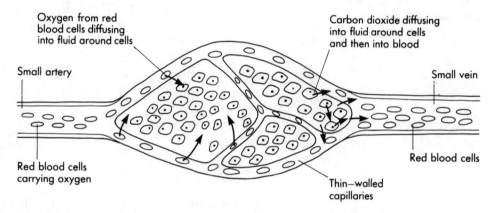

Fig 9.7 Oxygen diffuses into the

5 ❯ **RED AND WHITE BLOOD CELLS**

There are about 25 million million *red* blood cells in your body; their job is to carry oxygen from the blood capillaries around the lungs, to the body cells.

There are about 20 million *white* blood cells, whose function it is to protect the body against disease. Some of the white blood cells produce antibodies which kill bacteria, while others destroy bacteria by engulfing them.

Fig 9.8 White blood cells engulf and destroy bacteria in your body.

6 ❯ **THE HEART**

The heart is basically two muscular pumps which work side by side. Each side is divided into two chambers, an *upper atrium* and a *lower ventricle*. The *right atrium* takes in deoxygenated blood which has been round the body, and the *right ventricle* pumps the blood to the lungs, via the pulmonary artery. The *left atrium* takes in oxygenated blood from the lungs, via the pulmonary vein, and the more muscular *left ventricle* pumps the blood under great pressure around the body, via the aorta, the thick-walled main artery.

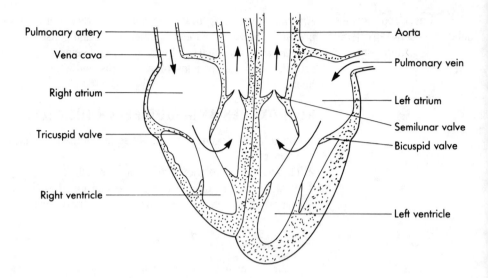

Fig 9.9a) The heart is a powerful pump which pumps blood round the body and to the lungs.

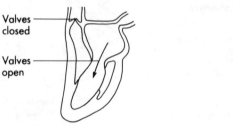

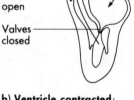

Fig 9.9b) The heart in action.

a) **Ventricle relaxed**: blood is forced from the atrium into the ventricle. Valves prevent blood flowing 'backwards'

b) **Ventricle contracted**: blood is forced from the ventricle and out of the heart. The atrium meanwhile re-fills with more blood

---

7 > BREATHING

> Large molecules are broken down to smaller molecules

At rest you are breathing about 15 times a minute. If you put your hands over your ribs and take a deep breath you can feel your chest cavity getting larger as you breathe in. The *intercostal* muscles, between your ribs, contract to pull your ribs up and out and the *diaphragm* muscle at the base of your chest flattens so that your chest cavity is made larger. Air outside your chest cavity is at greater pressure than air inside your chest, and this difference in pressure causes air to rush into your lungs.

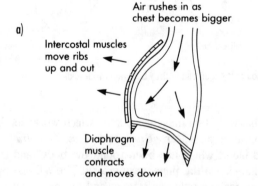

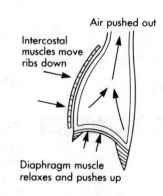

Fig 9.10 a) Breathing in.
b) Breathing out.

Your lungs are basically two sponge-like structures in your chest which fill up with air. Oxygen diffuses over the moist surface of the air sacs or *alveoli*, from the air into the blood in the capillaries, where it combines with haemoglobin in the red blood cells, to make a new substance called *oxyhaemoglobin*. The blood is pumped by the heart muscle to the rest of the body through arteries and eventually capillaries. The oxygen diffuses into your cells, and carbon dioxide from the cells diffuses into your blood and is carried back to the lungs. The intercostal muscles and diaphragm make your chest cavity smaller, therefore increasing the pressure in the lungs, so the air is pushed out.

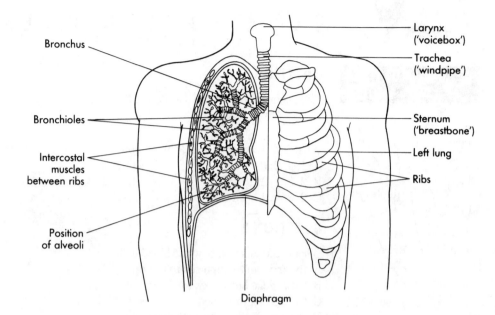

Fig 9.11 The human chest cavity.

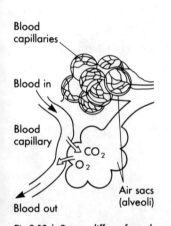

Fig 9.12a) Oxygen diffuses from the air sacs into your blood stream.

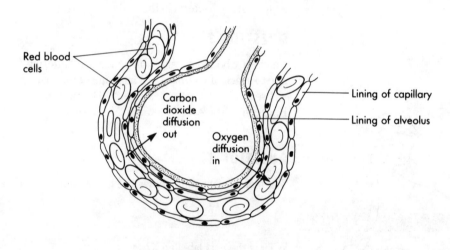

Fig 9.12b) Inside one alveolus.

8 > **THE EFFECT OF EXERCISE**

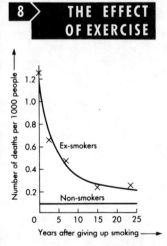

When your muscles are working harder during vigorous exercise they need more energy. Your heart rate increases to pump blood carrying glucose more quickly to your cells, and your rate of breathing increases so that more oxygen is taken in to release the energy from glucose. More carbon dioxide is produced which is removed by the increased rate of breathing.

People who are fit generally have a lower heart rate and therefore a lower pulse rate than people who are unfit, because exercise develops the heart muscle, just like any other muscle. Fit people and non-smokers get back to their resting pulse rate more quickly than unfit people and smokers. Regular exercise, eating a good, well-balanced diet without too much fat, and not smoking, can reduce the risk of heart disease.

Fig 9.13 You reduce the risk of dying from lung cancer if you are a non-smoker.

❝Your heart muscle gets stronger with more exercise❞

EXAMINATION QUESTIONS

MULTIPLE CHOICE

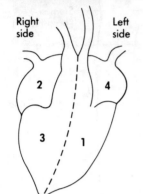

Right side

Left side

QUESTION 1

The diagram below shows a section through the heart.

What is the correct order of blood flow from the vena cava to the aorta?

A 1, 4, 2, 3   D 3, 2, 4, 1
B 2, 3, 1, 4   E 4, 1, 3, 2
C 2, 3, 4, 1

QUESTION 2

What is the function of white blood cells?
A to carry nerve impulses to the brain
B to produce hormones to clot the blood
C to help clot the blood
D to transport oxygen to the cells
E to destroy bacteria in the body

QUESTION 3

Children who have very soft bones are suffering from a deficiency disease called rickets, due to a lack of vitamin D. Which one of the following is a good source of vitamin D?

A bread   D oranges
B green cabbage   E sugar
C jam

QUESTION 4

The diagram opposite shows the human gut.

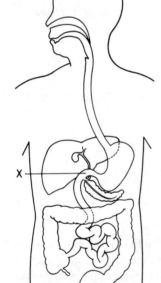

What is the part labelled X?
A the duodenum
B the ileum
C the large intestine
D the stomach
E the pancreas

QUESTION 5

In which part of the gut does the digestion of protein start?
A the mouth   D the small intestine
B the food tube   E the large intestine
C the stomach

QUESTION 6

What is the function of the excretory system?
A to break down food which you eat
B to get rid of undigested food from your body
C to remove harmful waste produced by your body
D to control all the organs in your body
E to take in oxygen and transport it to the cells

QUESTION 7

Which of the following is used for growth and repair of cells?
A starch   D proteins
B fats   E roughage
C minerals

QUESTION 8

The diagram below shows the chest cavity.

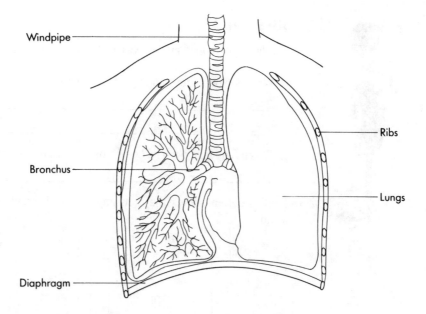

Windpipe

Ribs

Bronchus

Lungs

Diaphragm

Which one of the following contracts when you breathe in?

A bronchus   D ribs
B diaphragm   E windpipe
C lungs

STRUCTURED QUESTIONS

QUESTION 9

The label below shows the composition of a well-known breakfast cereal. Study the label and answer the questions which follow.   *(2)*

	Per 100g		Per 100g
Energy	1400kJ	Dietary Fibre	12.9g
		Vitamins:	
Protein	10.5g	Niacin	10.0mg
Fat	2.0g	Riboflavin (B₂)	1.0mg
Available		Thiamin (B₁)	0.7mg
Carbohydrate	66.8g	Iron	6.0mg

a) Which two food groups are carbohydrates?

   i) _____

   ii) _____

b) What use does the body make of   *(4)*

   i) carbohydrates _____

   ii) proteins? _____

c) The cereal supplies 1400 kJ of energy per 100 g; what does kJ stand for?   *(1)*

   _____

d) What is the total mass of vitamins the cereal contains per 100 g?   *(2)*

   _____ mg

e) To which food group does iron belong?   *(1)*

   _____

f) Which food group supplies dietary fibre?   *(1)*

_____

(NISEC; Specimen)

QUESTION 10

The illustration opposite shows a child suffering from malnutrition.

a) What do you understand by malnutrition?   *(2)*

_____

_____

b) Which food group would be of most benefit to the child shown in the picture?   *(1)*

_____

The histogram shows the consumption of different types of food in three areas of the world.

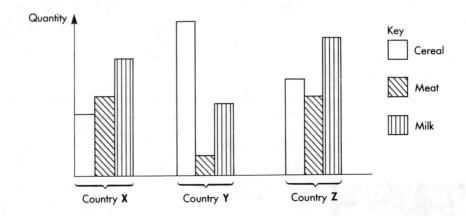

c) From the data given, from which country do you think it is likely that the child comes?
                                                                              (2)

_____

(NISEC; Specimen)

QUESTION 11

a) *Scurvy*, *rickets* and *anaemia* are illnesses which can affect different parts of the body. Match these illnesses to the part of the body they most affect:

   Part of body   *Illness it can be affected by*

   i) Bones   _____

   ii) Blood   _____

   iii) Skin   _____
                                                                              (3)

b) Each illness listed in (a) is caused by a particular substance missing from the diet. Name the substance and state **one** food which contains the substance.

Illness	Substance missing from diet	**One** food which contains missing substance
i) scurvy		
ii) rickets		
iii) anaemia		

                                                                              (3)
(WJEC; 1988)

QUESTION 12

A pupil was provided with samples of the following foods: starch, fat, sugar and protein.

The pupil selected **one** of these foods and placed equal amounts of it in each of three test tubes containing an enzyme in solution.

One test tube was kept at 10°C, one at 37°C, and the third was heated until the contents boiled.

A sample was removed from each test tube at intervals and tested for the presence of sugar.

The results are shown in the table below.

Test tube	Amount of sugar present			
	at 0 min	*after 5 min*	*after 10 min*	*after 20 min*
1	none	a little	a lot	a lot
2	none	none	a little	a lot
3	none	none	none	none

a) Which **one** of the following foods was placed in each of the three test tubes: starch, fat, sugar, protein?

_____

b) Name the enzyme which was present. _____

c) Which test tube was kept at 10°C? _____

d) In which test tube had the enzyme been boiled?

_____

e) Which test tube was kept at 37°C? Give a reason for your answer.

_____

_____

(6)

(LEAG; Specimen)

QUESTION 13

The table below gives information about the food values of 100 grams (g) of a number of foods.

Food	Energy measured in kilojoules (kJ)	Fat measured in grams (g)	Protein measured in grams (g)	Carbohydrate measured in grams (g)	Calcium measured in milligrams (mg)	Iron measured in milligrams (mg)
potato	370	0.0	2.0	21.0	7.0	0.7
fish	300	0.7	16.0	0.0	32.0	1.1
butter	3340	85.0	0.4	0.0	14.0	0.0
rice	1500	1.0	6.0	86.0	4.0	0.4
sugar	1620	0.0	0.0	100.0	0.0	0.0
soya	1810	24.0	40.0	13.0	210.0	7.0
orange	150	0.0	0.7	8.0	42.0	4.0
meat	1600	20.0	15.0	6.0	40.0	0.6

a) i) Which food listed in the table has the most fat?

_____

(1)

ii) Which food listed in the table only gives energy?

_____

(1)

iii) Suggest **one** food in the table which nearly gives a balanced diet. Explain your answer.

Food _____

(1)

Explanation _____

_____

_____

(2)

iv) Name **one** other important group of substances needed for a healthy diet which has been left out of the table.

_____

(1)

b) i) What pattern can you see between the fat content and the energy given by butter, rice, soya and meat?

_____

_____

_____

(2)

ii) Suggest **one** other food listed in the table which does not fit your pattern.

_____

(1)

c) Choose the **two** foods from the table which are most unsuitable for slimmers. Explain your answers.

Food 1 _____

(1)

Explanation _____

_____

(1)

Food 2 _____

(1)

Explanation _____

_____

(1)

d) Suggest **two** reasons why soya is now replacing meat.

Reason 1 _____

_____

(1)

Reason 2 _____

_____

(1)

e) Various forms of single-cell protein (SCP) are now being made and used instead of more usual food materials. *Mycoprotein* is an example. It is made from a fungus which is grown on glucose solution. The fungus grows as fibres that smell faintly of mushrooms. The length and texture of the fibres depend on their growing time. Mycoprotein can be dried to a powder or made to look and taste like chicken, fish or beef. It contains all the nutrients in beef but more fibre.

i) Suggest **two** reasons why foods such as these are being made.

Reason 1 _____

_____

(2)

Reason 2 _____

_____

(2)

ii) Suggest **two** problems which the makers will have to overcome if such food substitutes are to be accepted.

Problem 1 _____

_____

(1)

Problem 2 _____

_____

(1)
(LEAG; 1988)

QUESTION 14

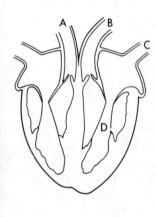

a) The figure alongside is a diagram of the heart.
Identify each of the four regions marked A, B, C and D.
i) left ventricle; ii) aorta; iii) pulmonary vein; iv) pulmonary artery. *(2)*

b) *Underline* the correct word in the following statements:
i) Arteries carry blood to/from the heart. *(1)*
ii) The blood vessels entering and leaving the heart on the right-hand side carry much/little oxygen. *(1)*

c) Explain why arteries have thicker walls than veins.

_____

_____

(1)

d) State the changes that take place in the blood as it passes through the lungs.
(4 lines available)

(2)
(WJEC; Specimen)

QUESTION 15

A simplified diagram of the heart, lungs and circulation system is shown below. The arrows show the direction of circulation.

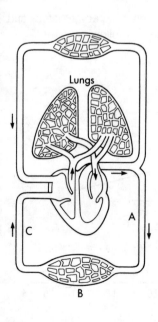

a) The three types of blood vessel labelled all vary in size, have different thickness of walls and in one case need valves along their length. With the help of diagrams, compare the blood vessels at points A, B and C.

A:

B:

C:

(6)

b) i) Using the previous diagram, explain how the heart works as a double pump to circulate blood round the body and also round the lungs. (4 lines available)

ii) Besides blood cells and plasma, what other materials would you expect to find in a sample of blood? (3 lines available) *(7)*

c) Doctors in Britain are increasingly concerned by the number of deaths from heart disease.

   i) How can exercise and a sensible diet help prevent heart disease? (5 lines available)

  ii) Discuss the evidence which indicates cigarette smoking is harmful. (7 lines available)

(7)

(Total marks 20)

(LEAG; Specimen)

QUESTION 16

The graph shows a person's breathing rate and volume of breathing at the start of a race, during the race and after the race. The following questions relate to this graph.

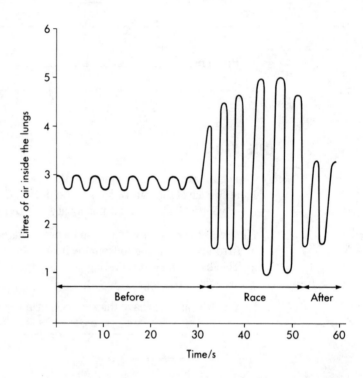

a) i) What was the maximum amount of air inside the athlete's lungs during the race?   *(1)*

  ii) What was the athlete's breathing rate per minute before the race started?

_____

(2)

Study the graph showing the pulse rates of a trained athlete, and of a person before and after starting to take regular exercise, and answer the questions that follow.

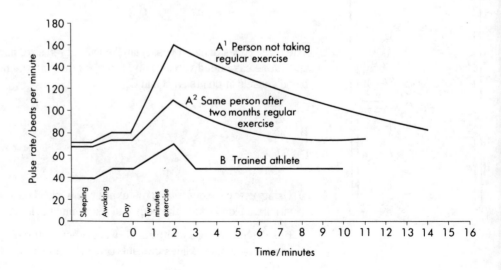

b) i) What is the difference between the sleeping pulse rates of A^1 and B?

_____

(1)

ii) What is the difference between the recovery times of A^1 and A^2?

_____

(2)

c) The illustration opposite shows two people who are very much overweight. They are said to be suffering from obesity.

i) Give **two** dangers to health that might follow from obesity.

1 _____

_____

2 _____

_____

(2)

ii) State one precaution other than exercise which might be taken to avoid obesity.

_____

_____

(1)
(NISEC; Specimen)

ANSWERS TO EXAMINATION QUESTIONS

MULTIPLE CHOICE

ANSWER 1

Key C. The vena cava brings blood from the body to the right atrium (2), and the blood is pumped to the lungs from the right ventricle (3), returning from the lungs via the left atrium (4) and then to the left ventricle (1).

ANSWER 2

Key E. Option D is a function of red blood cells. Option C, platelets, help to clot the blood.

ANSWER 3

Key B. All green vegetables are a good source of vitamins, especially vitamin D. Option D, oranges, are a good source of vitamin C.

ANSWER 4

Key A, the duodenum, the first part of the small intestine.

ANSWER 5

Key C, the stomach. The digestion of starch starts in the mouth, option A.

ANSWER 6

Key C. Be careful of option B, which is a function of the digestive system. Excretion is about removing waste produced by your body.

ANSWER 7

Key D, proteins. Option A, starch, and option B, fats, are used for energy.

ANSWER 8

Key B, diaphragm. Lungs have no muscle and do not contract, and ribs are moved by intercostal muscles.

ANSWER 9

a) i) sugar, (ii) starch,
b) i) to provide energy   ii) to build new cells for growth and repair
c) kilojoules
d) 11.7 mg
e) minerals
f) carbohydrate

ANSWER 10

a) lack of a balanced diet; all seven types of food must be eaten
b) protein
c) country Y

ANSWER 11

a) i) rickets   b) i) vitamin C, citrus fruit
   ii) anaemia   ii) vitamin D, green vegetables
   iii) scurvy   iii) iron, liver

ANSWER 12

a) starch
b) amylase
c) tube 2
d) tube 3
e) tube 1. Reason – the enzyme converted the starch to sugar after 10 minutes. Digestive enzymes work best at body temperature, 37°C.

ANSWER 13

a) i) butter
   ii) sugar
   iii) food – soya. Explanation – contains a proportion of all food types and is a good source of fat, protein, calcium and iron.
   iv) roughage
b) i) There is a general pattern which links the fat content and energy value of three of the four foods. The higher the fat, the greater the energy value. Butter has the highest amount of fat, and the highest energy value. Meat and soya have less than half the energy value of butter and only a quarter of the fat. Rice has less than half the energy value of butter and little fat.
   ii) Sugar has half the energy value of butter and contains no fat.
c) Food 1 – sugar. Explanation – contains a lot of carbohydrate, which produces a lot of energy which has to be used up.
   Food 2 – butter. Explanation – contains a lot of fat, which is stored in the body if not used up.
d) Reason 1 – soya is a plant, and it is more efficient to obtain food at the beginning of the food chain, as less energy has been lost.
   Reason 2 – soya is a better source of protein and calcium than meat, and many people are concerned about killing animals for meat.
e) i) Reason 1 – to provide a good source of protein and fibre for many more people than could be supplied with meat.
      Reason 2 – the food can be stored more easily than meat, as it can be dried and made into different types of meat as necessary.
   ii) Problem 1 – people will need to be convinced that the food substitute contains all the nutrients which were in meat.
      Problem 2 – the food will have to look and taste just like the meat it is replacing for it to be acceptable to meat eaters.

ANSWER 14

a) A pulmonary artery; B aorta; C pulmonary vein; D left ventricle.
b) i) Arteries carry blood *from* the heart.
   ii) The blood vessels entering and leaving the heart on the right side carry *little* oxygen.
c) The blood in arteries is under great pressure, so the artery walls are thicker.
d) The level of carbon dioxide in the blood is reduced as CO_2 diffuses into the air sacs. The level of oxygen in the blood is increased as O_2 diffuses into the blood.

ANSWER 15

a) A is an artery; B is a capillary; C is a vein.
b) i) The heart is divided by the septum, a thick wall which separates the blood going to the lungs from the blood going to the arteries. The ventricles on both sides contract at the same time. The right ventricle pumps blood to the lungs and the left ventricle pumps blood to the body.
   ii) water, salts, amino acids, urea, hormones, platelets.
c) i) exercise increases the efficiency of the heart in pumping blood around the body; a low fat diet reduces the risk of cholesterol building up and blocking the arteries.
   ii) Heavy smokers are more likely to die of heart disease than non-smokers, although the evidence is not conclusive; smoking reduces the oxygen-carrying capacity of the blood, and the heart has to work harder to pump the blood, so a heart attack is more likely.

ANSWER 16

a) i) 5 litres
   ii) 16 times per minute
b) i) 30
   ii) 6 minutes
c) i) 1 high blood pressure; 2 shorter life expectancy
   ii) balanced diet

A STUDENT'S ANSWER WITH EXAMINER'S COMMENTS

a) Give **two** functions of blood.

> Good, but include *to all cells* and *from cells* respectively.

   i) carry oxygen
   ii) remove carbon dioxide

(2)

b) Give the cause of

> Yes, but where? In coronary artery.

   i) coronary thrombosis a blood clot

(1)

> Good.

   ii) anaemia a lack of iron in the diet

(1)

c) Give **one** difference between a vein and an artery.

> Yes, but also state arteries do not.

   veins have valves

(1)

The following results were obtained in an investigation to find the relationship between heartbeat and exercise.

Time in minutes	0	1	2	3	4	5	6	7	8
Number of beats per minute	60	60	80	100	100	88	76	65	60

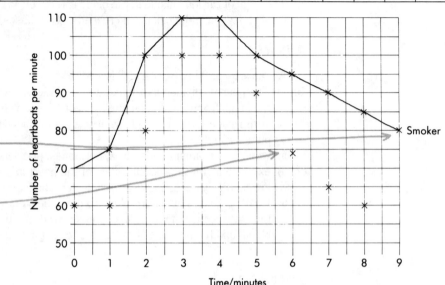

66 Good. This second graph is a line graph and you have followed the pattern of the first. 99

66 Good. 99

66 Error here. 73 should be 76. 99

66 Join points to show line. 99

d) On the graph paper above draw a *line graph* of the number of heartbeats per minute, plotted against time. (2)

e) Use your graph to answer the following questions.

i) Approximately when did the exercise start? between 1 and 2 minutes

ii) Approximately when did the exercise stop? between 4 to 5 minutes

66 Good answers. 99

iii) What was the heartbeat rate after 2½ minutes?

90 beats per minute

(1½)

f) i) Draw a second graph using the same axes to show the results that you would expect from a person 50 years of age who had been a heavy smoker through life. (1)

ii) Explain the graph you have drawn.

The pulse rate is higher as the heart works harder.
The pulse takes longer to get back to normal.

66 Well done. 99

(2)

g) Explain why regular exercise is considered to be good for the heart.

66 A bit vague; exercise develops the heart muscle. 99

to keep the person fit

(1)

h) Quite often people with breathing difficulties as a result of a heart attack are given pure oxygen. Give **one** reason for this.

66 Yes, the right idea here. 99

to get more oxygen into the blood.

(1)

(WJEC; 1988)

VARIATION, INHERITANCE AND EVOLUTION

GETTING STARTED

This chapter is all about 'changes' – and in today's world change is something we have all come to terms with; *new* models of familiar things appear every day! New cars, personal stereo players, compact discs and cameras keep appearing in the shops, all different in some way to those we have already, and tempting us to part with our money. It is now quite possible to imagine a machine which would behave much like a human, taking in energy, moving about and having enough artificial intelligence to make simple decisions and react appropriately to stimuli. What this machine, and the others listed above, would *not* be able to do is to *reproduce* – this is a unique characteristic of living things and so sets them apart from the machines we make.

Even more amazing is the way in which each generation of living things may be *different* from its parent generation. As we begin to understand the mechanisms of inheritance, this is no longer such a mystery, as we recognise that differences may simply be due to the reshuffling of *existing* genes and the creation of *new* ones by mutation. We think we can now explain how some 200 million different *species* of plants and animals have come into being on the Earth; according to the *theory of evolution*, organisms changed gradually from one generation to the next and, over many generations, new species have formed. To understand the *processes* that bring about evolution, it is essential to have an understanding of how living things *reproduce*, since this is the key to change.

ESSENTIAL PRINCIPLES

1 > REPRODUCTION

Reproduction is a characteristic of all living things. It may occur once, or many times, in an organism's lifetime. All life exists because previous generations have reproduced and the new individuals that survived have also reproduced. Because living things vary, they are not all equally well adapted to survive, so not all organisms which are born live long enough to reproduce. There seem to be many different *ways* of reproducing, but if we remove the details there are only two basic methods: *asexual* and *sexual.*

ASEXUAL REPRODUCTION

Asexual reproduction only involves one parent. This can be an advantage in that an isolated individual can reproduce on its own and produce offspring which are exact copies of the parent. If the parent is successful in coping with its environment, then it is important for the survival of the offspring that the parent's characteristics are passed on exactly. However, a lack of variation can cause problems if there is a sudden *change* in the environment – it may then be that none of the offspring will survive. A disease could destroy the whole population because there would be no resistant varieties.

> All the offspring are the same

Bacteria, yeasts and other single-celled organisms reproduce asexually by growing to a maximum size and then *dividing* into two smaller individuals. A single disease-causing bacterium could do this every twenty minutes, so that in only twenty-four hours some 4000 million bacteria would be produced, which could make you very ill indeed. Many different species of plants are able to reproduce asexually, and can also reproduce sexually, using whichever method is most advantageous for survival of the species.

Asexual reproduction in plants usually involves part of the plant becoming separated from the parent and developing into a new individual. Weeds in the garden do this when the gardener uses a mechanical cultivator, chopping up and replanting the weeds, thus accidentally increasing the weed problem. Gardeners are also able to grow new plants from their old favourites by taking cuttings, and to be sure that the new plants will be just like the original.

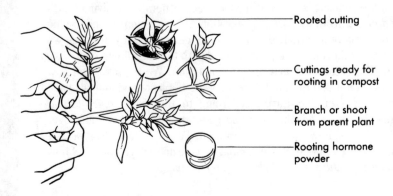

Rooted cutting

Cuttings ready for rooting in compost

Branch or shoot from parent plant

Rooting hormone powder

Fig 10.1 Cuttings being taken.

SEXUAL REPRODUCTION

> The offspring all differ from each other

Sexual reproduction usually involves two parents, although there are many organisms which have both female and male sex organs. Such plants and animals are called *hermaphrodites* and can make both male and female sex cells – these organisms usually exchange gametes with others of the same species. Common hermaphrodites include earthworms and buttercups.

Sexual reproduction always involves the fusion of two *gametes* – one male sex cell (sperm) and one female sex cell (egg). The new cell produced, the *zygote*, divides many times to form an *embryo* and eventually grows to become the young organism.

The first problem to be solved by organisms reproducing in this way is how to find a member of the opposite sex, and the second is how to get the sperm and egg together – both have been solved in many ways. In humans, fertilisation is *internal*, so the egg and sperm fuse inside the female's body. In frogs, fertilisation is *external*, with the sperm being shed over the eggs, which are laid in water. Usually offspring which are produced by internal fertilisation are better protected, as they develop either in an egg with a tough shell, or inside the mother, as in humans. The main advantage of sexual reproduction, as compared with asexual reproduction, is that the offspring will *vary* from each other and from the parents – variety can mean the difference between success or extinction for the species in a constantly changing environment.

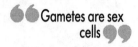

GAMETES

66 Gametes are sex cells 99

These special sex cells are *not* the result of the sort of cell division we call *mitosis*, like ordinary body cells. Cells produced by mitosis are identical to the parent cells, having exactly the same chromosomes.

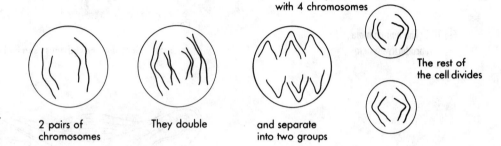

2 new cells, each with 4 chromosomes

The rest of the cell divides

Fig 10.2 Mitosis in a cell with four chromosomes.

2 pairs of chromosomes   They double   and separate into two groups

Gametes are produced by *meiosis*, or reduction division, which only happens in the sex organs. These new cells have *half* the number of chromosomes of the parent cell and so half of the information content. Two of these must fuse at fertilisation to produce the first normal cell of the offspring, one male and one female gamete. Female gametes are produced in the ovary, male gametes in a testis or stamen.

66 A zygote is a fertilised egg 99

At fertilisation, each gamete carries only one of each type of chromosome. When fusion has taken place the zygote has two full sets of chromosomes, which is normal for an ordinary body cell. An interesting outcome of meiosis is that all the gametes produced are different, but you would need to know much more about both meiosis and chromosomes to understand why.

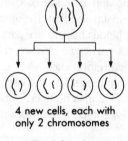

4 new cells, each with only 2 chromosomes

Fig 10.3 Meiosis in a cell with four chromosomes.

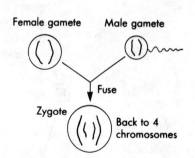

Female gamete   Male gamete

Fuse

Zygote

Back to 4 chromosomes

Fig 10.4 Fertilisation.

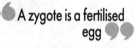

HUMAN REPRODUCTION

66 Sperm and egg join together to make a zygote 99

Male and female reproductive organs fit together during sexual intercourse in order to place the *sperm* (male gametes) well inside the female's body. Sperm are made in the testes and pass out of the male's body in a fluid (semen) through the penis during ejaculation. The sperm have only a short distance to swim to enter the uterus. They move across the uterus and travel along the fallopian tubes towards the ovaries. If there is an egg in the fallopian tube, *fertilisation* may take place. The fertilised egg travels to the uterus and embeds itself in the lining (endometrium). If fertilisation does not take place, the endometrium breaks down and is lost as part of the monthly menstrual cycle. Pregnancy (*gestation*) in humans is about 9 months; after birth, human offspring require a greal deal of parental care and attention.

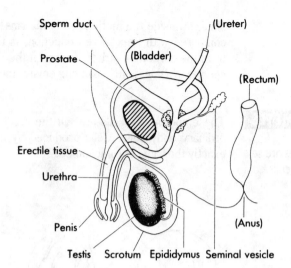

Fig 10.5 The human male
reproductive system.

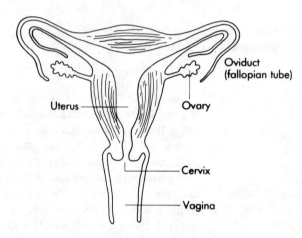

Fig 10.6 The human female
reproductive system.

4 ▷ CHROMOSOMES AND GENES

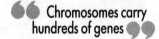
❝ Chromosomes carry
hundreds of genes ❞

Normal human body cells have 23 pairs of *chromosomes* in the nucleus, and every 23 pairs carries instructions for the whole human body. Each chromosome holds the information for many chemical reactions and is made of complex molecules of DNA (deoxyribonucleic acid). We believe, for instance, that the instructions for making the enzyme salivary amylase and the Rhesus blood antigens are part of the *same* chromosome.

The instructions for a particular characteristic, or trait, are called a *gene*. There are genes for all our characteristics such as eye colour, hair colour and blood type. Each chromosome carries many genes, each a certain length of DNA. We have two copies of each gene in every normal human body cell, one in each of a pair of chromosomes because we inherit one gene of each type – one from our father and one from our mother. These

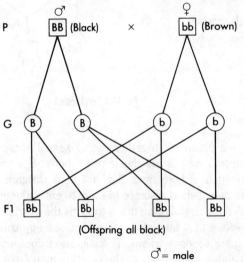

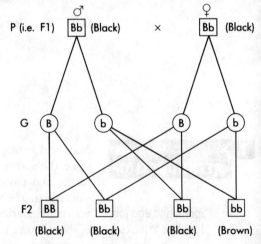

Fig 10.7 A typical monohybrid cross
for two generations.

♂ = male   ♀ = female
B = dominant (black) allele   × = crossing (mating)
b = recessive (brown) allele   G = gametes
P = parents   F1 = offspring in first generation ('first filial')

genes may be identical or have slightly different effects. For instance, we all have two genes for eye colour, if one is for blue eyes and one for brown eyes you will have brown eyes. We can't see genes, but their effects have been observed and patterns of inheritance discovered by scientists.

Over the 100 years or so since an Austrian monk, Gregor Mendel, established the basic laws of inheritance, the science of genetics has become well established. Our understanding of genetics has developed to a point where we can now create new organisms by genetic engineering, that is by transferring genes from one organism to another.

> 66 Look at the diagrams showing mono-hybrid cross 99

5 > MUTATIONS

When chromosomes are copied during mitosis and meiosis there is a possibility for mistakes to be made. These mistakes are known as *mutations* and can affect either single genes or whole chromosomes. Exposure to radiation and chemicals, such as mustard gas or LSD, can increase the rate of mutation. Mutation in body cells may result in cancer. Gene mutations are usually *harmful* and may cause genetic diseases. An example would be the albino gene; this mutation prevents the formation of the dark skin pigment melanin which protects against the sun's ultra-violet rays. Albino animals, therefore, are not protected. Some mutant genes are however *helpful* and can improve an organism's chance of survival. For instance, the sickle-cell gene, which affects the red blood cells in humans causing sickle-cell anaemia, can give some immunity to malaria. Other mutations seem to have no effect and are termed *neutral* – they appear not to affect survival.

The sickle-cell gene can however be harmful if a child gets it from *both* parents. This is one of some three thousand known genetic diseases, and we now have genetic counsellors to help affected people. About 5% of children admitted to UK hospitals are suffering from genetic diseases.

Chromosome mutations can also occur when chromosomes are altered during meiosis. Bits may be broken off or added to chromosomes, and sometimes whole chromosomes may be lost or gained. The faulty gametes which are produced may be fertilised and produce zygotes with *damaged* chromosomes, or *too few* or *too many* chromosomes. An extra number 21 chromosome in humans produces a Down's Syndrome child with a low mental age and very characteristic facial features which led to the previous name for this genetic disorder – *mongolism*. You may indeed know of a Down's person who has developed useful skills through special training and is a happy member of a family. Such diseases can now be detected in the early stages of pregnancy by taking a sample of fluid from the amniotic fluid in the womb and by examining some of the embryo's cells.

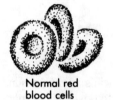
Normal red blood cells

'Sickle' cells

Fig 10.8 Sickle cells compared with normal red blood cells.

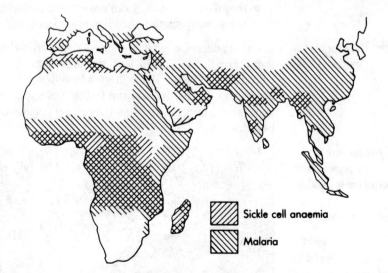

Fig 10.9 Distribution of sickle cell anaemia and malaria.

⬜ Sickle cell anaemia
⬜ Malaria

6 > HYBRIDS

If two different varieties of animals or plants are allowed to breed together, the offspring are known as *hybrids* and will possess the characteristics of both the varieties that were cross-bred. The technique of cross-breeding has been used to great advantage in producing disease-resistant plants and high-yielding crop plants. Hybrids such as varieties of corn were introduced to America in the 1930s and resulted in increased yields of up to 50%. You will find that seeds of hybrid flowers and vegetables are very expensive.

7 ▷ VARIATION

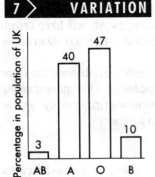

Fig 10.10 Discontinuous variation in human blood groups.

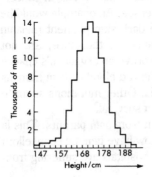

Fig 10.11 Continuous variation in humans: height.

8 ▷ NATURAL SELECTION

Think about these carefully

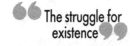
The struggle for existence

Fig 10.12 Pale and dark forms of the peppered moth.
a) Lichen covered tree in unpolluted area.
b) blackened tree in polluted area.

Fig 10.13 Increase in relative numbers of the dark form of the peppered moth in an industrial area.

	Percentage of each form	
Year	Dark	Pale
1848	1	99
1894	99	1

Organisms *vary* even within the same family. The variations are the result of new genes (mutations) and new mixtures of genes (sexual reproduction). There are two *types of variation* between individuals of the same species:

1 *Discontinuous variation.* This enables us to separate individuals into distinct groups; one of the most used examples is blood grouping. We all belong to one of the four main groups. The groups are A, B, AB and O; there are no in-between groupings such as AO. The information in the genes accounts for most of this form of variation, and the environment affects it very little.
2 *Continuous variation.* This refers to characteristics that do *not* allow us to separate individuals into distinct groups. Your height and weight are good examples of this sort of characteristic. Many genes may influence height and weight, but the environment can be important also. In any large population you would get a whole range of heights and weights.

SPECIES

This is the word we use to describe organisms that are related closely enough to breed successfully, which means that the offspring must be able to reproduce themselves when they mature. It is possible for horses and donkeys to mate and produce offspring called mules, but these are sterile and cannot breed. Of all the groups that we use to classify living things, the *species*, or breeding group, is the smallest.

Natural selection is the theory we use to explain evolution. Darwin's voyage around the world in the 1830s aboard *HMS Beagle* provided the key for him to develop and refine his theory in the years that followed. Darwin's observations were that:

- organisms produce large numbers of offspring;
- the offspring vary considerably;
- many offspring die before adulthood;
- many offspring do not survive to breed;
- they die because they can't overcome problems – starving, being eaten by predators, being fatally injured, suffering disease, etc.

Darwin described this as a *struggle for survival* against a harsh environment. Scientists today term the difficulties 'selection pressures'. It is these pressures that determine which individuals survive. Those best adapted survive to pass their genes on to the next generation. Hares that can run fastest will escape the fox, and so genes for powerful leg muscles will be 'selected' and over many generations the performance of the species will be enhanced.

If the environment *changes*, the process of natural selection allows the species to adapt to the new situation, the most advantageous variations surviving to breed. Without variation, a species is very likely to become extinct. The Peppered Moth is a good example in that the colour of the moths has changed in recent times, the darker mutant ones becoming more common in industrial areas as the Industrial Revolution blackened the environment. However, they were still rare in the countryside where the lighter form was dominant. Camouflage is the key to understanding this; predators could easily find light-coloured moths in sooty cities, and so selection favoured the dark genes. In the countryside the reverse was true. Now that industrial pollution is less severe the situation should change again.

9 > ARTIFICIAL SELECTION

This is selective breeding, and humans have taken many species from the wild and controlled their evolution, with amazing results. All the different varieties of dog have been produced by *artificial selection* of the wolf, a single wild species. Our domesticated cattle breeds, poultry, sheep and cereal crops have all been bred from wild species by generations of farmers. Plant and animal breeding is now big business, and so breeders are always on the look-out for wild varieties that could be useful.

EXAMINATION QUESTIONS

MULTIPLE CHOICE

QUESTION 1

In a species of pea plant, red flowers were dominant to white flowers.

Pure-breeding, red-flowered pea plants are crossed with pure-breeding, white-flowered pea plants. What proportion of red- and white-coloured plants will be produced in the F_1 generation?

A all white-flowered plants
B equal numbers of white-flowered plants and red-flowered plants
C a 3:1 ratio of red-flowered plants to white-flowered plants
D a 3:1 ratio of white-flowered plants to red-flowered plants
E all red-flowered plants

QUESTION 2

Which one of the following organs in the body forms gametes?

A the brain   D the uterus
B the penis   E the vagina
C the testes

QUESTION 3

How many sperm are needed to fertilise a human egg cell?
A 1; B 10; C 100; D 1000; E 1 000 000

QUESTION 4

Which one of the following is an example of discontinuous variation?

A blood group   D shoe size
B head size   E weight
C height

QUESTION 5

Which one of the following processes takes place when the sperm fuses with an egg?
A fertilisation   D menstruation
B intercourse   E selection
C ovulation

**STRUCTURED
QUESTIONS**

QUESTION 6

a) In sexual reproduction, new offspring are formed after fusion (fertilisation) of eggs and sperms.
   i) In the space below, draw diagrams of an egg and sperm and then show what happens during fertilisation:

   egg   *sperm*   *fertilisation*

                                                                                                   (3)

   ii) Explain, in words or diagrams, how:
      1 non-identical twins are formed   *(2)*
      2 identical twins are formed   *(2)*

b) A boy had two rabbits. The male was grey and the female was white. He allowed them to mate so that he could make some money from selling baby rabbits. **ALL** the baby rabbits were grey.

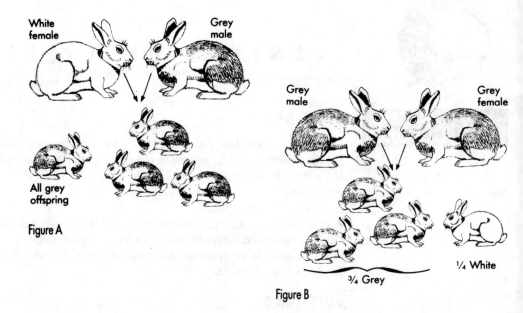

Figure A

Figure B

When the baby grey rabbits had grown he let two of them mate several times. One quarter of their babies turned out to be white.

   i) Which coat colour was dominant? _____
                                                                                                   (1)
   ii) Explain why:
      1 the first two rabbits (shown in Figure A) did not have any white babies;   *(2)*
      2 the grey offspring were able to have white babies (see Figure B).   *(2)*
   iii) White rabbits are easier to sell, and fetch a higher price than grey rabbits. Suggest how the boy could arrange mating so that only white babies were produced. (4 lines available)   *(2)*

c) i) In vegetative (asexual) reproduction, new plants can be made from just one parent. Choose from the examples in Figure C (or any other examples you may know about) and describe how you could produce **two** identical plants from one parent.

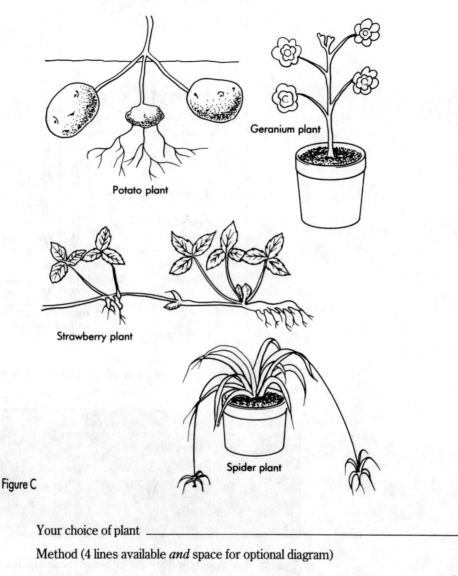

Potato plant

Geranium plant

Strawberry plant

Spider plant

Figure C

Your choice of plant _____

Method (4 lines available *and* space for optional diagram)

(2)

ii) Plant growers use methods based on **asexual** reproduction to produce many beautiful plants for sale to the public. Give **two** reasons why they prefer to use these methods rather than the normal sexual reproduction (pollination–seeds–growth).

1 _____

_____

2 _____

_____

(2)
(Total marks 18)
(LEAG; GCSE 1988)

QUESTION 7

a) It is believed, from fossil evidence, that the horse evolved from a small, dog-sized organism into a large, strong organism.

Examine Figure A showing the evolution of the horse and then answer the questions which follow.

Explain the environmental factors that may have led to the changes in the horse in Figure A. (6 lines available)   *(4)*

Figure A

b) Table 1 below shows some external characteristics of two organisms which look very similar.

	Honey bee	Hoverfly
Body	3 segments	3 segments
Legs	3 pairs	3 pairs
Wings	2 pairs	1 pair
Colour	yellow and black stripes	yellow and black stripes
Length	1.5 cm	2 cm
Sting	present	absent

Table 1

A predator of insects will not eat either of these organisms, even though the hoverfly is harmless.
  i) Explain the reason for the predator's behaviour. *(3)*
  ii) What is the meaning of the term 'genetic mutation'? *(1)*
  iii) Explain how genetic mutations in the ancestors of the hoverfly account for the similarities between it and the bee. (3 lines available) *(2)*
  iv) Mutations in disease-causing bacteria are a serious medical problem. Suggest a reason for this. *(1)*

c) In 1884, in the Manchester area, a very dark variety of the peppered moth was found. Usually this moth is greyish-white in colour with black dots. By 1895 about 95% of the peppered moths in the same area were of the very dark form.
  i) Explain very carefully how it is possible to have had only one very dark peppered moth in 1884, but for 95% of the population to be very dark in 1895. (5 lines available) *(3)*
  ii) Nowadays, pollution is being removed from the environment. Explain very carefully what effect the removal of pollution would have on the population of peppered moths in Manchester. *(4)*

(Total marks 18)
(LEAG; GCSE 1988)

A N S W E R S   T O
E X A M I N A T I O N   Q U E S T I O N S

MULTIPLE
CHOICE

ANSWER 1

Key E, all red-flowered plants. The red colour is dominant to white, so option A is wrong. The parents are both pure-breeding, so the recessive gene is not present in the red-flowered parent; this invalidates options B, C and D.

ANSWER 2

Key C, the testes. The uterus and vagina are involved in reproduction but not in formation of sex cells.

ANSWER 3

Key A, one sperm. Although millions are produced, only one fertilises the egg.

ANSWER 4

Key A, blood groups. All the others show a gradual change and are therefore continuous variation.

ANSWER 5

Key A, fertilisation. Option C, ovulation, is when an egg is released, and option D, menstruation, is the release of the extra lining of the womb.

STRUCTURED
QUESTIONS

ANSWER 6

a) i)

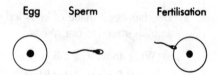

    ii) 1 Two different sperm fertilise two ova at the same time to produce non-identical twins.

       2 When a sperm has fertilised the ovum or egg, the fertilised egg then divides and forms two zygotes. A new individual is formed from each zygote, each having identical chromosomes, so the twins are identical.

b) i) grey

    ii) 1 The grey gene was dominant over the white gene. The male carried two dominant grey genes and was homozygous, or pure-bred.

       2 Each offspring carried one dominant grey gene and one recessive white gene, so when they mated the recessive white genes combined to produce a white offspring.

    iii) He could only breed from white rabbits.

c) i) Geranium

    Take two or more small cuttings from part of the geranium stem where there are side shoots, and put them into some soil.

    ii) 1 Plants are produced which are identical to the parent

       2 The process is quicker than using seeds.

ANSWER 7

a) There may have been a change in availability of food, so that the horses with better-adapted teeth would survive.

   A change in the type of predator may have favoured larger horses which could run more quickly.

b) i) The hoverfly mimics the bee, which has a sting. The predators have learnt that the bee has a sting and therefore avoid another insect with the same warning colours.

   ii) A genetic mutation occurs when there is a mistake in the way in which the genes are copied in the nucleus, so the number or type of genes is different to the parent.

   iii) The hoverflies which may have been produced as mutations with the yellow and black stripes of the bee survived, and those which did not look like the bee were eaten. The genes from the successful hoverflies would be passed on to the next generation.

   iv) Bacteria can become resistant to antibiotics and other drugs used to kill bacteria. Mutations are produced at a rapid rate and pass on their resistance to the next generation.

c) i) The dark-coloured moth survived against the dark-coloured bark of the polluted trees. This moth passed on its chromosomes to the next generation, so more dark-coloured moths were produced. The light-coloured moths were eaten as they showed up on the bark.

   ii) As the bark of the trees becomes lighter, the dark moths will show up and be eaten. Any light-coloured moths will have an advantage and will survive, so the population may change to that of 1884.

A STUDENT'S ANSWER WITH EXAMINER'S COMMENTS

a) Use has been made of knowledge of genetics and inheritance to breed plants and animals suited to our needs.

   i) What do we call this process?

   <u>artifical selection</u>

   (1)

   ii) Explain how a farmer could use this knowledge to breed cows which produce a lot of milk.

   <u>The farmer only breeds from the cows which</u>
   <u>produce the most milk.</u>

   (2)

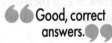 66 Good, correct answers. 99

b) Genes are units of inheritance found on chromosomes in cells.

   i) How many chromosomes are found in a human embryo cell?

   <u>46</u>

   (1)

   ii) How many chromosomes are found in a human egg or sperm cell?

   <u>23</u>

   (1)

iii) Using diagrams, show what happens to these numbers of these chromosomes:
    1 At the formation of sperm cells in the testes

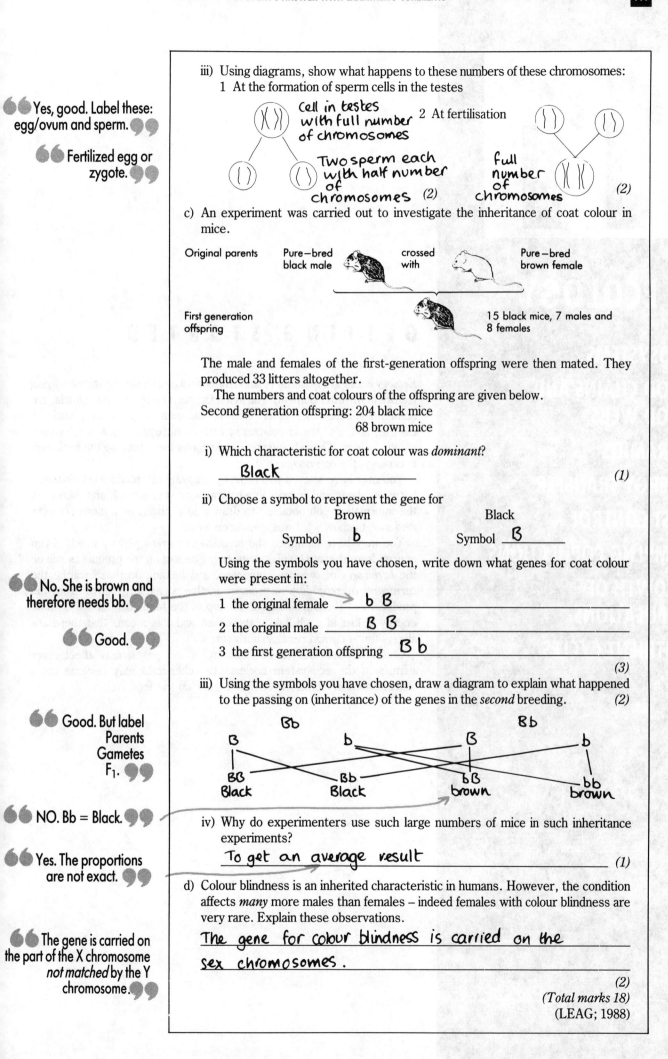

Yes, good. Label these: egg/ovum and sperm.

Cell in testes with full number of chromosomes

2 At fertilisation

Two sperm each with half number of chromosomes *(2)*

full number of chromosomes *(2)*

Fertilized egg or zygote.

c) An experiment was carried out to investigate the inheritance of coat colour in mice.

Original parents   Pure–bred black male   crossed with   Pure–bred brown female

First generation offspring   15 black mice, 7 males and 8 females

The male and females of the first-generation offspring were then mated. They produced 33 litters altogether.

   The numbers and coat colours of the offspring are given below.

Second generation offspring: 204 black mice
                           68 brown mice

i) Which characteristic for coat colour was *dominant*?

    Black   *(1)*

ii) Choose a symbol to represent the gene for

                Brown   Black

        Symbol   b   Symbol   B

Using the symbols you have chosen, write down what genes for coat colour were present in:

No. She is brown and therefore needs bb.

1 the original female   b B

Good.

2 the original male   B B

3 the first generation offspring   B b

                                   (3)

iii) Using the symbols you have chosen, draw a diagram to explain what happened to the passing on (inheritance) of the genes in the *second* breeding. *(2)*

**Good. But label
Parents
Gametes
F₁.**

Bb   Bb

B   b   B   b

BB   Bb   BB   bb
Black   Black   brown   brown

NO. Bb = Black.

iv) Why do experimenters use such large numbers of mice in such inheritance experiments?

    To get an average result   *(1)*

Yes. The proportions are not exact.

d) Colour blindness is an inherited characteristic in humans. However, the condition affects *many* more males than females – indeed females with colour blindness are very rare. Explain these observations.

    The gene for colour blindness is carried on the

    sex chromosomes.

The gene is carried on the part of the X chromosome *not matched* by the Y chromosome.

                                    (2)
                            (Total marks 18)
                            (LEAG; 1988)

C H A P T E R

11

ECOLOGY

ECOSYSTEMS

FOOD CHAINS AND
FOOD WEBS

PYRAMIDS

ENERGY TRANSFER

PEST CONTROL

SAMPLNG POPULATIONS

GROWTH OF
POPULATIONS

NUTRIENT CYCLES

GETTING STARTED

Ecology is the study of the relationships between the living and non-living factors in the environment. The living factors, the plants and animals, are sometimes called the *biotic* factors; the non-living factors, such as climate, soil, and the circulation of carbon, nitrogen and water, are the *abiotic* factors. These living and non-living factors make up the basic unit in ecology, the *ecosystem*.

You may have started this topic by studying the feeding relationships between plants and animals in a habitat near your school, and then used the information you obtained to draw a food chain, or a more complex *food web*, to show what was feeding on what.

You may have identified the *producers* or *green plants*, which obtain energy from the sun by *photosynthesis*. Feeding on the producers will be the *herbivores* or *primary consumers*, and feeding on those will be the *carnivores* or *secondary consumers*. In this way energy flows from the producers to the consumers at the top of the food chain or web. Some energy is lost at each link in the chain, and this means that there are always fewer carnivores than herbivores.

Chemical pesticides, used to control insect pests, may affect other animals in the ecosystem because the chemicals may become more concentrated in animals which are higher up the food web.

ESSENTIAL PRINCIPLES

66 Use information from your own field studies where possible 99

You may have been out of school on a 'field trip' as part of your science course, in order to study an *ecosystem* such as a woodland, a rocky shore, or a pond. You may have just done some field work in the immediate area around your school, and looked at a rotting log, or a hedgerow. During your studies you will probably have noted the living (biotic) and non-living (abiotic) factors which made up the ecosystem which you were studying.

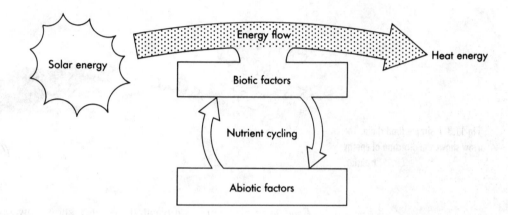

Fig 11.1 How the biotic and abiotic factors interact in an ecosystem.

For any ecosystem the non-living (abiotic) factors will include rainfall, temperature, wind and light intensity, as well as factors which affect the soil, such as the presence of minerals, air and humus.

The living (biotic) factors will include the community of animals and plants which are found in the ecosystem. You may have counted the numbers in a population of just one species of animal or plant. You may also have noticed how different populations are not always competing for food, space, light, etc., and are therefore able to live together in the same ecosystem.

COLONISATION

66 A mature woodland is a 'climax' community 99

Part of your own study about ecology may have involved finding out how a community of plants and animals becomes established within a particular habitat by the process of *succession*. Succession happens when different species move into a new area and begin to be established. For example, dandelion seeds are sometimes blown on to an area of bare soil, where they become established very quickly. Each plant or animal which settles in a new area helps to stabilise the soil and release nutrients, and may help to provide a habitat for other species. Gradually the numbers of different plants and animals which occupy the area increase, until a stable and balanced community of animals and plants is reached. This is known as a *climax community*. Figure 11.2 shows how the numbers of species increase with time.

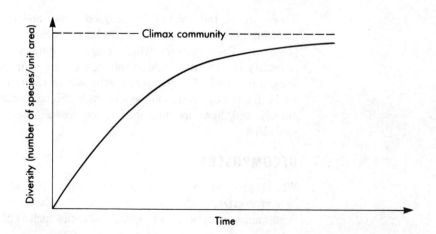

Fig 11.2 The number of species increases over a period of time.

2   FOOD CHAINS AND FOOD WEBS

When you studied an ecosystem, you were probably able to identify the main species of plants and animals, and to find out what was feeding on what. A *food chain* simply shows how an animal obtains its food directly from another animal or plant. The arrows show the *direction* of transfer of energy.

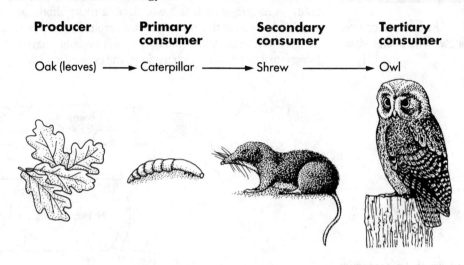

Producer	Primary consumer	Secondary consumer	Tertiary consumer
Oak (leaves) ⟶	Caterpillar ⟶	Shrew ⟶	Owl

Fig 11.3 A simple food chain. The arrow shows the direction of energy transfer.

Food webs are more complicated, as they show how one animal may be feeding on several others to obtain food, or how one plant may have several different animals feeding on it.

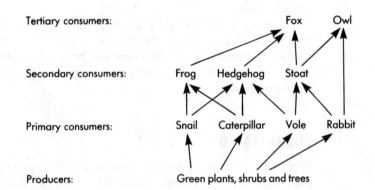

Fig 11.4 In a food web one animal feeds on more than one source of food.

Tertiary consumers: Fox   Owl

Secondary consumers: Frog   Hedgehog   Stoat

Primary consumers: Snail   Caterpillar   Vole   Rabbit

Producers: Green plants, shrubs and trees

PRODUCERS

At the start of all food chains and webs are the green plants, called the *producers*. Green plants make their own food by using solar energy from the sun in the process of *photosynthesis*. Plants convert carbon dioxide and water into carbohydrates, which are then converted into plant protein, oils and fats.

CONSUMERS

These are all the animals in the food chain, and can be divided into herbivores and carnivores. The *herbivores* are the *primary consumers*, which feed directly on the plants or producers. The *carnivores*, which obtain their energy by feeding on the herbivores, are the *secondary consumers*. Some carnivores obtain their energy from *other* carnivores, and these are described as *tertiary* or *third level consumers*; for example, a hawk or fox which feeds on other carnivores in the food chain. Some animals feed on a *mixed diet* of plants and animals, and these are described as *omnivores*. They feed at more than one level in the food chain.

DECOMPOSERS

When plants and animals die, all the nutrients which are stored in their bodies are recycled by *decomposers*, such as bacteria and fungi. These organisms break down the bodies of dead animals and plants, and release nutrients such as nitrogen into the soil.

3 >	PYRAMIDS

PYRAMID OF NUMBERS

Figure 11.5 shows how energy is *lost* at each stage of the food chain. This means that there is a decrease in the number of organisms at each stage of the food chain, as there is less energy available. The *pyramid of numbers* in Figure 11.5 indicates how the number of producers supports fewer herbivores, which in turn support fewer carnivores, supporting still fewer tertiary consumers. However the pyramid of numbers can also look like Figure 11.6!

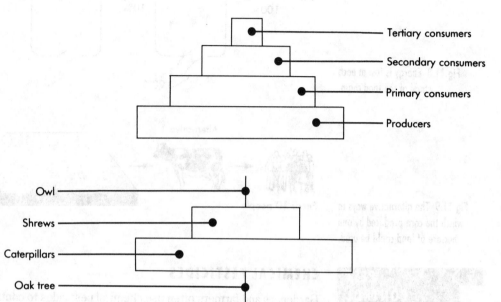

Fig 11.5 Pyramid of numbers.

— Tertiary consumers
— Secondary consumers
— Primary consumers
— Producers

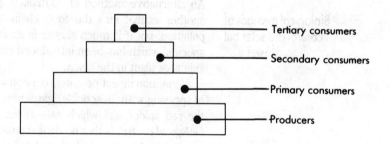

Fig 11.6 A pyramid of numbers based on one oak tree.

Owl
Shrews
Caterpillars
Oak tree

This shows how *one organism*, an oak tree, provides energy for many caterpillars, which provide energy for a few shrews, which in turn provide energy for just one owl.

PYRAMID OF MASS

The total mass or biomass of organisms in a population decreases along the food chain, because less energy is available at each stage. The *pyramid of biomass* may look like Figure 11.7.

— Tertiary consumers
— Secondary consumers
— Primary consumers
— Producers

Fig 11.7 Pyramid of biomass.

4 >	ENERGY TRANSFER

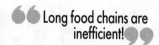

Long food chains are inefficient!

Energy is *transferred* at each stage of the food chain, from the plant producer to the herbivores and then to the carnivores. Only about 10% of the available energy is transferred at each stage of a food chain. The other 90% is lost by life processes such as respiration, excretion and movement. The amount of living material or *biomass* is therefore reduced at each stage of the food chain.

For example, when a cow eats grass, the cow excretes about 60% of the energy taken in from the grass. Another 30% is used up by the cow in respiration, growth and movement. When the cow is eaten by man, only about 10% of the energy originally taken in by the cow is available for food.

Figure 11.8 shows how one hectare of land can produce either enough food for cows to feed 10 people, or enough grain to feed 100 people. It is evidently much more efficient for man to obtain food from *producers* instead of from *consumers* who have wasted so much energy.

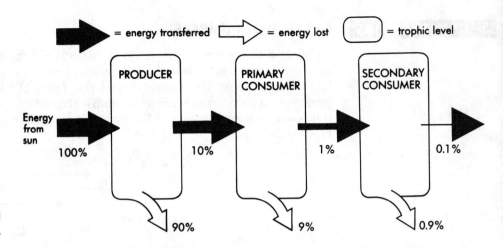

Fig 11.8 Energy is lost at each stage of the food chain.

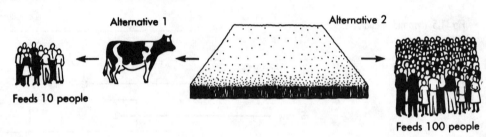

Fig 11.9 The alternative ways in which the corn produced by one hectare of land could be used.

Feeds 10 people

Feeds 100 people

5 > PEST CONTROL

Chemical pesticides can build up in the food chain

CHEMICAL PESTICIDES

Gardeners and farmers often use chemical pesticides to control insects which are damaging crops and other plants. The advantage of using chemical pesticides is that they are very effective and fast-working. Herbicides are also used to kill unwanted plants which otherwise affect the yield of crops. Although these chemicals may be used only in very small quantities, the concentration of chemical may build up at each stage of the food chain, and accumulate in the top carnivore: for example, a bird of prey such as an owl or hawk. The chemicals would affect each organism in the food chain, but the top carnivore, which receives the highest concentration, would be affected the most, and may even be killed or have very low rates of reproduction.

BIOLOGICAL CONTROL

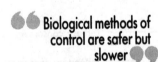

Biological methods of control are safer but slower

An alternative method of controlling pests without the use of chemicals is to introduce another animal into the food chain which will feed on the pest. This method avoids pollution, but it is much slower in its effects than using chemical pesticides. Also the 'new species' which has been introduced can itself become a pest if it starts to feed on another animal or plant in the chain.

A common insect pest in greenhouses is a tiny red spider which damages plants. Instead of spraying with insecticide, gardeners can introduce another insect which is a predator on the red spider and which eats about 20 red spiders a day! An advantage of using such *biological control* is that no dangerous chemicals have to be used and strains of insects that are resistant to chemicals do not develop.

6 > SAMPLING POPULATIONS

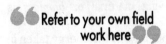

Refer to your own field work here

When you studied an ecosystem you may have been involved in estimating the *population* of a particular species of animal or plant. One of the techniques which you may have used is *random sampling*, as outlined below.

RANDOM SAMPLING

1 Measure the whole area of study.
2 Use a quadrat of known size, eg $0.25m \times 0.25m = \frac{1}{4}m^2$.
3 Place the quadrat at random.
4 Count the numbers of a particular species of animal, or assess the proportion of the quadrat which is covered by a particular plant.
5 Record your result.
6 Repeat stages 3, 4 and 5 until data has been collected from 10 quadrats.

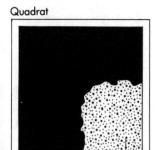

Quadrat

Species A   Species B

Fig 11.10 Using a quadrat to estimate percentage cover.

7 Find the average numbers of the species, or average percentage cover of a plant per square metre.
8 Multiply by the total number of square metres to find the total population of the area.

MARK–RELEASE–RECAPTURE

Another commonly used method of counting a population is *mark–release–recapture*. This method could be used to count a population of snails, for example, and would involve using a special non-toxic paint or marker pen.

1 Capture, count and mark a representative sample of a population.
2 Release the animals in the same area.
3 At a later stage, when the marked animals have mixed with the rest of the population, recapture and count the numbers of animals, and record how many of the marked animals are in the second sample.
4 Use the formula below to estimate the total population:

$$\frac{\text{number in first sample} \times \text{number in second sample}}{\text{number of marked animals recaptured}}$$

7 ▷ GROWTH OF POPULATIONS

Simple ecological methods can be used to study how populations change in size. Figure 11.11 shows a typical growth curve for a population.

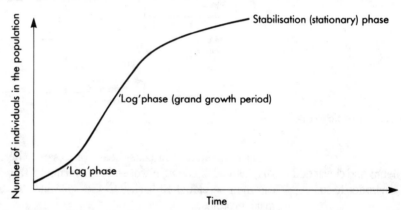

Fig 11.11 The graph shows a typical growth curve for a population.

As you can see, a new population starts with very low numbers in the 'lag' phase, and then shows a very rapid increase in number in the 'log' phase. When resources limit growth, then a *stabilisation phase* is reached and the population remains fairly constant. This continues until there is a *change* in one of the limiting factors, such as availability of food, space or disease. Remember that a population is *all* the members of the *same species* in an area.

COMPETITION

When two organisms both require the same resource, such as food, space, light and water, they can be said to be *competing* with each other. Sometimes competition occurs between members of the same species, and sometimes between members of different species. Figure 11.12 shows how the population of a *predator* increases and decreases as the population of the *prey* goes up and down.

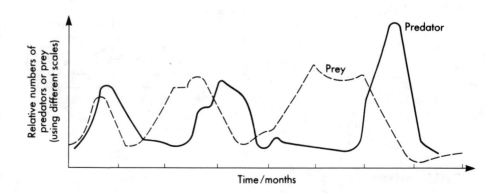

Fig 11.12 The population of the prey affects the numbers of the predator.

8 >	NUTRIENT CYCLES

The recycling of nitrogen, carbon and water forms an essential link between the living and non-living factors in the ecosystem.

THE NITROGEN CYCLE

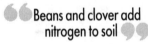
Trace the cyclical path taken by each substance in the three cycles

Plants such as peas, beans and clover are able to absorb nitrogen gas from the air through special lumps on their roots called *nodules*. These nodules contain nitrogen-fixing bacteria which take in or 'fix' the nitrogen as nitrates. The nitrates are then used by plants to make proteins. The proteins are taken in by animals when they eat the plants, and are returned to the soil when animals and plants are decomposed by bacteria and fungi which live in the soil. The decomposers form ammonium compounds, which are converted into nitrates by nitrifying bacteria.

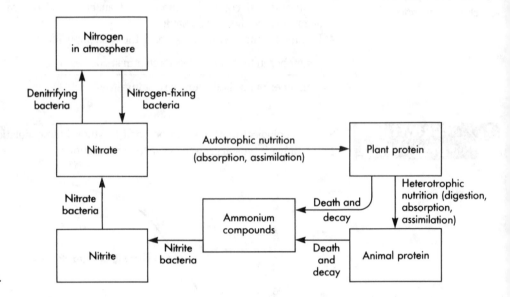

Fig 11.13 The Nitrogen cycle.

Beans and clover add nitrogen to soil

Farmers often plant peas, beans or clover to help increase the amount of nitrates in the soil, instead of adding nitrogen in the form of nitrate fertilisers. The peas, beans and clover can then be ploughed back into the soil, and the nitrates can be used by other plants to make proteins.

Some nitrates are lost from the soil when denitrifying bacteria convert the nitrates into nitrogen gas, which is released into the air. However some nitrates are added to the soil when lightning converts nitrogen, oxygen and water in the air to acids in rain.

THE CARBON CYCLE

Carbon is breathed out, as carbon dioxide, by all animals and plants. Whenever fossil fuels, such as coal, oil or gas, are burnt, carbon dioxide is also released into the atmosphere.

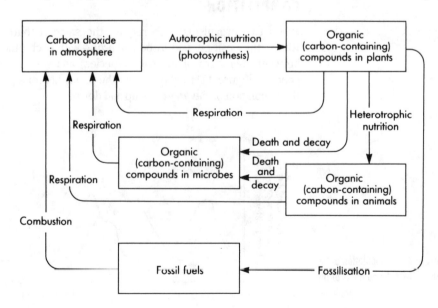

Fig 11.14 The Carbon cycle.

Green plants take in carbon dioxide during the daytime, and combine the carbon dioxide with water to make carbohydrates. This process is known as *photosynthesis*, and it releases oxygen as a waste product.

The plants are eaten by animals, and the carbon, in the form of carbohydrates, proteins and fats, is used to make the cells of the animals. As the animals respire, the carbohydrates are broken down to form carbon dioxide and water. The carbon is released as carbon dioxide into the atmosphere.

THE WATER CYCLE

Water in the ocean is continuously being evaporated by the heat of the sun, and this vapour condenses to form clouds. When the clouds are blown over hills and mountains, they release the condensation as rain. Some of the water drains through the ground and back to the sea by rivers, and some of it is absorbed through the roots of plants, and is evaporated from the leaves in the process of *transpiration*. Rain also dissolves some of the poisonous gases in the air, such as sulphur dioxide, and forms dilute sulphuric acid, which falls as acid rain.

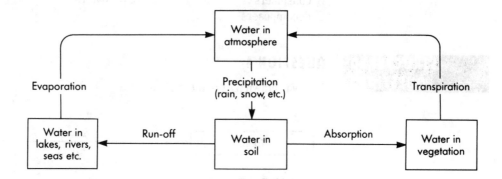

Fig 11.15 The Water cycle.

EXAMINATION QUESTIONS

MULTIPLE CHOICE

QUESTION 1

The diagram below shows a food web.

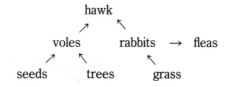

Which of the following is a primary consumer?
A fleas   D seeds
B grass   E voles
C hawks

QUESTION 2

Look at the following simple food chain.

oak tree → caterpillars → small birds → buzzard

Which of the following diagrams shows the pryamid of *mass* for this food chain?

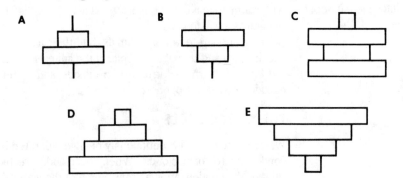

Fig 11.16

QUESTION 3

What are the organisms called which first occupy a newly formed sand dune?
A colonisers   D herbivores
B consumers   E predators
C decomposers

STRUCTURED
QUESTIONS

QUESTION 4

Below is drawn part of the carbon cycle.

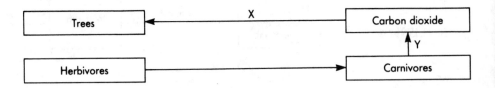

a) Name the processes represented by X and Y.

X is _____ Y is _____

(2)

b) Could fungi be used instead of trees? Give one reason for your answer.

_____

_____

(1)
(WJEC; 1988)

QUESTION 5

a) The curves below show how the population of rabbits and foxes changes over a two-
year cycle. Use the curves to answer the questions which follow.

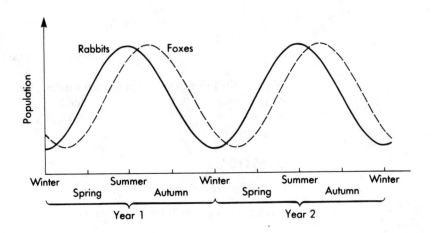

  i) At what time of year is the rabbit population lowest?

  _____

                                                                    (1)

  ii) At what time of year does the rabbit population rise most rapidly?

  _____

                                                                    (1)

  iii) Why do you think that the fox population falls each year?

  _____

                                                                    (1)

b) Use the information given in the simple food web below to answer the questions which follow.

  Name:
  i) a major predator _____
                                                                    (1)

  ii) a herbivore _____
                                                                    (1)

  iii) a carnivore _____
                                                                    (1)

  iv) a producer _____
                                                                    (1)

c) Complete the following food chain.

  cabbage ⟶ rabbit ⟶ _____
                                                                    (1)

d) What would be the effects of removing the foxes?

  _____

  _____

                                                                    (3)

e) Many rosegrowers need to protect their crops from greenfly attack. Suggest **two** ways of controlling greenfly.

  1 _____

  _____

                                                                    (1)

  2 _____

  _____

                                                                    (1)
                                                          (MEG; Specimen)

QUESTION 6

The diagram below shows how different living things depend on others.

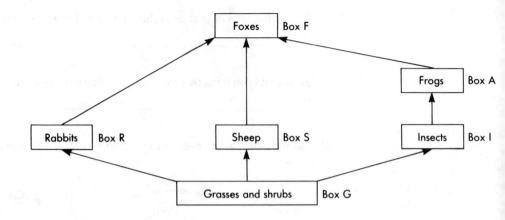

After each group or 'box' there is a code letter. Use this code letter to answer some of the questions where indicated.

a) What is the name or term given to this type of diagram?   *(1)*

b) Which group or 'box' would contain
   i) the *smallest number* of individual living things?
   ii) the *greatest total weight* of living things?   *(2)*

c) i) Which box contains the primary producers?
   ii) Where do these primary producers get their energy from?   *(2)*

d) If the rabbit population was killed off by disease, what **two** effects could this have on sheep-farming in the area?

   i) _____

   _____

   ii) _____

   _____

                                                                                              (2)
                                                                                        (WJEC; 1988)

QUESTION 7 (EXTENSION QUESTION)

The diagram at the top of page 131 shows the energy pathway through a simple food chain.

a) i) In the diagram, **X** and **Y** represent energy losses from living organisms. Suggest **one** process for each which could illustrate the loss.   *(2)*
   ii) Calculate the percentage of the Sun's energy absorbed by plants.   *(2)*

b) i) What happens to most of the Sun's energy falling on grassland?   *(1)*
   ii) Explain why it is more efficient for man to obtain his energy from grassland (eg wheat) rather than meat (eg cow).   *(2)*

c) In the Arctic, human communities have difficulty in growing food crops.
   i) Suggest **two** factors that are mainly responsible for this.   *(2)*
   ii) What would be the probable effect of lack of food on the size of the human communities?   *(1)*
                                                                                        (MEG; Specimen)

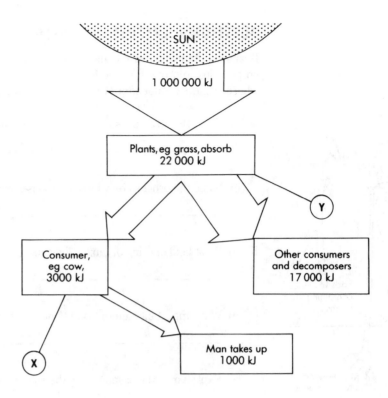

QUESTION 8 (EXTENSION QUESTION)

The diagram below shows the position of a sewage outflow pipe at a local beach.

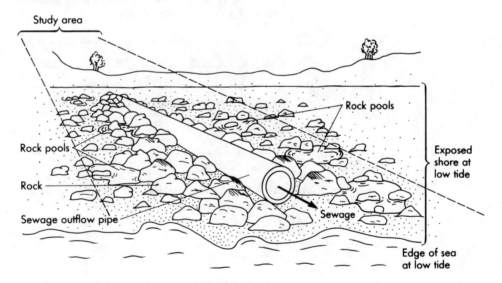

The whole beach is covered in different types of seaweeds, growing on rocks and in rock pools. The main species of animals are snails, crabs, mussels, barnacles, limpets and fish. The animals live in the rock pools.

There is concern that the animals and plants are being affected by the sewage from the pipe.

You and a group of friends decide to investigate the situation by collecting some information about the different types of animals and plants.

a) Describe how you would measure the size of the population of **one** of the types of animals found in the study area on the beach.   (4)

b) Describe how you would compare the seaweeds growing in the study area on this beach with those growing on a beach where there was no sewage pipe.   (4)

c) Suggest **three** factors, other than the presence of the sewage pipe, which could affect the types of plants and animals found on the two beaches.   (3)

(MEG; 1988)

QUESTION 9 (EXTENSION QUESTION)

Beans are important in the diet of many people in the world. In addition, growing bean crops helps improve the soil fertility. This can be very important in parts of the world where farmers cannot afford expensive fertilisers.

a) i) Name the structures at **A** through which the plants lose water to the atmosphere.

_____

(1)

ii) Name the process by which plants lose water to the atmosphere.

_____

(1)

b) i) What kind of living organism lives inside the bean root nodules?

_____

(1)

ii) What important element is obtained for the plant through the root nodules?

_____

(1)

iii) Explain how the organisms in the root nodules help the plant to obtain this element.

_____

_____

(1)

iv) After harvesting the beans, farmers dig in the roots of beans. They do not remove them. Explain why they do this.

_____

_____

(1)

v) Explain how growing beans can help to improve soil fertility.

_____

_____

(2)

c) Write a paragraph to explain why in some underdeveloped countries beans may be an important part of the diet of the people.

_____

_____

_____

_____

(3)
(LEAG; 1988)

Diagram labels: A, Pods containing beans, Soil level, Root nodules

ANSWERS TO EXAMINATION QUESTIONS

ANSWER 1

Key E, voles; remember primary consumers are herbivores which feed from the green plants or producers in the food chain. The hawks and fleas are secondary consumers.

ANSWER 2

Key D; remember pyramid of mass means the amount of biomass in a food chain, not the number of organisms. Option A shows a pyramid of number for this food chain, one oak tree and one buzzard, represented by a single line, with many caterpillars and fewer small birds.

ANSWER 3

Key A, colonisers; the other options are all organisms involved in food chains but not in colonisation of a new area.

ANSWER 4

a) X is photosynthesis, Y is respiration.

b) No, because green plants are needed in the carbon cycle to carry out photosynthesis and to make carbohydrates. Fungi are not green plants as they do not have chlorophyll. They obtain their energy from decaying animals and plants.

ANSWER 5

a) i) in the winter (note the rabbit population is the solid line).
    ii) in the spring
    iii) The foxes feed on the rabbits. When there are fewer rabbits the number of foxes declines.

b) i) fox (or cat)
    ii) slug, rabbit or greenfly (all acceptable)
    iii) mole, tit, thrush, fox, cat (all acceptable)
    iv) cabbage (or rose)

c) cabbage → rabbit → *fox*

d) The numbers of rabbits and moles would increase, the numbers of cabbages and slugs may decrease.

e) 1 putting more ladybirds on the rose bush to eat the greenfly
   2 adding chemical pesticide to the rose bush to kill the greenfly.

ANSWER 6

a) food web

b) i) box F
    ii) box G

c) i) box G
    ii) the Sun

d) i) more grasses and shrubs available for the sheep, so the numbers of sheep could increase
    ii) the foxes may eat more sheep as they cannot feed on rabbits, so the numbers of sheep may decrease.

ANSWER 7

a) i) Energy loss X could be excretion and respiration.
       Energy loss Y could be reflection and transpiration.
    ii) 2.2%

b) i) Most of the energy is reflected, some is used to evaporate water, some goes into
       the soil.
    ii) Energy is wasted at each level of the food chain, so it is more efficient for man to
        obtain energy as close to the start of the food chain as possible.

c) i) low temperatures, short growing season, poor soil
    ii) population size may be reduced in number.

ANSWER 8

a) 1 Measure the total area of the beach to be studied.
    2 Using a $\frac{1}{4}m^2$ quadrat, place the quadrat at random and count the numbers of
      individuals in that small area.
    3 Record results and repeat until 10 quadrats have been sampled.
    4 Add all results together; divide by 10 to find average result.
    5 Multiply by total area of beach to find total population.

b) Using random quadrats, sample the proportion of a particular species of seaweed on the
   two different areas of beach. Repeat for different species. Observe differences in colour,
   size, etc., of seaweeds of the same species on the two different beaches.

c) 1 exposure of the beach to strong waves and wind.
    2 amount of human interference on the beach, eg tourism, boating, etc.
    3 different types of pollution such as oil and other chemicals in the seawater.

ANSWER 9

a) i) stomata
    ii) transpiration
b) i) bacteria
    ii) nitrogen (as nitrates)
    iii) bacteria in the nodules absorb the nitrogen from the air in the soil, and combine it
         with other elements.
    iv) the bacteria can live freely in the soil to fix nitrogen
    v) beans increase the nitrogen content of the soil. Nitrogen is required by plants to
       make plant protein.
c) Beans provide a good source of proteins, minerals and vitamins. They are at the
   beginning of the food chain, so it is a more efficient use of the total energy which is
   available, rather than having cattle grazing on the land and converting the plants into meat

A STUDENT'S ANSWER WITH EXAMINER'S COMMENTS

1 A group of students were investigating the ecology of a stream near their school. They observed the following feeding relationships:

Animals	What the animals were eating
caddis fly larvae	leeches, water lice, mayfly nymphs
swallow	alderfly larvae
leeches	midge larvae
mayfly nymphs	diatoms (small green plants)
alderfly larvae	caddis fly larvae
water lice	rotting plants
midge larvae	diatoms (small green plants)

a) Name the **two** animals from the table which are competing for the same food.

“OK two marks.”

1 ⟶ Mayfly nymphs ✓

2 ⟶ Midge larvae ✓

(2)

b) Suggest **two** factors which may limit the growth of the diatoms (small green plants).

“Only one factor given here, ie 'being eaten'. You could suggest the amount of light, space or pollution as a second factor.”

1 being eaten by midge larvae ✓

2 ⟶ being eaten by mayfly larvae ✗

(2)

c) Complete the food web below, using the information from the table.

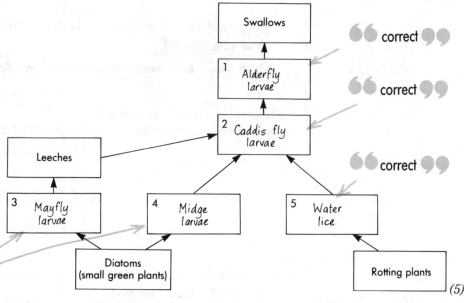

“correct”

“correct”

“correct”

“Be careful. These two are reversed.”

(5)

d) At the end of the investigation the students observed that all the mayfly nymphs had changed to adult mayflies and had flown away. Suggest **two** effects that this change would have on the ecology of the stream.

“Yes.”

1 numbers of leeches would decrease ✓

“No – the caddis fly would feed on midge larvae and water lice instead.”

2 ⟶ number of caddis fly larvae would decrease

(2)

e) A local gardener accidentally allowed a small amount of chemical pesticide to flow into the same stream. The pesticide was absorbed by the diatoms (small green plants) and eventually affected the swallows more than the other animals in the food web. Suggest why the swallows were most affected by the chemical pesticide.

the swallows feed on all the other animals in the ✓

food chain indirectly so the (amount) of pesticide

increases. ✗

66 Yes. 99

66 No. The concentration of pesticide increases. 99

(2)
(MEG; 1988)

2 The diagram below shows part of a food web.

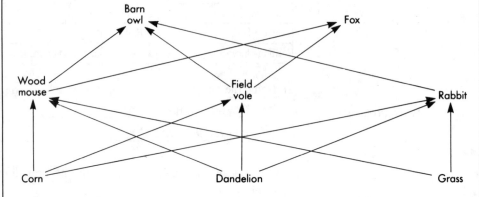

Suppose all the field voles were suddenly killed by disease.

a) Why would the number of dandelions be likely to increase?

not being eaten by voles

(2)

b) Why would the number of foxes be likely to decrease?

less voles to eat

owls may eat more mice so less for fox

66 Good. 99

(2)

The label below shows the chemical composition of a rose fertiliser.

Analysis
COMPOUND FERTILIZER 10.5–7.5–10.5
NITROGEN (N) Total   10.5%
PHOSPHORUS PENTOXIDE
(P$_2$O$_5$) Total   7.5%
of which Soluble in water   4.5%
Insoluble in water   3.0%
POTASSIUM OXIDE
(K$_2$O) Total   10.5% (K8.7%)
MAGNESIUM (Mg)   2.7%
1.2 kg 2.65 lb.

c) Why is it necessary to put substances such as nitrogen back into the soil?

It is lost from the soil

66 Yes, but state how plants use up nitrogen to make proteins. 99

(2)

d) Explain briefly the dangers to the environment of fertilisers which are readily soluble in water.

They are washed into lakes and cause algae to grow.

66 Good. Also fish die from lack of oxygen when algae are decomposed. 99

(3)
(NISEC; 1988)

THE SOLAR SYSTEM, THE WEATHER, AND ROCKS

GETTING STARTED

Every day the Sun rises and sets, at night the stars 'appear' in the sky, and the Moon seems to change its shape during the month. To understand how some of these events take place you need to know how the Earth orbits around the Sun, and how the Moon orbits around the Earth.

To investigate conditions in outer space, man has sent both manned and unmanned rockets on voyages of discovery. One day it is possible that people could be living in a space station instead of living on Earth.

Satellites are already in everyday use for observing the Earth and its atmosphere, and making a major contribution to weather forecasting. In Britain, as in many countries, a very common topic of conversation is the weather. People generally enjoy warm, sunny weather more than cold, wet weather. Although the weather in Britain seems very changeable, we are not usually affected by the extremes experienced in some parts of the world, where floods, droughts, earthquakes and volcanoes cause great suffering to many people.

ESSENTIAL PRINCIPLES

1 ⟩ THE SUN

The Sun is one of billions of stars which make up a galaxy known as the Milky Way. There are billions of galaxies like the Milky Way in the universe. The Sun is about half-way through its life cycle of 9600 million years and is about a million times larger than the Earth. It is made of hydrogen and helium gas, and its temperature is about 6000°C at its surface. At the centre of the Sun the temperature is much higher, and this is where nuclear fusion is taking place as the hydrogen is being converted to helium. Figure 12.1 shows the life cycle of a star such as the Sun.

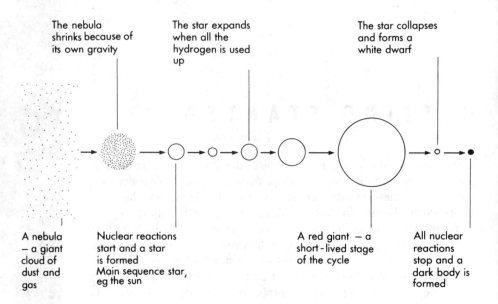

Fig 12.1 The life cycle of a star.

2 ⟩ THE SOLAR SYSTEM

Nine planets, of which Earth is one, orbit around the sun, which is at the centre of our *solar system*. Figure 12.2 shows the arrangement of the *planets* (not to scale).

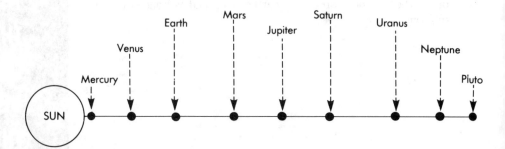

Fig 12.2 How the planets are arranged.

Figure 12.3 shows you some data about the *nine planets in the Solar system*.

Try and understand general patterns in the planets

There are two basic groups of planets. The planets *nearer* the Sun – Mercury, Venus, Earth and Mars – have small diameters and high density; the planets *further away* – Jupiter, Saturn, Uranus, Neptune and Pluto – have large diameters but low density. Planets which are further away from the Sun take longer to orbit the Sun and generally have lower mean surface temperatures than planets nearer the Sun.

PROBLEMS OF COLONISATION

When considering the problems of living on any planet other than Earth, you have to think about factors such as the availability of oxygen and water, temperature, pressure and radiation. Conditions on the surface of the planets, with the exception of the Earth, are generally fairly hostile. For example, *Jupiter*, the largest planet in the solar system, has a solid rock core surrounded by layers of liquid hydrogen, and is covered in a thick layer of hydrogen gas. The atmosphere is very cold since the planet is so far away from the Sun, and the planet is surrounded by zones of radiation. Trying to colonise this planet would cause astronauts several problems, such as protecting themselves from radiation and from the low temperatures, carrying sufficient oxygen to breathe, and moving about.

Would you like to live there?

| | 1 Diameter (Earth=1) | 2 Mass (Earth=1) | 3 Surface gravity (Earth=1) | 4 Density, in Kg m⁻³ | 5 Period of spin | | | 6 Angle of tilt between axis and orbit | 7 Average distance from Sun (Sun-(Earth=1) | 8 Period of orbit, in years | 9 No. of moons (*=plus rings) |
Body					days	hours	minutes				
Sun	109.00	333 000.00	28.00	1400	25	9		97°			
Mercury	0.40	0.06	0.40	5400	58	16		90°	0.4	0.2	0
Venus	0.95	0.80	0.90	5200	244	7		267°	0.7	0.6	0
Earth	1.00	1.00	1.00	5500		23	56	113°	1.0	1.0	1
Moon	0.27	0.01	0.17	3300	27	7		91°	1.0	1.0	0
Mars	0.53	0.10	0.40	4000		24	37	114°	1.5	1.9	2
Jupiter	11.18	317.00	2.60	1300		9	50	93°	5.2	11.9	16*
Saturn	9.42	95.00	1.10	700		10	14	116°	9.5	29.5	15*
Uranus	3.84	14.50	0.90	1600		10	49	187°	19.2	84.0	5*
Neptune	3.93	17.20	1.20	2300		15	48	118°	30.1	164.8	2
Pluto	0.31	0.0025	0.20	400	6	9	17	?	39.4	247.7	1

THE MAIN MEMBERS OF THE SOLAR SYSTEM

Fig 12.3 Some data about the planets in the solar system.

3 ▷ THE EARTH Some important facts:

- A year is the time taken for the Earth to orbit the Sun, about 365 days.
- A day is the time taken for the Earth to spin on its own axis, about 24 hours.

Figure 12.4 shows how the Earth is tilted as it orbits the Sun.

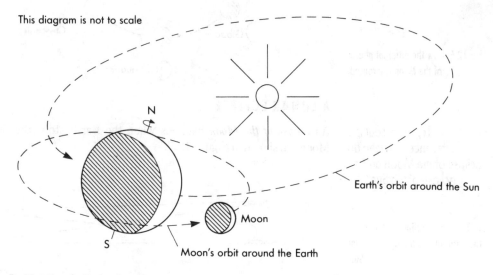

Fig 12.4 How the Earth orbits the Sun.

THE SEASONS

The 23° tilt of the Earth's axis means that different parts of the world get different amounts of sunlight, and this causes the seasons. Winter occurs in the half of the Earth which is tilted *away* from the Sun; summer occurs in the half of the Earth which is tilted *towards* the Sun. When it is summer in the Northern hemisphere, it is winter in the Southern hemisphere (see Figure 12.5).

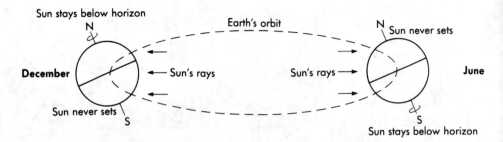

Fig 12.5 How the seasons are caused.

4 ▷ THE MOON

The Moon is a *satellite* of the Earth which takes 28 days to orbit the Earth. This is known as a *lunar month*. The Moon also rotates on its own axis every 28 days, so the same side of the Moon faces the Earth all the time.

Figure 12.6 shows how the different phases of the Moon appear when the Moon is viewed from Earth. When the Earth is between the Sun and the Moon we can see all the light from the Sun which is reflected by the Moon, and the Moon therefore appears to be a full Moon.

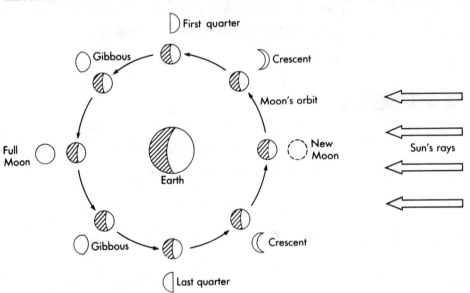

Fig 12.6 How the different phases of the Moon are caused.

A LUNAR ECLIPSE

> Try to sort out the difference between an eclipse of the Moon and an eclipse of the Sun

An *eclipse of the Moon* happens when the Earth stops the Sun's rays from reaching the Moon, as shown in Figure 12.7.

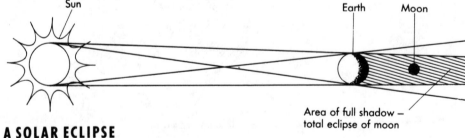

Fig 12.7 In an eclipse of the Moon, the Earth blocks the light from the Sun.

A SOLAR ECLIPSE

An *eclipse of the Sun* happens when the Moon passes between the Sun and the Earth, so the Sun appears to be covered, as shown in Figure 12.8.

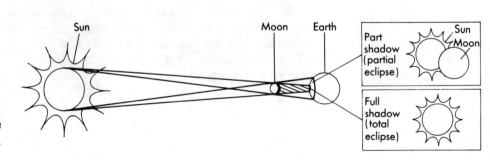

Fig 12.8 In an eclipse of the Sun, the Moon blocks the light from the Sun.

THE TIDES

The Moon exerts a gravitational pull on the water on the Earth's surface. The effect of this on the side nearest the Moon is to pull the water towards the Moon and thereby produce a high tide. Another high tide happens on the side of the Earth furthest away from the Moon. Owing to the rotation of the Earth, these high tides happen every 12 hours.

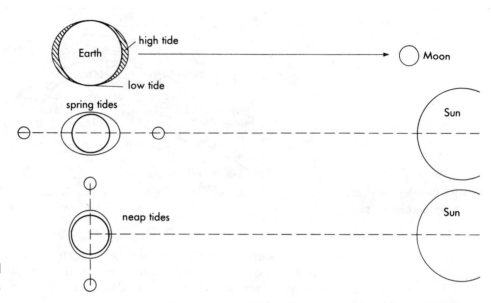

Fig 12.9 How 'spring' tides and 'neap' tides are caused.

Spring and neap tides

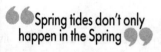
Spring tides don't only happen in the Spring

Although the Sun is much further away from the Earth, it too has a gravitational pull on the Earth. When the Sun and Moon are *in line*, about twice a month, their combined gravitational pull causes a very high tide or 'spring' tide. These tides have very large tidal ranges, this means that they have 'very high' high tides and 'very low' low tides.

When the Sun and Moon are *at right angles* with each other, which happens about twice a month, the gravitational effect is cancelled out and weak tides, called 'neap' tides, with small tidal ranges, are produced. These tides have 'low' high tides.

5 > THE WEATHER

The surface of the Earth is surrounded by the *atmosphere*, a thick layer of gases which are constantly changing to produce the effects which are described as the 'weather'.

GASES IN THE ATMOSPHERE

The proportion of the gases in the atmosphere is shown below:

- nitrogen about 79%;
- oxygen about 20%;
- carbon dioxide about 0.03%;
- noble gases about 1%;
- impurities such as dust particles, gases such as sulphur dioxide, nitrous oxides;
- water vapour.

WATER VAPOUR

The amount of *water vapour* in the air varies from none to about 5%. Warm air can hold more water vapour than cold air. Usually we cannot *see* water vapour until it condenses and falls as rain, or when windows steam up. We *feel* the effects of water vapour because when there is a high moisture content the air feels sticky and damp, and we find it difficult to cool down.

AIR PRESSURE

The Earth's gravitational pull holds the layer of gases around the surface of the Earth, and the weight of air above any part of the Earth is described as *air pressure*. For example, the weight of air pressing down on 1 centimetre square is 10 Newtons. Atmospheric pressure is therefore about 10 N/cm^2. This unit is also described as *one bar* or 1000 millibars.

Look at the weather map shown in Figure 12.10.

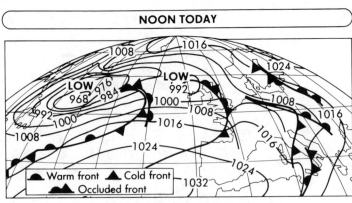

NOON TODAY

Information supplied by **London Weather Centre**

Fig 12.10 The isobars link places which have equal pressure.

> Watch the weather news on TV to help you understand weather maps

The lines on the weather map are pressure contours called *isobars*, which join points of equal pressure. When the isobars are close together, the pressure gradient is steep, and winds will be very strong. Wind generally moves from an area of high pressure to an area of low pressure.

You can see the isobars or pressure bars on the map. For instance, those labelled as 1024 millibars indicate a 'high' pressure of just over 10 N per centimetre square. Pressure is usually measured with a barometer, but in an aeroplane a pilot uses a sensitive barometer, called an *altimeter*, which measures atmospheric pressure and height.

Increasing and decreasing pressure

If air is compressed, the molecules are closer together in a smaller space; as the air becomes denser in this way, the pressure is increased. Pressure decreases with altitude because as you go higher up, there is less air above you pressing down on you. If you go about 6 kilometres high, the pressure drops to about half as the air molecules thin out.

6 >	CLOUDS

HOW CLOUDS ARE FORMED

1 When air passes over water, the air picks up water vapour which has evaporated from the surface.
2 When the air has absorbed the *maximum amount* of water vapour which it can hold at that temperature, it is said to be *saturated*. Colder air can hold less water vapour than warmer air.

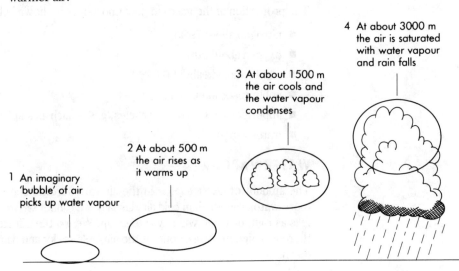

4 At about 3000 m the air is saturated with water vapour and rain falls

3 At about 1500 m the air cools and the water vapour condenses

2 At about 500 m the air rises as it warms up

1 An imaginary 'bubble' of air picks up water vapour

Fig 12.11 How clouds are formed.

3 The energy from the Sun heats up masses of air and causes the air molecules to spread out, so that the air becomes less dense and rises.
4 As the air rises, it cools down; any water vapour in the air begins to condense and form clouds.
5 When the cloud rises higher, the air in the cloud becomes saturated with water vapour, which is then released as rain.

Britain is covered by a network of stations whose function is to detect falling rain by radar. In the near future it is hoped that these will be linked with radar stations across Europe. Meteorologists can then predict where rain is likely to fall in the next few hours. This is of especial benefit to people such as air traffic controllers, farmers and organisers of outdoor events, such as Wimbledon tennis.

> **"A good example of technological application"**

DIFFERENT TYPES OF CLOUDS

The chart below shows information about three common types of cloud: cumulus, cirrus, and stratus clouds.

Name	Height ('000m)	Description
cirrus	8	wispy white threads
cumulus	2.5	thick white clouds with flat base and rounded tops
stratus	0.5–2.5	continuous sheet of low cloud

7 › GLOBAL WEATHER

A number of different factors affect how air masses move around to cause global weather patterns. However, two important factors are as follows:

1 The air at the Equator is heated up more than the air at the Poles, as the Equator receives more of the Sun's radiation.
2 The Earth spins on its axis, at a speed of approximately 2 000 km per hour at the Equator, but at a speed of zero at the poles. This means that as air moves *towards the Poles* the air speed is slowed down, but as air moves *towards the Equator* the air speed is increased.

Figure 12.12 shows the net effect of these two factors on how air masses move around. The winds move in a clockwise direction in the Southern hemisphere, and in an anticlockwise direction in the Northern hemisphere.

Fig 12.12 Global weather patterns.

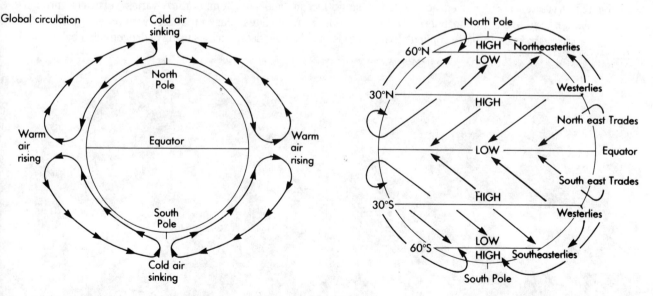

COLD FRONTS AND WARM FRONTS

Figure 12.12 shows a belt of low pressure at about 50°N. This region of low pressure is the boundary between two large air masses: the cold, dry *Polar Continental* and the warm, moist *Tropical Maritime*. The warm air is less dense than the cold air and rises over it, creating a front called the *Polar Front*. Figure 12.13 shows how 'kinks' develop in this Polar Front, creating warm and cold fronts.

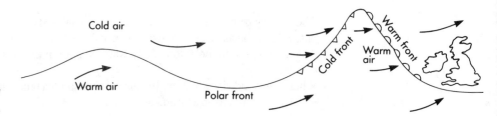

Fig 12.13 An imaginary aerial view
of the polar front.

A *warm front* develops as warm, moist air rises over the cold, dry air. A *cold front* develops as cold, dry air pushes underneath the warm, moist air.

The weather map in Figure 12.14 shows a typical depression or LOW, with a cold front and a warm front.

Fig. 12.14 A typical depression or
LOW will bring rain to Britain.

As the *warm front* passes over, the weather pattern will show increasing wind and cloud cover, light rain or drizzle and a fall in pressure. As the *cold front* passes, the rain becomes much heavier, the wind becomes very strong and the temperature drops. The pressure then rises and the rain ceases as the sky clears.

WEATHER FORECASTING

Satellite pictures, like the ones shown in Figure 12.15 and on the TV weather news, are able to show the position and speed of the changing weather patterns. For example, a satellite could show the development of a cold front, or the position of a depression as it moved across the Atlantic Ocean, and how temperature varies vertically through the atmosphere. The information from satellites is used together with other information from more conventional methods of collecting data, such as using hydrogen-filled balloons which

Fig. 12.15 A satellite picture
showing a frontal system
approaching Britain

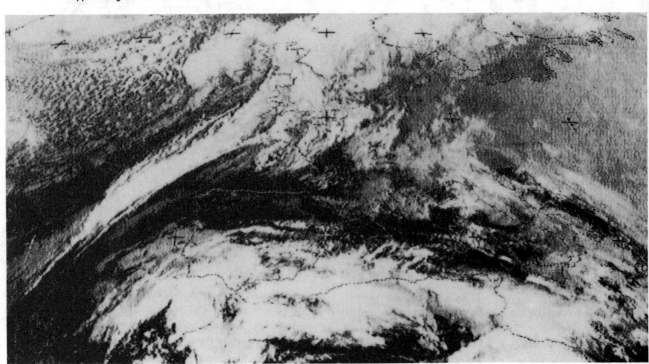

float in the atmosphere, and computer weather forecasts. Meteorologists are then able to pass information to national and local news stations as well as to aeroplanes and shipping.

The type of satellite used is a *geostationary satellite* whose speed is the same as that of Earth. The satellite is held in orbit by the Earth's gravitational field. Some satellites are able to use both infra-red and visible light to collect data. This means that data can be collected during a 24-hour period as a frontal system develops.

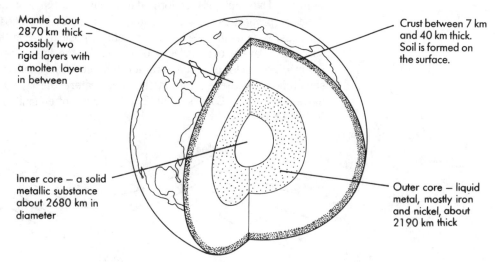

Figure 12.16 shows the main layers of the Earth.

Mantle about 2870 km thick — possibly two rigid layers with a molten layer in between

Crust between 7 km and 40 km thick. Soil is formed on the surface.

Inner core — a solid metallic substance about 2680 km in diameter

Outer core — liquid metal, mostly iron and nickel, about 2190 km thick

Fig 12.16 The structure of the Earth.

THE CRUST, VOLCANOES AND EARTHQUAKES

The *crust* consists of large plates of rock, forming the continents, which are floating on the molten mantle. Mountains can be created and volcanoes can occur when two of these plates *meet*, whereas earthquakes can happen when the plates *slide past* each other.

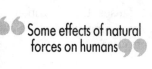

Fig 12.17 The large plates of rock which form the Earth's crust.

Some of the visible effects of earthquakes are buildings falling down and large cracks appearing in the roads. In mountainous regions earthquakes can be responsible for causing avalanches of snow, and in the oceans very large tidal waves can be produced.

Some of the effects of volcanoes are the destruction of towns and villages, and the removal of agricultural land and forests. The *magma*, which flows out on the surface at a temperature of 1000°C, is a mixture of lava and volcanic gases. Some eruptions produce large amounts of volcanic dust particles, which enter the atmosphere and cause cloud formation.

In the crust are many different types of rocks which contain minerals. The minerals either exist as pure elements, such as gold, or as mineral *ores*, such as malachite (copper carbonate).

SEDIMENTARY ROCKS

The rocks in the crust are broken down or eroded in many different ways:

1 by the action of moving water;
2 by wind, ice and frost;
3 by changes of temperature;
4 by chemical action, such as acidic rainwater on limestone;
5 by the action of living organisms, such as worms and plant roots.

The result of erosion is to break down the rocks into smaller particles, which eventually form soil. Different soils are formed from different types of rocks, so soils will differ in their drainage properties, texture, acidity, and mineral composition. Rivers carry the fine particles, such as gravels and sands, and deposit them on the sea bed, where they form successive layers over millions of years. As the layers become compressed, layers of *sedimentary rocks* or *strata* are formed, such as sandstone and limestone. You can sometimes see these strata at the coast where the layers may have been lifted up by movements of the Earth's crust. The strata are often faulted and folded, as you can see in Figure 12.18.

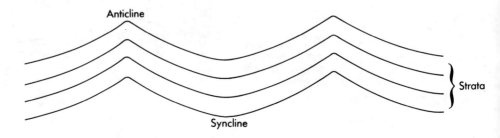

Fig 12.18

IGNEOUS ROCKS

> **Look at some samples of rocks such as granite. Can you see the crystals?**

Igneous rocks are formed when molten magma from the mantle cools and solidifies. The size of the crystals which can be seen in igneous rocks indicates the rate of cooling of the magma. Small crystals are formed when the magma cools rapidly. Volcanoes occur when the molten rock forces its way to the surface, often through a weak part of the crust. Granite and basalt are examples of igneous rocks.

METAMORPHIC ROCKS

Very high temperature and pressure in the Earth's crust causes the formation of *metamorphic rocks* from both igneous and sedimentary rocks. For example, limestone can be changed into marble, and compressed mud can be changed into slate.

THE ROCK CYCLE

Over millions of years rocks change from one type to another, as shown in Figure 12.19.

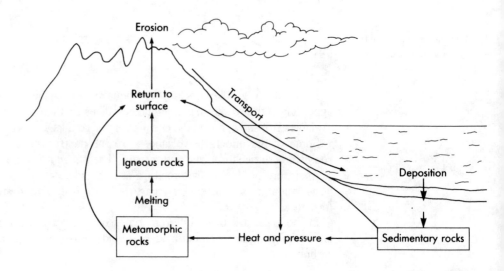

Fig 12.19

EXAMINATION QUESTIONS

MULTIPLE
CHOICE

QUESTION 1

What is a year?
A the time taken for the Earth to rotate on its axis
B the time taken for the Moon to orbit the Earth
C the time taken between two solar eclipses
D the time taken for the Earth to orbit the Sun
E the time taken between summer and winter.

QUESTION 2

The flow chart below shows the possible life cycle of our Sun, a middle-aged star.

clouds of dust and gas → star contracts → main sequence star → star expands → X
→ white dwarf → dark body

Which one of the following should be at X?
A black hole   D neutron star
B galaxy   E red giant
C nebula

QUESTION 3

Which one of the following phases of the Moon occurs during a 'spring' tide?
A crescent moon   D gibbous moon
B first quarter   E last quarter
C full moon

QUESTION 4

What happens during a total eclipse of the Moon?
A The Moon goes behind the Sun.
B The Moon is between the Earth and the Sun.
C Mars moves between the Sun and the Moon.
D The Earth is between the Sun and the Moon.
E The Sun is between the Earth and the Moon.

QUESTION 5

The diagram below shows the approximate percentage of gases in the atmosphere.

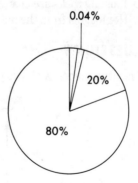

What gas is present in the largest percentage?
A carbon dioxide   D nitrogen
B hydrogen   E sulphur dioxide
C oxygen

QUESTION 6

The diagram below shows a weather map.

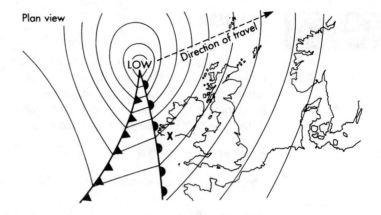

What type of weather is happening at area X?
A cold with very heavy rain
B cold with clear blue skies
C a very strong wind
D warm, sunny, dry weather
E warm and raining.

QUESTION 7

The diagram opposite shows the structure of the earth.

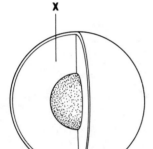

What does area **X** represent?

A crust	D outer core
B inner core	E continental plates
C mantle	

QUESTION 8

Which one of the following describes how igneous rocks are formed?
A Existing rocks are broken down by changes of temperature.
B Existing rocks are eroded by the action of water.
C An earthquake cracks the Earth's crust.
D Existing rocks are changed by high temperature and pressure.
E Hot magma from the mantle cools and solidifies.

QUESTION 9

The diagram below shows the rock cycle.

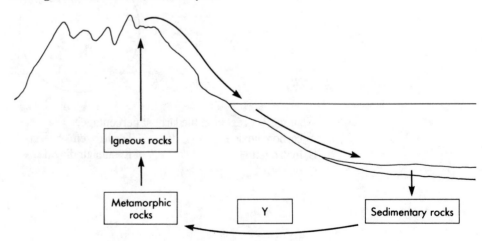

Which one of the following should be in box Y?
A deposition   D melting
B erosion   E heat and pressure
C evaporation

STRUCTURED QUESTIONS

QUESTION 10

The diagram below, which is not drawn to scale, shows the relative positions of the Sun, Moon and Earth.

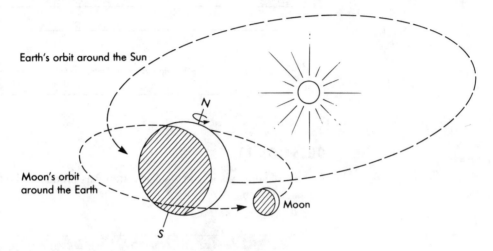

a) State how the motion of the Moon and Earth gives us

i) a year

_____

_____

(1)

ii) a lunar month

_____

_____

(1)

iii) a day

_____

_____

(1)

b) Draw labelled diagrams showing the positions of the Sun, Moon and Earth when:

i) spring tides occur _____

(1)

ii) neap tides occur _____

(1)

iii) What phase of the Moon would you expect to see when there are spring tides?

_____

(1)

c) A list of planets is given below.
    Mercury
    Pluto
    Mars
    Saturn
    Venus
    From the list choose which planet

i) has the most moons _____

(1)

ii) is the smallest planet _____

(1)

iii) has the longest year _____

(1)

d) If you attempted to live on Venus, describe **two** problems you might encounter other than those of getting there.

1 _____

_____

(1)

2 _____

_____

(1)
(MEG; 1988)

QUESTION 11

A study of some planets in a solar system has produced the following observations. They are listed in Table A.

PLANET	Mass compared with Earth	Atmosphere	Nature of surface	Average temperature (°C)
A	one tenth	None	Very hard and rocky	−25
B	half	Traces of oxygen. Little carbon dioxide. Little clouds.	Soft sand, some water	2
C	four times	Traces of oxygen. Nitrogen. Dense clouds.	Mainly water. Swamp land.	28

Table A

a) i) Suggest which planet may have the highest gravity.

_____

(2)

ii) Give a reason. (3 lines available)   *(2)*

b) i) Suggest which planet may support plant life.

_____

(1)

ii) Give **two** reasons. (7 lines available)   *(2)*

c) i) Which planet is **most unlikely** to support life?

_____

(1)

ii) Give **two** reasons. (7 lines available)   *(2)*

d) i) What would happen to water spilled by an astronaut on planet A?

"Oh dear!"

Astronaut drops insulated flask of water

Flask stopper comes off

_____

_____

(1)

ii) Give a reason for your answer.

_____

_____

(1)

e) Describe **five** benefits of space exploration to society. (10 lines available)

(5)

f) State **two** disadvantages of space exploration.

1 _____

_____

2 _____

_____

(2)
(Total marks 19)
(LEAG; 1988)

QUESTION 12

Figure 1 is a map of California showing the San Andreas fault.

a) i) What is meant by a 'fault' in the Earth's surface?

_____

_____

(1)

ii) The San Andreas fault is known as a 'tear' fault. Draw a labelled diagram to illustrate how such a fault occurs in the Earth's surface.

iii) Explain why earthquakes are common in this area. (6 lines available)   *(3)*

iv) Explain why volcanic eruptions are likely in areas of the Earth's crust like this. (6 lines available)   *(3)*

b) Earthquakes and volcanoes can give rise to destruction and enormous loss of human life. However, the San Andreas fault is in an area which is densely populated by people. Much of San Francisco was destroyed in 1906, and there is constant fear of further major earthquakes, yet still it is a densely populated region.

Write a scientific account of why such active regions of the Earth's crust are still attractive for humans to live in. (12 lines available)   *(6)*

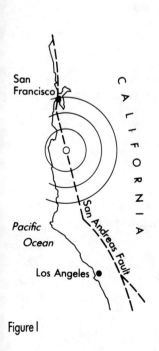

San Francisco

CALIFORNIA

Pacific Ocean

San Andreas Fault

Los Angeles

Figure 1

ANSWERS TO EXAMINATION QUESTIONS

MULTIPLE
CHOICE

ANSWER 1

Key D. Option A is a day, option B is a lunar month.

ANSWER 2

Key E, red giant. Option C, nebula, is the name of the gas cloud at the start of the life cycle. Option B is the name for a collection of many stars. Option D, a neutron star, is formed by some massive stars when they have exploded after becoming red supergiants, but the question refers to the Sun.

ANSWER 3

Key C, full moon.

ANSWER 4

Key D. Remember, the Moon never goes behind the Sun as in option A, as the Moon is a satellite of the Earth.

ANSWER 5

Key D, nitrogen. Option C, oxygen, is only present about 20%.

ANSWER 6

Key E, warm and raining. This type of weather is typical of a warm front. Option A is typical of a cold front.

ANSWER 7

Key C, the mantle.

ANSWER 8

Key E describes the formation of igneous rocks. Options A and B are both descriptions of sedimentary rocks, and option D describes metamorphic rocks.

ANSWER 9

Key E. Heat and pressure lead to the formation of metamorphic rocks.

STRUCTURED
QUESTIONS

ANSWER 10

a) i) A year is the time taken for the Earth to go once around the Sun.
    ii) A lunar month is the time taken for the Moon to go once around the Earth.
    iii) A day is the time taken for the Earth to spin once on its own axis.
b) i) diagram with the Sun, Moon and Earth in line
    ii) diagram with the Moon at right angles to line of Earth and Sun
    iii) full or new Moon
c) i) Saturn
    ii) Mercury (or Pluto)
    iii) Pluto
d) 1 no oxygen for breathing, so I would have to carry oxygen in cylinders
    2 very hot, so I would have to wear protective clothing

ANSWER 11

a) i) planet C
   ii) four times the mass of Earth
b) i) planet C
   ii) 1 traces of oxygen for respiration
       2 temperature similar to Earth
c) i) planet A
   ii) 1 no atmosphere
       2 very low temperatures
d) i) It would freeze.
   ii) temperature below freezing point of water, 0°C
e) 1 minerals may be discovered
   2 more space available for people to live
   3 new sources of food may be discovered
   4 alternative energy sources may be found
   5 better understanding of effects of gravity if research carried out where there is
     little gravity
     (Any similar answers acceptable.)
f) 1 very expensive, the money could be used to cure diseases on Earth
   2 dangerous: rockets explode and kill astronauts

ANSWER 12

a) i) The pressure of the Earth causes the rocks in the crust to break or fault.
   ii)

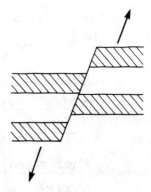

iii) Earthquakes happen near large faults, as two plates in the Earth's crust move past
     each other, aided by lubrication of a small proportion of molten material. Sudden
     fracturing releases energy, causing vertical and horizontal vibrations.
iv) Volcanic eruptions occur at weak places in the Earth's crust, as molten rock forces
    its way to the surface. In this area, lava runs from long fractures or fissures to form
    basalt plateaus.
b) The region may be very fertile and produce good crops. Other safer areas may be less
   fertile. The region may be on the coast and be accessible for trading, whereas other
   safer areas may be inland. There may be valuable minerals in the area which can offer
   employment to people involved in mining industries. The risk factor of earthquakes is
   being reduced, owing to their predictability. Buildings are being constructed to with-
   stand the shockwaves.
   (Any valid scientific suggestion would be acceptable here.)

A STUDENT'S ANSWER WITH EXAMINER'S COMMENTS

Some facts about four planets in a different solar system are given in the table below.

Planet	Temperature range °C	Atmosphere	Surface conditions	Mass compared with Earth = 1
Helios	0 to 50	Nitrogen, oxygen, some carbon dioxide and cloud	Water and sandy soil	1.4
Rheagos	−25 to −10	Hydrogen, some CO_2. No cloud	Very hard rock with some powdered material	4.6
Solos	−10 to 12	Mainly CO_2 with a lot of cloud	Swampland and water	3.2
Carmel	−45 to 40	None	Very hard rock	0.9

a) Study the table and then answer the following questions.

   i) Which planet is most likely to support plant and animal life as we know it?

   Helios ✓

   (1)

   ii) Give **three** reasons for your answer to part i).

   1 water available on Helios

   (1)

   2 the temperature is like Earth ✓

   (1)

   3

   (1)

   iii) Which planet has the greatest temperature variation?

   Helios X

   (1)

   iv) Why do you think Solos has a lot of cloud in its atmosphere?

   due to the CO_2, and water.

   (1)

   (WJEC; 1988)

"Good."

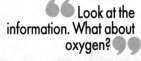**"Look at the information. What about oxygen?"**

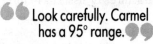**"Look carefully. Carmel has a 95° range."**

GETTING STARTED

Materials can be grouped in a variety of ways for different purposes:

- solid/liquid/gas;
- metals/non metals;
- element/compound/mixture;
- ionic/covalent.

Each form of classification has its uses. However if we want to understand why materials are placed in one group or another and why materials have the properties they do, then we need to understand something about the internal structure of matter.

The kinetic theory is a model (an idea) that takes the view that:

- all substances are made of particles;
- these particles have energy and are constantly moving – they have **kinetic energy**.

This idea can help us understand and explain many properties, such as expansion, melting, evaporation, diffusion, osmosis.

Atomic structure. Another useful idea is to imagine that atoms are themselves made of particles, which are found in the nucleus (centre) and as electrons orbiting the nucleus.

- A knowledge of the nucleus helps us understand radioactivity.
- A knowledge of the electrons and how they fit into an atom helps us understand how and why chemical reactions take place.

ESSENTIAL PRINCIPLES

All matter can be classified as either **solid**, **liquid**, or **gas**. These are called the three *states of matter*. The view that matter (solid, liquid or gas) is made up of particles which are in constant motion is called the *kinetic theory*. This idea can help us explain several properties of solids, liquids and gases.

The particles in a *gas* are moving very fast (they have a lot of kinetic energy) and are a great distance apart. The particles in a *liquid* are moving more slowly and are closer together. In a *solid* the particles are very close together and are 'vibrating' rather than moving freely. This idea is often shown by a piece of equipment similar to that in Figure 13.1. The motor turning very fast (providing a lot of energy) makes the metal spheres imitate a gas, but when it is moving more slowly (providing less energy) the spheres imitate a liquid.

66 Make sure you read
this carefully and try to
understand these ideas 99

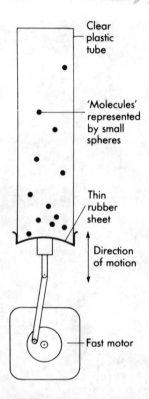

BROWNIAN MOTION

Brownian motion was first seen by a scientist called Robert Brown. He noticed that when he looked at pollen grains in water through a microscope they were 'jiggling' around in a random way. This was explained in later years by another scientist, who said that the strange movement was due to the very much smaller water particles (water molecules) hitting the pollen grains and making them move. This can also be seen in a 'smoke cell', where the particles of smoke are being moved by the air molecules striking them. The water or air molecules cannot be seen, even with the most powerful microscope; they are far too small, but the effect they have on the much, much larger pollen grains or smoke particles is very obvious.

This odd movement could only be explained by assuming that air (gas) and water (liquid) were made of particles and that these particles were moving.

Fig 13.1 This equipment imitates
the movement of particles.

Diffusion means *mixing*; gases, liquids and even solids can mix together or *diffuse* if left alone (even without anyone stirring them!). Diffusion provides *evidence* for the kinetic theory.

DIFFUSION IN GASES

a) When the top is removed from a bottle containing ammonia solution, you can smell the ammonia (which is a *gas*) even if you are some distance away. The ammonia has mixed with the air and spread out.

66 Ammonia molecules are
• moving faster than
hydrogen chloride 99

b) When the equipment in Figure 13.2 is set up and left for a short time, a white ring appears in the tube. This white substance is ammonium chloride, which is formed when the gas ammonia meets the gas hydrogen chloride. This could only happen if the gas particles had *kinetic energy* and were able to spread out and mix. Notice the white ring where the gases meet is *not* in the centre. Which gas spreads out the faster? Does this tell you which has the lighter particles?

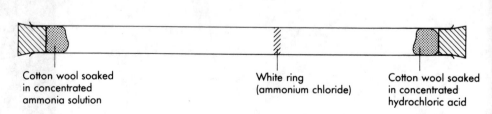

Fig 13.2 Diffusion in gases.

Cotton wool soaked
in concentrated
ammonia solution

White ring
(ammonium chloride)

Cotton wool soaked
in concentrated
hydrochloric acid

DIFFUSION IN LIQUIDS

Molecules move more slowly in solids

Diffusion can also occur in *liquids*, eg between ink and water. This can be shown by leaving a layer of water in contact with a layer of ink (see Figure 13.3a). The diffusion takes place more slowly than between gases because the particles have less energy. They are moving more slowly and are closer together.

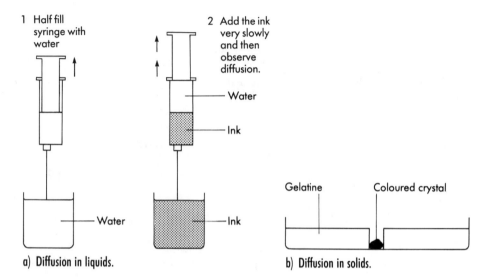

Fig 13.3   a) Diffusion in liquids.   b) Diffusion in solids.

DIFFUSION BETWEEN SOLIDS

Diffusion can take place between *solids*, although this takes place even more slowly. In Figure 13.3b a coloured crystal is placed in some gelatine; after a day or two the colour has spread throughout the gelatine.

The only way to explain these results is to assume that substances are made of *particles* and that these particles have kinetic energy (are moving).

Diffusion in action

Gas exchange in the alveoli of the lungs takes place by diffusion (see Figure 13.4). Diffusion of particles takes place from where there is a higher concentration to where there is a lower concentration. Particles will diffuse until they are evenly distributed.

Diffusion can also be a nuisance; it is because of diffusion that pollutant gases, eg from car exhausts, power stations and aerosols, can spread throughout the atmosphere.

	Concentration of gas in blood flowing to alveoli	*Concentration of gas in air in alveoli*
oxygen	low	high
carbon dioxide	high	low

Fig 13.4 Concentration of gases in the lung.

3 > EXPANSION

In general, when matter is heated it *expands*, though some substances expand more than others. Again, this can be understood if we imagine all substances to be made of particles. In Figure 13.5 we see that heating transfers energy to the substance, increasing the kinetic energy of its particles.

A common mistake is to say that the particles themselves get bigger; this is not so, it is the **gaps** between the particles that increase.

Expansion can be seen in action in many ways. For example:

Check up here with Chapter 8 on feedback and control

1 *Bimetallic strip*: this consists of two metals with different expansion rates (*coefficients of expansion*) stuck together. When heated, the strip bends. Bimetallic strips are often used in thermostats as a switching device, as well as for flashing light bulbs.
2 *Gaps* are left between the end-joints of rails on railways to allow for expansion.

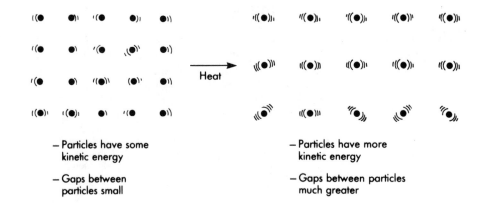

– Particles have some
  kinetic energy

– Gaps between
  particles small

– Particles have more
  kinetic energy

– Gaps between particles
  much greater

Fig 13.5 Expansion is caused by
increased kinetic energy of particles.

COMPARING SOLIDS, LIQUIDS AND GASES

In Figure 13.6 we see the relationships between the particles in solids, liquids and gases.

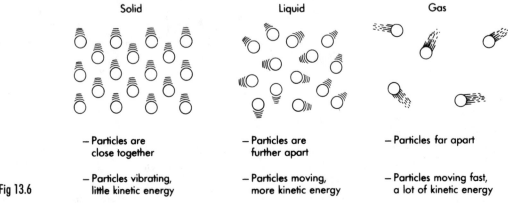

Solid

– Particles are
  close together

– Particles vibrating,
  little kinetic energy

Liquid

– Particles are
  further apart

– Particles moving,
  more kinetic energy

Gas

– Particles far apart

– Particles moving fast,
  a lot of kinetic energy

Fig 13.6

By adding more energy to the system (by **heating**), we can change a **solid** to a **liquid** to a **gas**. Similarly, by taking energy away from the system (by **cooling**), we can change a **gas** to a **liquid** to a **solid**.

MORE ABOUT GASES

The particles in a *gas* are moving very fast. When these particles hit something they exert a *force* on that object. The combined effect of the many millions of particles in a gas acting on an area is its *pressure*:

Pressure = force per unit area

Pressure is expressed in Newtons per square metre (N/m^2).

The pressure of a gas can be *increased* by *increasing its temperature* (heating). The gas particles will have more kinetic energy and so will be moving faster and striking the sides of a container harder and more often.

The pressure of a gas can also be *increased* by *reducing the volume* of that gas. The particles in the gas will be closer together, so they will strike the walls of the container more often.

Remember: the volume of a gas is equal to the volume of the container.

These ideas help to explain the 'gas laws' or 'gas patterns':

■ Pressure α temperature (provided the volume remains the same),

  or P/T = a constant.

■ Pressure α 1/volume (provided the temperature remains the same),

  or P × V = a constant.

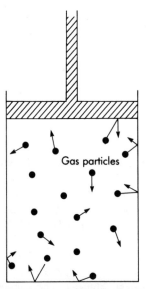

Fig 13.7 Particles striking the sides of a container create pressure.

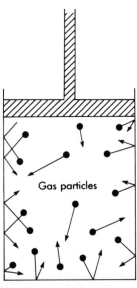

Fig 13.8 Increasing temperature increases pressure.

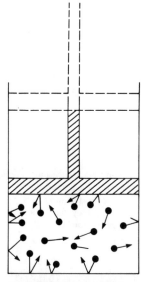

Fig 13.9 Decreasing volume increases pressure.

In order to make calculations using these gas 'laws', temperatures are measured on the *Kelvin* scale of absolute temperature, where 0K (Kelvin) is equal to –273° Celsius. 0K is known as *absolute zero*, or the temperature at which particles have no kinetic energy.

5 > CHANGING LIQUIDS TO GASES

What's happening when water boils?

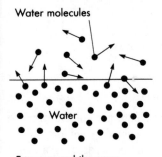

Every second the same number of molecules leave the water as return to the water

Fig 13.10 Equilibrium between a liquid and its vapour.

EVAPORATION

In a beaker of a liquid (eg water) the particles (water molecules) will have different energies. Some fast-moving molecules will have enough energy to escape the surface of the water. This is called **evaporation**. When the molecules escape the surface they bump into air molecules and some may even travel back into the liquid. The more molecules escape the surface and become vapour (gas form), the more chance there is that any newly escaped molecules will be knocked back into the water.

The *rate* of evaporation can be *increased* by:

■ blowing across the surface of the water, so that the vapour molecules are removed as they are formed;

■ heating, thereby giving more molecules the energy to escape. If enough energy is transferred to the water, *all* the molecules will be able to escape. We call this *boiling*. Water boils at 100°C at sea level.

■ by reducing the air pressure, thereby allowing the molecules to escape more easily. (This is why water boils at a lower temperature on mountains, where the air pressure is less than at sea level.)

Evaporation in action

1 Pressure cookers will cook food more quickly, because they allow the water to boil at a higher temperature. The increased pressure prevents the high-energy water molecules escaping from the surface of the water.

2 Aerosol cans contain liquids under pressure that are normally gases at atmospheric pressure (these liquids have boiling points just below room temperature). Pressing the nozzle releases the pressure, allowing some of the liquid (called the *propellant*) to evaporate, carrying the substance to be sprayed with it. Much concern has been shown recently because of some of these propellants, called chlorofluorocarbons (CFCs). These have been shown to damage the ozone layer of the Earth's atmosphere.

3 We cool down more quickly if our skin is wet. This is because our body heat evaporates the water molecules on our skin, taking the heat energy with them.

Manufacturers are now making 'ozone friendly' chemicals

FRACTIONAL DISTILLATION

A technological application

Let us return to liquids and consider *fractional distillation*. This is a process used in industry to separate liquids of different boiling points. Fractional distillation is used in the

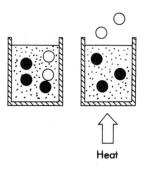

When the mixture is heated, the lighter molecules (O) move more quickly than the heavier molecules (●)

Fig 13.11

chemical industry to separate crude oil into 'fractions', ie mixtures of liquids with similar boiling points. The liquids with high boiling points have large, heavy particles, whereas those with low boiling points have small, light particles. The *heavier* particles need *more energy* to help them escape the surface of the liquid. The *forces* which attract the heavier particles to each other are greater than the forces between the lighter particles.

Fractional distillation in action

1 Fractional distillation can also be used to separate other liquids of differing boiling points, such as alcohol from wine.
2 It can also be used to purify zinc. When zinc is extracted from zinc ore it often contains a small amount of lead. These can be separated by fractional distillation, since the boiling point of zinc (908°C) is much lower than that of lead (1651°C).

6 > SOLUTIONS

Solutions can be made by *dissolving* substances. The substance that is dissolved is called the **solute**. The substance that does the dissolving is called the **solvent**.

Solvent + solute → solution

A *solvent* is normally a liquid (it could be a gas). Water is a very good solvent. A *solute* can be solid, liquid or gas.

A *concentrated* solution can be made by dissolving a large amount of solute in a small amount of solvent. A *dilute* solution can be made by dissolving a little solute in a large amount of solvent.

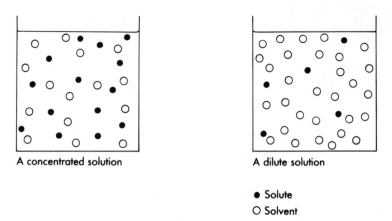

A concentrated solution   A dilute solution

Fig 13.12

● Solute
O Solvent

The *concentration* of solutions can be measured as grams of solute per cubic decimetre of solution (g/dm^3) or as moles of solute per cubic decimetre of solution (mol/dm^3). (The mole is a measure of the amount of substance; it relates to the number of particles present; see page 204.)

A *saturated* solution is one which contains the maximum amount of dissolved solute.

7 > OSMOSIS

One feature of particles is their size; for example, water particles are much smaller than sugar molecules. This difference in size can have some interesting effects.

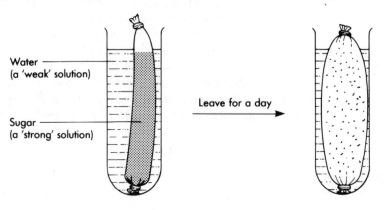

Water
(a 'weak' solution)

Leave for a day

Sugar
(a 'strong' solution)

Fig 13.13

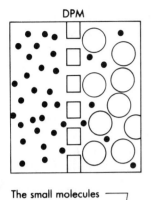

DPM

The small molecules of water pass through the membrane

The large molecules of sugar cannot pass through

Fig 13.14 Osmosis.

A concentrated sugar solution is placed in a bag made of visking tubing (a material like cellophane). The bag and its contents are then placed in a beaker of water. After a short time the bag will be seen to be much bigger. Why?

The effect is due to the visking tubing acting as a sort of particle sieve. The tubing material contains tiny holes or pores, just big enough to let the small water particles pass into the bag, but *not* to let the large sugar particles out. As a result, the volume of the bag increases.

The movement of water from a dilute to a concentrated solution is called *osmosis*. Materials such as visking tubing are called *differentially permeable membranes* or DPMs. If the process were allowed to continue, water would pass through the tubing walls until the concentration of the solutions inside and out were the same. Using a differentially permeable membrane to separate the substances is called *dialysis*.

DPMs in action

1 Cell membranes act as DPMs, allowing water to enter cells. Water passes into root hairs (special cells on the tips of roots) by osmosis. The cells contain a solution of sugars, salts and other solutes; water can enter through the cell membrane because the solution inside the cell is more concentrated than outside.

2 Kidney machines, which can take over when some people's kidneys fail because of disease, also use DPMs (flat tubes of cellophane). Harmful substances are removed from the blood by osmosis.

3 Some methods of food preservation work with help from DPMs and osmosis. All the bacteria (which cause food to decay) are single-celled organisms; whole cell membranes act as DPMs. Fruit can be preserved by placing it in a concentrated sugar solution. Since the solution outside the cell is more concentrated than the solution inside, water moves out of the cell and the bacteria are dehydrated and killed. Food preservation by 'salting' can be explained in the same way.

8   ATOMS, MOLECULES AND IONS

The *particle* is the building block of all matter. There are three types:

THE ATOM

This is the simplest particle; there are just over 100 different atoms. It is from these atoms, and combinations of these atoms, that the other two types of particles can be made. Each atom has its own name and symbol to represent it.

Atom	Symbol
Hydrogen	H
Oxygen	O
Carbon	C
Copper	Cu
Chlorine	Cl
Sodium	Na

Each chemical symbol is either a single capital letter (eg H) or else a capital letter followed by a small letter (eg Cl). Atoms are not generally found on their own.

THE MOLECULE

This is a particle that contains two or more atoms chemically joined together. Molecules can contain the same type of atom or different atoms chemically joined (bonded). Each molecule has a name and a chemical formula to represent which atoms are joined together.

Molecule	Name	Formula
(H)(H)	hydrogen	H_2
(H)(O)(H)	water	H_2O

Fig 13.15 Each molecule can be represented by a formula.

The numbers show the proportions of atoms present in the molecule. They refer to the atoms immediately before the number, and are always written below the line (subscript).

For example, glucose (a sugar), $C_6H_{12}O_6$ contains 6 atoms of carbon, 12 atoms of hydrogen and 6 atoms of oxygen.

THE ION

Ions have either lost or gained electrons

This is a particle that carries an electrical charge, which may be positive or negative. Each ion has a name and formula. Ions can be derived from single atoms or from combinations. The charge on the ion is shown as a number above the symbols (superscript). The size of the charge is indicated as a number, for example, $1+, 2+, 3+,$ or $1-, 2-, 3-$.

Ion	Formula
oxide	O^{2-}
chloride	Cl^-
copper	Cu^{2+}
carbonate	CO_3^{2-}

Not all possible combinations of atoms produce molecules and ions. There are rules governing their formation. This makes life a lot easier; these ideas are explained further in the next section (atomic structure).

9 ELEMENTS, COMPOUNDS AND MIXTURES

All substances can be classified according to the types of particles they contain and how these particles are joined (chemically bound or not). Substances can be classified as:

- **elements;**
- **compounds;**
- **mixtures.**

ELEMENTS

Try to understand the difference between element, compound and mixture

Elements are substances that contain only **one** type of atom. For example *copper* is an element containing copper atoms, *hydrogen* is also an element. Hydrogen gas contains hydrogen molecules. Elements cannot be broken down into simpler chemical substances.

COMPOUNDS

Compounds are substances which contain *more than one* type of atom chemically joined. The particles in a compound may be molecules or ions. A compound can be chemically split into simpler substances.

Water is a compound. It consists of water molecules. Each water molecule contains two atoms of hydrogen and one atom of oxygen. Water can be split by electrolysis into hydrogen and oxygen. *Sodium chloride* is also a compound. It consists of sodium ions and chloride ions. There is one sodium ion for every chloride ion. It can be split by electrolysis into sodium atoms and chlorine molecules.

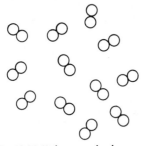
Fig 13.16 Hydrogen molecules.

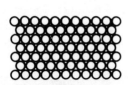
Fig 13.17 Copper atoms.

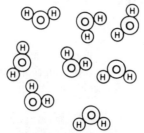
Fig 13.18 Water molecules.

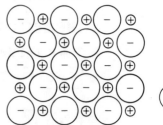
⊖ Chloride ion
⊕ Sodium ion

Fig 13.19 Sodium chloride.

MIXTURES

Mixtures are substances which can contain various amounts of elements and/or compounds *mixed together*. They can easily be physically separated. For example, a mixture of iron and sulphur can easily be separated with a magnet.

10 ATOMIC STRUCTURE

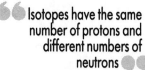

Cloud of electrons

Protons Neutrons

Nucleus

Fig 13.20 Particles which make up the atom.

❝ Learn the difference between atomic number and atomic mass ❞

Electron shells

Na

Nucleus   Electron (e)

Fig 13.21 The sodium atom.

❝ Isotopes have the same number of protons and different numbers of neutrons ❞

SUB-ATOMIC PARTICLES

Atoms themselves are made up of particles (often referred to as *sub-atomic particles*). These sub-atomic particles are:

- protons ⎫
- neutrons ⎭ found in the nucleus

- electrons   found orbiting the nucleus

The differences in these particles are shown in the table:

Sub-atomic particle	Mass (u)*	Charge
proton	1	+1
neutron	1	0
electron	very small ($\frac{1}{2000}$)	−1

*(u = atomic mass unit)

PATTERNS FOR ATOMS

- The number of protons in an atom is called the **atomic number**. Atoms have atomic numbers of 1 to 107.

- There are **always** the *same number* of electrons and protons, so every atom is electrically neutral. Charges on the electrons and protons 'cancel out'.

- Electrons are arranged in a series of *shells* around the nucleus. Each shell can only contain a limited number of electrons. For elements with an atomic number up to eighteen the *maximum* numbers in the first 3 shells are shown; thereafter the arrangement becomes more complex.

    1st shell   maximum 2 electrons
    2nd shell   maximum 8 electrons
    3rd shell   maximum 8 electrons

For example, in the sodium atom, which has 11 electrons, the arrangement is:
2 (in 1st shell); 8 (in 2nd shell); 1 (in 3rd shell)

The total number of protons and neutrons in the nucleus is called the **mass number** (each proton and neutron has a mass of 1u). There are usually about the same number of protons as of neutrons in a nucleus. You can work out the structure of an atom from the atomic number and the mass number:

Atomic number = number of *protons* (= number of *electrons*)

Mass number = number of *protons* + number of *neutrons*

These numbers can be added to the chemical symbol for the atom as follows:

Mass number A
                    ← chemical symbol
Atomic number Z

For example, in the sodium atom, $^{23}_{11}$ Na:

the atomic number = 11, therefore there are 11 protons and 11 electrons;
the mass number = 23 = number of protons + number of neutrons;
the number of neutrons = mass number – atomic number
                    = 23 – 11 = 12

Therefore, sodium has 11 protons, 12 neutrons and 11 electrons. We can show the electron configuration (arrangement of electrons in their shells) for sodium as Na:2,8,1. Figure 13.22 shows the patterns for the atoms of some common elements.

ISOTOPES

The type of atom is determined by its atomic number (number of protons). Carbon is carbon because it has 6 protons. Chlorine is chlorine because it has 17 protons. It is

Element	Number of protons in the nucleus (atomic number)	Number of protons and neutrons (mass number)	Number of electrons in each shell			
			Shell 1	Shell 2	Shell 3	Shell 4
Hydrogen	1	1	1			
Helium	2	4	2			
Lithium	3	7	2	1		
Beryllium	4	9	2	2		
Boron	5	11	2	3		
Carbon	6	12	2	4		
Nitrogen	7	14	2	5		
Oxygen	8	16	2	6		
Fluorine	9	19	2	7		
Neon	10	20	2	8		
Sodium	11	23	2	8	1	
Magnesium	12	24	2	8	2	
Aluminium	13	27	2	8	3	
Silicon	14	28	2	8	4	
Phosphorus	15	31	2	8	5	
Sulphur	16	32	2	8	6	
Chlorine	17	35.5	2	8	7	
Argon	18	40	2	8	8	
Potassium	19	39	2	8	8	1
Calcium	20	40	2	8	8	2

Fig 13.22

possible, however, for atoms such as these to have *different* mass numbers. This means that they contain different numbers of neutrons in their nucleii. Such atoms, which are chemically the same, but differ in their mass numbers, are called **isotopes**.

Chlorine has two isotopes: chlorine 35 (with a mass number of 35), and chlorine 37 (with a mass number of 37). Both these atoms behave in identical ways in chemical reactions (they have the same number of protons and electrons), but they have different numbers of neutrons in their nucleus. This is shown in Figure 13.23. In chlorine gas the proportion of these isotopes is always the same. There are 3 chlorine-35 atoms for every 1 chlorine-37 atom. The average number of protons and neutrons in a chlorine nucleus is therefore

$$\frac{35u + 35u + 35u + 37u}{4} = 35.5u \text{ (where u = 1 atomic mass unit)}$$

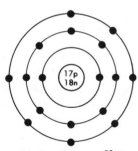

Chlorine—35 atom, $^{35}_{17}$Cl
2e.8e.7e

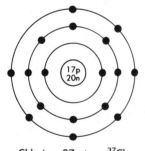

Chlorine—37 atom, $^{37}_{17}$Cl
2e.8e.7e

Fig 13.23 Isotopes of chlorine.

RELATIVE ATOMIC MASS

Different elements have different proportions of isotopes (some of which may be radio-active; see page 165). The **relative atomic mass** of an element is based on the average mass of all the atoms in the element (taking the isotope carbon 12 as the standard) and will not be a whole number. This is the number that is usually quoted in a list of atomic masses or given in the periodic table.

DETECTING ATOMS – FLAME TESTS

It is not always easy to know which atoms are present in a compound. Some, although not *all*, give distinct colours to flames, a fact used widely in making fireworks. In the laboratory, substances can be tested by placing a small amount on a clean wire in a 'blue' bunsen flame. The colour of the flame indicates the atom present.

Colour of flame	Atom present
apple green	barium
orange (brick red)	calcium
green	copper
blue flashes	lead
lilac	potassium
yellow	sodium
red	strontium

Radioactivity is the result of the breakdown of some nuclei in atoms. Some isotopes are unstable and will emit energy in the form of heat and radiation to become more stable, for example, carbon 14 and uranium 235. Some of these isotopes are naturally occurring, like the two examples given, whilst others, such as plutonium 239, can be manufactured. Naturally occurring radioactive isotopes are usually found in the heavier elements, or are the isotopes of lighter elements which have more neutrons present in their nuclei.

RADIOACTIVE DECAY

When the nucleus in radioactive materials breaks down it can emit different types of radioactivity:

- **Alpha** (α) particles: these are fast-moving helium nuclei (groups of 2 protons and 2 neutrons). They are easily stopped by a sheet of paper and will not travel very far through the air. They are weakly deflected by a magnetic field.

- **Beta** (β) particles: these are very fast-moving electrons which travel further through the air than α particles and are more difficult to stop. They can be stopped by thin sheets of metal, and are deflected by a magnetic field.

- **Gamma** (γ) rays: these are not particles at all, but a form of electromagnetic radiation of very short wavelength. They are very penetrating and are much more difficult to stop. They can be stopped by thick sheets of lead, but are not deflected by a magnetic field.

> Learn the characteristics of each type of radioactivity

When radioactive atoms **decay** and emit particles they change into other atoms. For example, when uranium 238 loses an α particle: $^{238}_{92}U \rightarrow ^{234}_{90}Th + ^4_2He$

Similarly, when carbon 14 loses a β particle: $^{14}_6C \rightarrow ^{14}_7N + ^0_{-1}e^-$

Radioactive atoms can be created by bombarding non-radioactive atoms with other particles. These could be α particles, β particles, or more often fast-moving neutrons.

DETECTING RADIOACTIVITY

Radioactivity was first discovered because of its ability to 'fog' photographic plates – in the same way as light affects photographic film. This is the way X-ray photographs are taken today (X-ray was the first name given to radioactivity). Radioactivity, however, also has the ability to ionise gases that it passes through, and it is this property that forms the basis of radiation detection technique today. The Geiger-Müller tube is an example. The tube is filled with a gas that is mainly argon. When radiation passes into the tube, some of the gas atoms are ionised. This causes a tiny electric current to flow, the size of which can be measured and is proportional to the amount of ionisation produced (ie the radiation present).

HALF-LIFE

Over a period of time, any radioactive material will decay and become stable (non-radioactive). *When* any particular nucleus will decay and release its radiation and energy cannot be predicted. They decay in a *random* way. However, different substances decay at different rates, and the rate of decay of all radioactive material is measured in **half-lives**.

The half-life is the time taken for the radioactivity to reduce by half. For a particular radioactive material the half-life is constant, whatever the conditions. Radioactive decay is unaffected by temperature or pressure. Half-lives can be very long or very short (thousands of years to less than a second). If you plot a graph for the decay of any radioactive material it will always follow the same pattern, as in Figure 13.24.

NATURAL RADIATION

We are constantly exposed to radioactivity from natural sources. This is referred to as *background radiation*. It arises from cosmic rays penetrating the atmosphere, soil, rocks (particularly granite in this country) and building materials, and from the food we eat (mainly owing to a radioactive isotope of potassium). In addition to these we receive small doses of radiation from medical treatment, such as chest and dental X-rays.

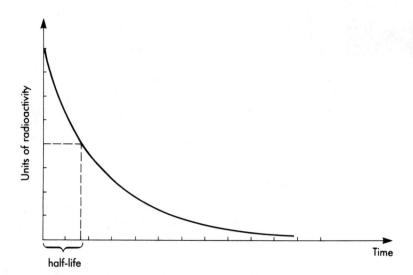

Fig 13.24 The decay curve for radioactive materials.

BIOLOGICAL EFFECTS OF RADIOACTIVITY

The effect of radiation on living tissue depends on several factors:

1 the strength of the radiation;
2 the length of exposure;
3 how much of the tissue (how many cells) is exposed.

The results of such exposure vary. There may be no serious effect if only a few cells are damaged, but in animals cancer may develop if the radiation dose is high enough. Radiation can also cause genetic mutations, so that future offspring are different in some way. In extreme cases, if enough cells are killed, the plant or animal may die.

USES OF RADIOACTIVITY

Radioactive isotopes can be used in a variety of ways, for example in industry, in medicine, for food production and for radiocarbon dating.

1 Manufacturers can check the thickness of metal containers, or the amounts of materials in packages, by measuring the amount of radiation that passes through. An example is measuring the amount of toothpaste in a tube.
2 All living things contain a large amount of carbon. Most of the carbon atoms are of the isotope carbon 12, but a small proportion are of the radioactive isotope carbon 14. This proportion of carbon 12 to carbon 14 is the same for all living things whilst they are alive. When the organism dies, the amount of carbon 14 decreases (half-life 5736 years). By measuring the amount of radioactive carbon *left*, one can date the item by reference to the half-life curve. This technique of carbon 14 dating was recently used to date the Turin Shroud.
3 Small amounts of radioisotopes can be introduced into underground water systems. Geiger counters can then be used to detect the position of leaks.
4 Food irradiation is a method of preserving food by directing radiation (usually gamma rays) on to fresh food. Such irradiation of food can destroy bacteria and prevent the growth of moulds, sterilise the contents of sealed packets, reduce the sprouting of vegetables or prolong the ripening of fruits. This irradiation does NOT make the food radioactive. However, it is not suitable for all food since it can change the taste.
5 Radiation can be used to control pests. Male insects are reared in the laboratory and are sterilised by being exposed to a controlled dose of gamma rays. They are then released into the wild, where they mate, competing with normal males. The females with which the sterilised males mate do not reproduce, so the insect population is quickly reduced.

EXAMINATION QUESTIONS

QUESTION 1

If fine pollen grains on the surface of water are examined under a microscope, it will be seen that the pollen grains are in random motion, frequently changing direction. The movement is most likely to be due to:

A air draughts blowing on the water
B chemical reaction between the pollen and the water
C attraction and repulsion between charged particles
D collisions between water molecules and pollen grains
E electrolysis of pollen grains

(LEAG; Specimen)

QUESTION 2

When ice is changing from a solid to a liquid at its melting point:
A heat is given out
B its particles become more ordered
C its particles gain energy
D its temperature increases

(SEG; Specimen)

QUESTION 3

When water changes into steam, the molecules become:
A much larger   D separate atoms
B more widely spaced   E much smaller
C less in mass

QUESTION 4

The separation of a liquid into different substances with similar boiling points is called:
A chromatography   D filtration
B distillation   E heating
C evaporation

QUESTION 5

When copper forms an ion it loses two electrons. This can be shown by:
A Cu; B Cu^-; C Cu^{2-}; D Cu^+; E Cu^{2+}

QUESTION 6

Phosphorous has an atomic number of 15 and a mass number of 31. How many protons does it have?
A 3; B 15; C 16; D 31; E 46

QUESTION 7

Chlorine has two isotopes. What is different about the atomic structure of the isotopes?
A the number of electrons
B the number of protons
C the number of neutrons
D the number of protons plus electrons

QUESTION 8

Which type of radiation would be stopped by a few sheets of paper?
A alpha particles
B beta particles
C gamma radiation
D X-rays
E sound waves

QUESTION 9

A radioactive substance has a half-life of 15 years. What proportion of the substance would be left after 30 years?

A a half   D a sixth
B a third   E an eighth
C a quarter

QUESTION 10

The graph below shows how the activity of a radioactive substance changes with time.

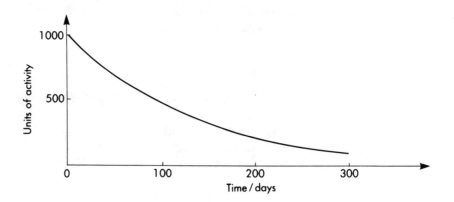

What is the half-life of this substance?
A 50 days; B 100 days; C 200 days; D 500 days; E 1000 days

**STRUCTURED
QUESTIONS**

QUESTION 11

When a teacher discovers an unlabelled radioactive source, she uses the apparatus below to find out the activity of the source and type (or types) of radiation being emitted.

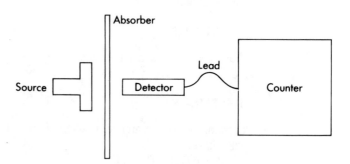

a) What does 'activity of the source' mean?

_____

(1)

The number of counts with **no** absorber is recorded. When a thin piece of tissue paper is used as an absorber the number of counts drops noticeably.

b) What type of radiation has the tissue paper absorbed?

_____

(1)

A sheet of lead 2 cm thick is now used as an absorber, but some radiation is still detected.

c) i) What is this radiation? _____

(1)

ii) Give **one** example of how this radiation can be used in either medicine or industry.

_____

_____

(1)
(MEG; 1988)

QUESTION 12

Tubes for toothpaste are filled as shown.

The empty tube is placed between a radioactive source and a detector.

Paste is put into the tube and, when the tube is full, it is moved along the production line for sealing.

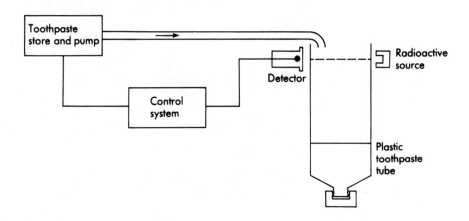

a) When the tube is full what effect will this have upon the beam of radiation reaching the detector?

_____

(1)

b) What instruction will the detector pass to the filling mechanism?

_____

(1)

c) What type of radiation would most likely be used for this purpose?

_____

(1)

d) Name a suitable detecting device.

_____

(1)

e) i) This is an example of a feedback control system. Which of the two kinds of feedback, negative or positive, is being used here?

_____

(1)

ii) Give one reason for your answer.

_____

(1)

iii) Some years ago toothpaste tubes were made of lead. Why could this system not have been used then?

_____

(1)
(MEG; Specimen)

QUESTION 13 (EXTENSION QUESTION)

The table below refers to the radius of some common atoms and their ions.

Element	Radius of atom	Radius of ion
Lithium	1.3	0.7
Sodium	1.5	1.0
Calcium	1.4	1.0
Tin	1.4	0.9
Oxygen	0.7	1.3
Sulphur	1.0	1.8
Bromine	1.1	2.0
Iodine	1.3	**X**

a) What pattern do you observe about the relative sizes of an atom and its ion when comparing metals and non-metals?   *(2)*

b) Predict the size of the radius of the iodine ion, **X**.   *(1)*

c) Name **two** elements from the above list which form negative ions.   *(2)*

Look at the periodic table in Chapter 14, and identify the position of sodium and lithium.

d) What is the size of the charge on these ions?   *(1)*

e) Sodium chloride has the following properties: high melting point, solid, dissolves in water to become an electrolyte.

   i) State the type of bonding which holds together the sodium and chloride ions.   *(1)*

   ii) Describe, with the help of diagrams, how the bonding between sodium and chloride ions differs from the bonding between two chlorine atoms.   *(3)*

(MEG; 1988)

A N S W E R S   T O
E X A M I N A T I O N   Q U E S T I O N S

MULTIPLE CHOICE

ANSWER 1

Key D. It is the water molecules moving about which make the pollen appear to be moving on its own.

ANSWER 2

Key C, the particles gain energy. Option B is incorrect because the particles are gaining energy and moving about more quickly. Option D, temperature rise, does not occur when ice is changing state from a solid into a liquid.

ANSWER 3

Key B, more widely spaced. Options A and E are wrong because the molecules do not change in size, they just have more space.

ANSWER 4

Key B, distillation. Option A is separating different coloured substances using paper.

ANSWER 5

Key E, Cu^{2+}. Electrons are negatively charged, so the ion has a positive charge as it has lost the electrons.

ANSWER 6

Key B, 15 protons: the atomic number.

ANSWER 7

Key C. The number of neutrons varies, the protons and electrons stay the same.

ANSWER 8

Key A, alpha particles, are stopped by paper; Option B, beta particles, are stopped by thin sheets of metal, and option C, gamma radiation, is stopped by thick sheets of lead.

ANSWER 9

Key C, a quarter. In 15 years a half would be left, so in another 15 years, a quarter of the original is left.

ANSWER 10

Key B. It has taken 100 days for the activity to reduce from 1000 units to 500 units (from the graph).

STRUCTURED QUESTIONS

ANSWER 11

a) the number of particles emitted per second by the source
b) alpha radiation
c) i) gamma radiation
    ii) to irradiate foods to kill bacteria

ANSWER 12

a) It will stop the beam.
b) to stop the filling mechanism
c) beta radiation
d) a Geiger-Müller tube
e) i) negative feedback
    ii) it stops the tube from becoming too full
    iii) beta radiation would be stopped by lead

ANSWER 13 (EXTENSION QUESTION)

a) The diameter of the metal atoms is larger than the diameter of the metal ions. The diameter of the non-metal atoms is smaller than the diameter of the non-metal ions.
b) 2.3
c) any two non-metals, eg oxygen and sulphur
d) 1
e) i) ionic bonding
    ii) In the bonding between sodium and chloride ions, an electron has moved from the outer shell of the sodium atom, so forming a positively charged sodium ion. The electron has joined the outer shell of the chlorine atom, so forming a negatively charged chloride ion. The two ions are attracted to each other.

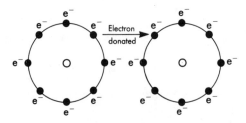

Positively charged
sodium ion:
full outer shell

Negatively charged
chloride ion:
full outer shell

In the bonding between two chlorine
atoms, one electron from each atom is
shared between the two atoms.

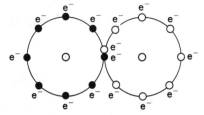

Each chlorine
atom now appears
to have a full
outer shell: shared electrons

A STUDENT'S ANSWER WITH EXAMINER'S COMMENTS

(with acknowledgements to 'The Observer')

Following the Chernobyl disaster in April 1986, the government in Britain started measuring the levels of radioactivity in sheep meat.

a) Why was it considered important to measure the radioactivity in sheep meat?

The sheep would have eaten the grass which
had radiation on it.

(2)

> **❝❝** Yes and state also that the radiation levels in meat had to be below a safe level for human consumption. **❞❞**

b) State **two** methods of detecting radiation from the meat.

1 Using a GM tube
2 Using photographic film

(2)

c) Complete Table 4 below about two radioactive particles.

> **❝❝** No. Thin metal sheets. **❞❞**

Name of particle	Description	Charge (+ or −)	How to identify each particle
Alpha	(i) helium nuclei	(ii) +	(iii) stopped by paper
Beta	(iv) electrons	(v) −	(vi) stopped by lead

Table 4

d) The number of counts per minute from a radioactive source is recorded once every half hour. The results are shown in Table 5.

Time/minutes	Corrected counts per minute
0	121
30	86
60	60
90	44
120	29
150	21
180	15

Table 5

i) What is the meaning of the term 'half-life'?

time taken for radioactivity to be half

 Good.

(2)

ii) Use the results in the table to calculate the half-life of the source. (Show your working.)

Approx 60 seconds to go from 120-60

∴ half life = 60 seconds

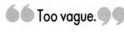 Good.

(2)

e) Name **two** sources of background radiation.

1 Rocks

2 TV sets

 TV sets are not usually regarded as a source of background radiation.

(2)

f) Discuss the advantages and disadvantages of using radioactive materials in industry and medicine.

They can be dangerous and harm people.

They can kill cancer cells inside people.

X rays are used to see broken bones. They

can sterilise equipment.

Too vague.

Good points here.

 State which are advantages/ disadvantages.

(4)

(LEAG; 1988)

CHAPTER

14

THE PERIODIC TABLE

PERIODS AND GROUPS

BONDING AND THE
PERIODIC TABLE

GIANT STRUCTURES

MACROMOLECULES

VALENCY AND
WRITING FORMULAE

TRENDS AND THE
PERIODIC TABLE

GETTING STARTED

The periodic table is a useful way of grouping together *different elements* which have *similar properties*: for example, metals and non-metals. The elements are arranged in order of their *atomic number* (proton number) and approximately in order of *relative atomic mass*.

The periodic table can be used as a basis for predicting the physical and chemical properties of different elements. The position of an element in the table enables you to predict its melting point, density and reactivity, and the formulae of any compounds which the element may form.

Across the periodic table are *periods* or rows, and down the table are the *groups* or columns.

ESSENTIAL PRINCIPLES

1 ▷ PERIODS AND GROUPS

The periodic table is a complete list of all the elements and hence the atoms that exist. It is more than just a list because it is arranged in a definite grid or pattern of rows and columns. Each *row* is called a *period*, and each *column* is called a *group*. The simplest atom (the lightest) appears at the top left, and the most complex (the heaviest) appears at the bottom right. The atoms are arranged in *increasing* order of mass.

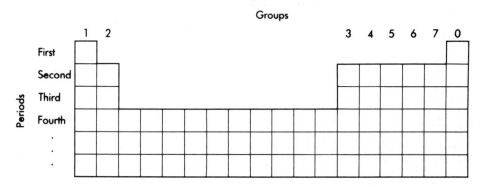

Fig 14.1

PERIODS

Each period corresponds to an electron shell. As you move across the *first period* you are filling the *first* electron shell:

atom:	H	He
atomic number:	1	2
electron configuration:	1	2

As you move across the *second period* you are filling the *second* electron shell:

atom:	Li	Be	B	C	N	O	F	Ne
atomic number:	3	4	5	6	7	8	9	10
electron configuration:	2,1	2,2	2,3	2,4	2,5	2,6	2,7	2,8

In the *third period* you are filling the *third* electron shell:

atom:	Na	Mg	Al	Si	P	S	Cl	Ar
atomic number:	11	12	13	14	15	16	17	18
electron configuration:	2,8,1	2,8,2	2,8,3	2,8,4	2,8,5	2,8,6	2,8,7	2,8,8

This means that as you go *across* the table the atoms are getting *heavier* (more protons and neutrons). As you go *down* the table the atoms are getting *bigger* (more electron shells which take up more space).

GROUPS

The groups can be considered to consist of 'families' of elements that behave in similar ways in chemical reactions. You will notice that as you go *down a group*, the atoms have the *same number of electrons in their outer shell*.

For example, in group 1:

atom	electron configuration
H	1
Li	2, 1
Na	2, 8, 1
K	2, 8, 8, 1

This is important since it is the *arrangement* of electrons in their shells which determines the way in which atoms behave in chemical reactions.

BONDING AND THE PERIODIC TABLE

There is a stable arrangement for electrons in atoms. This occurs when an atom has a **filled outer shell**. All the atoms in group 0 have filled outer shells. These atoms do not react with other substances except for a very few special cases.

All other atoms react in order to fill their outer electron shells. They can do this in two ways:

- ionic bonding;
- covalent bonding.

IONIC BONDING

In the reaction between sodium and chlorine atoms, electron transfer has occurred to form ions:

$$Na + Cl \rightarrow Na^+ + Cl^-$$

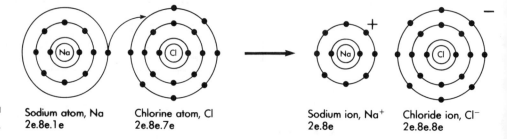

Fig 14.2 Formation of ions when sodium reacts with chlorine.

Sodium atom, Na
2e.8e.1e

Chlorine atom, Cl
2e.8e.7e

Sodium ion, Na$^+$
2e.8e

Chloride ion, Cl$^-$
2e.8e.8e

The sodium atom has *lost* an electron to become a sodium ion: we show this as Na$^+$.
The chlorine atom has *gained* an electron to become a chlorine ion: we show this as Cl$^-$.
Both the ions that are formed have filled outer shells.

Once these two ions have been formed, they will attract each other because of the opposite charges of the ions. (Like charges repel; unlike charges attract.) The reason the electron transfer takes place in this direction is that any transfer of electrons takes energy. It is easier to take 1 electron from sodium than 7 from chlorine. This results in the general rule:

- Metals form **positive ions**.
- Non-metals form **negative ions**.

A positive ion is called a *cation*; a negative ion is called an *anion*.

Metal atoms	Group	Electrons lost	Ion formed
lithium	1	1	Li$^+$
sodium	1	1	Na$^+$
potassium	1	1	K$^+$
magnesium	2	2	Mg^{2+}
calcium	2	2	Ca^{2+}
aluminium	3	3	Al^{3+}
Non-metal atoms	Group	Electrons gained	Ion formed
oxygen	6	2	O^{2-}
sulphur	6	2	S^{2-}
chlorine	7	1	Cl$^-$
bromine	7	1	Br$^-$
iodine	7	1	I$^-$

Fig 14.3 Some atoms and their ions.

Also, as a general rule:

- Group 1 elements form ions with **one positive** charge (they have one electron to lose).

- Group 2 elements form ions with **two positive** charges (they have 2 electrons to lose).
- Group 3 elements form ions with **three positive** charges (they have 3 electrons to lose).
- Group 7 elements form ions with **one negative** charge (they have one space to fill).
- Group 6 elements form ions with **two negative** charges (they have two spaces to fill).

Properties of ionic compounds

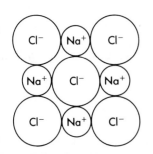

Fig 14.4 The sodium chloride lattice.

Try to understand the differences between ionic and covalent bonding

The formation of ions in this way (from the reaction between metal and non-metal atoms) results in positively and negatively charged particles which have a strong attraction for each other. These ions form a giant ionic lattice, in which each ion is surrounded by as many ions of the opposite charge as possible, similar to that in Figure 14.4.

These strong forces of attraction mean that ionic substances have high melting points and high boiling points and are solids at room temperature. Ionic substances will also usually dissolve in water. Since ionic compounds contain charged particles they will conduct electricity, but only if the ions are free to move. This can happen if:

- the compound is heated until it is molten;
- the compound is dissolved in water.

Electrolysis

The process of ionic substances conducting electricity is called *electrolysis*. During this process the ions are turned back into atoms. This is illustrated by the electrolysis of molten sodium chloride.

The two rods that extend into the liquid are called the *electrodes*. The positive electrode is called the *anode* and attracts the negative ions (*anions*). The negative electrode is called the *cathode* and attracts the positive ions (*cations*).

At the anode the chloride ion loses electrons and turns back into atoms. The atoms join in pairs to form chlorine molecules. At the cathode the sodium ions gain electrons and turn back into sodium atoms.

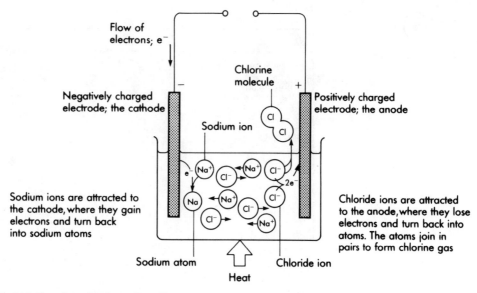

Fig 14.5 Electrolysis of molten sodium chloride.

COVALENT BONDING

Atoms have stable arrangements if their outer electron shells are filled. This can happen by the *sharing* of electrons. Non-metal atoms combine to form molecules by sharing electrons in their outer shells. The exception to this is the atoms in Group 0, which have stable electron arrangements already.

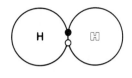

or H – H

Fig 14.6 The hydrogen molecule.

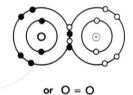

or O = O

Fig 14.7 The oxygen molecule.

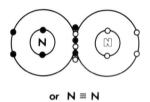

or N ≡ N

Fig 14.8 The nitrogen molecule.

Fig 14.9 It is only the non metal atoms which form molecules.

Two hydrogen atoms will join together to form a hydrogen molecule, by sharing their electrons. Each atom can then be considered to have a filled electron shell (2 electrons). The shared pair of electrons is called a *covalent bond* and can be shown as a line between the two atoms H–H. The molecule is represented as H_2.

An oxygen molecule is formed in a similar way, but because each oxygen molecule has 6 electrons in its outer shell (electron configuration 2,6) it has two 'spaces' to be filled. It does this by each atom sharing **two** of its electrons; this forms a *double covalent bond*. The molecule is represented as O_2.

Similarly, nitrogen atoms will pair up to form nitrogen molecules, but this time by forming a *triple* covalent bond. Each covalent bond is a shared pair of electrons. The nitrogen molecule is represented as N_2.

Non-metal atoms exist in the free state as *molecules* (see Figure 14.9) because in this way they can have *stable electron arrangements*.

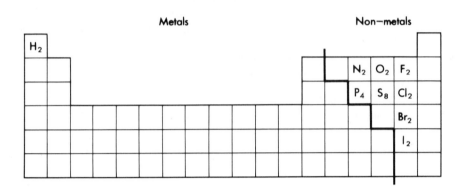

SOME COMMON COVALENT COMPOUNDS

Non-metal atoms will combine with other non-metal atoms to form *covalent compounds*: for example, water (H_2O).

Remember, each line represents a shared pair of electrons, or in other words, a covalent bond.

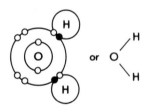

or O

Fig 14.10 Water molecule.

Name	Formula	Structure
carbon dioxide	CO_2	O = C = O
ammonia	NH_3	
methane	CH_4	
ethane	C_2H_6	
ethene	C_2H_4	
ethyl alcohol	C_2H_5OH	

Fig. 14.11 Some common covalent compounds

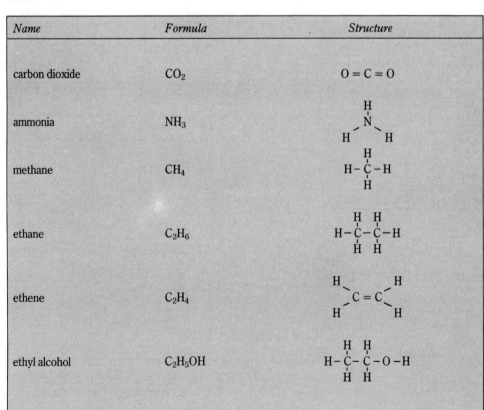

PROPERTIES OF COVALENT COMPOUNDS

Although the covalent bonds holding together the atoms in a molecule are *strong*, the forces holding the molecules themselves are *weak*. This means that covalently bonded substances are often gases or liquids, or solids with relatively low melting points and low boiling points. They do not conduct electricity and do not usually dissolve in water.

COMPARING COVALENT AND IONIC COMPOUNDS

	Ionic compounds	*Covalent compounds*
relation to periodic table	formed between metal atoms and non-metal atoms	formed between non-metal atoms
melting point	high >250°C	low <250°C
boiling point	high >500°C	low <500°C
electrical conductivity	good conductor when molten or in solution	non-conductors
solubility in water	usually soluble	usually insoluble

WATER AS A SOLVENT

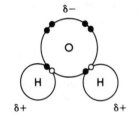

Fig 14.12 The polar water molecule.

Water dissolves ionic substances. The reason is that the water molecule is *polar* – it has a slight negative charge ($\delta-$) at one end and a slight positive charge ($\delta+$) at the other. This is a result of the oxygen atoms attracting the electron pairs of the bonds with the hydrogen atoms more strongly. Water can therefore dissolve ionic substances. Water is not the only polar molecule (although it is more polar than most). Water will also dissolve other molecular compounds which are themselves slightly polar, eg ethanol.

---

3 ▷ GIANT STRUCTURES

METALS AS GIANT STRUCTURES

Metals are giant structures. The metal atoms are 'bonded' together in an unusual way. The metal atoms lose some of their outer electrons and so become, in effect, positive ions. These electrons then move around the atoms freely. The metal atoms/ions are in a sea of electrons. The electrons are free to move and are shared by all the atoms. This idea helps to explain many of the properties of metals.

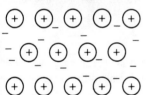

Fig 14.13 Metals are giant structures.

- *High boiling points and melting points:* the attraction between the 'ions' and electrons is strong, so usually the metals will have high melting points and boiling points and will be strong and hard.

- *Conduction of electricity:* the ease of movement of electrons will mean that metals will easily conduct electricity when a potential difference is applied across the metal.

---

4 ▷ MACRO-MOLECULES

Some covalently bonded molecules do not have the properties indicated above, because their molecules are *very large*. They have a large number of covalent bonds and form giant molecules, or *macromolecules*.

ELEMENTS

Carbon is an example of an element which forms large numbers of covalent bonds between its atoms. It can do this in two ways, to form *diamond* or *graphite*. These two forms of carbon are called *allotropes*. Some other elements have different allotropic forms, but not necessarily forming giant molecules (eg sulphur).

Diamond is very strong because each carbon atom is linked to four other carbon atoms. A diamond crystal is one giant molecule. Graphite is very strongly bonded, but in layers; each layer is a giant molecule. However, the forces holding the layers together are weak, so they slide over each other. This property is made use of in pencils; the pencil 'lead' is really graphite.

Silicon is in the same group as carbon; it too has similar abilities to form giant structures. The structure of silicon is the same as that of diamond. Silicon dioxide, a compound of silicon, has a giant structure, the atoms being bonded by covalent bonds. We come across this substance quite often; it appears as sand and as quartz in rocks and it can be made into glass. Silicon is in fact the second most common element found in the Earth's crust (28%), the first being oxygen.

Diamond   Graphite

Fig 14.14   Allotropes of carbon.

COMPOUNDS OF CARBON

There are many *compounds* of carbon that form very large molecules. They exist because of carbon's ability to form long chains (as well as rings) of covalently bonded carbon atoms. These macromolecules are called *polymers*; some exist naturally, and some are man-made. Examples of these are starch, wool, polythene, and nylon. These compounds contain atoms other than carbon, but it is the carbon atoms that provide the ability to form large molecules.

Although the polymers have large molecules which contain many thousand atoms, the giant molecules of carbon and silicon contain many *billion* atoms.

PROPERTIES OF MACROMOLECULES

The *giant* molecules, such as carbon, have very high melting points and boiling points, will not dissolve in water and generally will not conduct electricity. Graphite, one form of carbon, is an exception. Silicon will also weakly conduct electricity, and is regarded as a 'semi-conductor'; it is this property that makes silicon valuable for use as 'microchips' in computer technology.

The *large* molecules (polymers), such as starch, have higher melting points and boiling points than ordinary molecules, but not as high as giant molecules or ionic compounds (which are also giant structures). They are not very soluble in water (most are insoluble) and will not conduct electricity.

<table>
<tr><td>5 ></td></tr>
</table>

5 > VALENCY AND WRITING FORMULAE

> Check back to the beginning of the chapter

A *formula* for a compound shows the ratio of atoms present in that compound, whether it is ionic or covalent. Each atom has a 'combining power', which is called the *valency*. The valency of an atom depends on the number of electrons in it outer shell and hence its position in the periodic table. For example, atoms in group 1 have a valency of 1; atoms in group 2 have a valency of 2.

In general as one moves *across* the periodic table the valency gradually *increases* to a maximum of 4, then gradually decreases to 0. This is not always the case, and there are some important exceptions, but it is a good 'rule of thumb'.

Atom	Na	Mg	Al	Si	P	S	Cl	Ar
Outer shell electrons	1	2	3	4	5	6	7	8
Group no	1	2	3	4	5	6	7	0
Valency	1	2	3	4	3	2	1	0

The reason for this of course is that if we consider atoms reacting to form ions, one atom has to lose electrons, whereas the other atom has to gain electrons. Those atoms (non-metals), like sulphur, which have 6 electrons in their outer shell can be considered to have 2 spaces (to complete the full set of 8). It is easier to fill 2 spaces than it is to remove 6 electrons. When atoms join up to form ions, the number of electrons *leaving* one atom must match the number of electrons being *gained* by the others. How can this happen? It often helps to imagine the atoms to have hooks representing their valencies (electrons to be donated or accepted).

Example 1: *Sodium will react with chlorine to form a compound, sodium chloride*

Na has a valency of 1 (Na)

Cl has a valency of 1: we can represent it as (Cl)

When these atoms combine *all* hooks must be attached:

(Na)⌒(Cl)

So the formula is NaCl.

Example 2: *Magnesium will react with chlorine to form magnesium chloride*

Magnesium: valency 2: (Mg)

Chlorine: valency 1: (Cl)

When they join, *all* hooks must be attached, so we need an extra Cl to take care of the otherwise spare hook:

(Cl)
(Mg)
(Cl)

The formula is therefore MgCl$_2$. The 2 as subscript refers to 2 atoms of what is immediately in front, ie Cl atoms.

Example 3: *The formula of aluminium oxide*

Aluminium: valency 3 (Al)

Oxygen: valency 2 (O)

When they join, *all* hooks must be attached:

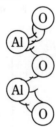

So the formula is Al$_2$O$_3$.

Sometimes we can regard a collection of atoms, referred to as a *radical*, as having a valency. For example:

sulphate SO$_4$$^{2-}$: valency 2
nitrate NO$_3$$^-$: valency 1
carbonate CO$_3$$^{2-}$: valency 2
hydroxide OH$^-$: valency 1

Example 4: *The formula of copper nitrate*

Copper: valency 2 (Cu)

Nitrate: valency 1 (NO$_3$$^-$)

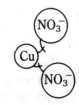

Formula Cu(NO$_3$)$_2$

Notice the use of brackets with the 2 as subscript outside. This means 2 of whatever is inside the brackets.

You will not be expected to remember all the valencies for these atoms or radicles, but it is worth remembering how they are related to the *position* in the periodic table.

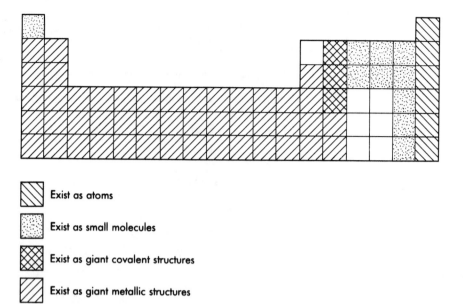

Exist as atoms

Exist as small molecules

Exist as giant covalent structures

Exist as giant metallic structures

Fig 14.15 Trends and the periodic table.

TRENDS DOWN A GROUP: FAMILIES OF ELEMENTS

Each group in the periodic table contains elements which behave in similar ways in chemical reactions. This is because they have the *same number of electrons in their outer shells*. They do, however, differ by degrees in their intensity of reaction as you travel 'down the group'. Examination syllabuses require only a detailed study of:

- group 1 – the alkali metals (a group of metals);
- group 7 – the halogens (a group of non-metals);
- group 0 – the inert gases (a special group).

Group 1 – the alkali metals

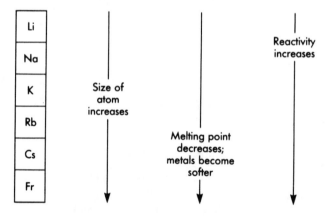

Fig 14.16 The alkali metals.

■ **Reaction with air:** lithium, sodium and potassium react with air to form oxides. When the metal is cut with a knife its surface quickly tarnishes. The speed of reaction increases as you move down the group. If any of the alkali metals are represented by M, the general reaction is:

$$4M + O_2 \rightarrow 2M_2O$$

Formulae of oxides formed: Li_2O, Na_2O, K_2O. These oxides dissolve in water to produce alkaline solutions.

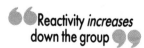Reactivity *increases* down the group

■ **Reaction with water:** lithium, sodium and potassium react quickly with water. Lithium when placed on water 'fizzes' and quickly reacts. Sodium will buzz around on the surface of the water giving the odd spark. Potassium reacts more violently, producing a lilac flame. Reactivity increases as you move down the group. Each produces a strong alkaline solution with water. The general reaction is:

$$2M + 2H_2O \rightarrow 2MOH + H_2$$

Formulae of hydroxides produced: LiOH, NaOH, KOH.

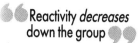

66 Reactivity *decreases* down the group **99**

■ **Reaction with halogens:** each will react with halogens to form compounds called halides. The reactivity will increase as one moves down the group. For example, the reaction with chlorine:

$$2M + Cl_2 \rightarrow 2MCl$$

Formulae of halides formed: LiCl, NaCl, KCl.

■ **Reactivity trends:** the atoms react to form ions which have a charge of $1+$. In forming these ions, eg Na^+, an electron has to be removed from the outer shell. Those atoms which have outer shells *further away* from the positive nucleus (the bigger atoms) will require *less energy* to remove that electron, and so will tend to be *more reactive*; hence reactivity *increases* as you move down the group: $Cs>Rb>K>Na>Li$.

Group 7 : The halogens

■ **Reaction with metals:** the halogens will react with metals to form metal halides. For example, iron with chlorine:

$$2Fe + 3Cl_2 \rightarrow 2FeCl_3$$

The reactivity of the halogens decreases as you move down the group.

■ **Reaction with water:** the halogens will react with water to form acidic solutions which also act as bleaches. The reactivity decreases as you move *down the group*, as does the bleaching power of the solutions. The solutions produced from iodine and bromine are weak acids, whereas chlorine and fluorine will produce strong acids. For example:

$$H_2O + Cl_2 \rightarrow HCl + HOCl \text{ (chloric acid – bleach)}$$

■ **Reactivity trends:** when halogens react with metals they do so to form ions:

F^-, fluoride ion; Cl^-, chloride ion; Br^-, bromide ion; I^-, iodide ion

The ease with which these atoms form ions depends on the number of electron shells the atom has. In order to form an ion, the atom has to gain an electron. The atom with its outer shell closer to the positive nucleus will find this easiest, because of the strong pulling power of the positive nucleus. The *larger* the atom, the *further away* the outer electron shell, so the less influence the nucleus will have. Thus we would expect fluorine to be much more reactive than iodine, which is indeed the case.

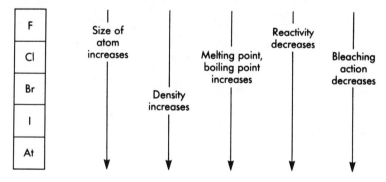

Fig 14.17 The halogens.

Group 0 : The inert gases

These gases show no reactivity (with a very few exceptions), because they have stable filled outer orbitals. They do not form molecules but exist as separate atoms (see Figure 14.18).

Fig 14.18 The inert gases.

TRENDS ACROSS A PERIOD

As one moves across a period of the periodic table, there is a gradual change in the properties of the elements. Remember, as you move *across* a period you are *adding one more electron* to the outer shell of the atom each time. For example, Figure 14.19 compares the elements of the third period; Figure 14.20 summarises the overall trends.

Metal/non-metal	Na m	Mg m	Al m	Si n/m	P n/m	S n/m	Cl n/m	Ar n/m
Outer shell electrons	1	2	3	4	5	6	7	8
Valency	1	2	3	4	3	2	1	0
Oxidation no.	+1	+2	+3	+4	−3	−2	−1	0
Melting point/°C	98	650	660	1410	44	113	−100	−189
Boiling point/°C	880	1100	2470	2355	280	444	−35	−186
Oxide nature	basic	basic	amphoteric	acidic	acidic	acidic	acidic	–
Formula of oxide	Na_2O	MgO	Al_2O_3	SiO_2	P_2O_3	SO_2	Cl_2O	–
Formula of chloride	$NaCl$	$MgCl_2$	$AlCl_3$	$SiCl_4$	PCl_3	S_2Cl_2	Cl_2	–

m = metal: n/m = non-metal

Note: Similar trends in properties occur across the second period from lithium to neon. It is a valuable exercise to draw up a table for this period using a data book for the numerical data.

Fig. 14.19 Trends across the 3rd period

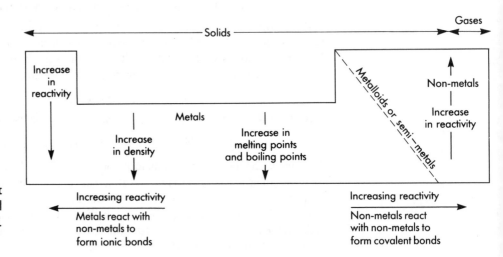

Fig 14.20 Trends in the periodic table. *Remember*, these are general trends – there are exceptions.

E X A M I N A T I O N   Q U E S T I O N S

**MULTIPLE
CHOICE**

Questions 1, 2 and 3 refer to the periodic table shown below.

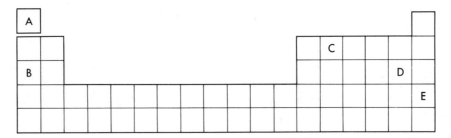

QUESTION 1

Which letter represents the lightest element?

QUESTION 2

Which letter represents a halogen?

QUESTION 3

Which letter represents a very reactive metal?

Questions 4 and 5 refer to the diagram opposite showing the atomic structure of sodium.

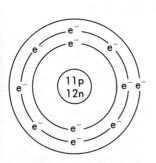

QUESTION 4

What is the atomic number of sodium?
A 1; B 7; C 11; D 12; E 23

QUESTION 5

What is the valency of sodium?
A 1; B 2; C 3; D 11; E 23

**STRUCTURED
QUESTIONS**

QUESTION 6

1								2
H								He

3	4		5	6	7	8	9	10
Li	Be		B	C	N	O	F	Ne
11	12		13	14	15	16	17	18
Na	Mg		Al	Si	P	S	Cl	Ar
19	20							
K	Ca							

Figure 1

Figure 1 shows the first 20 elements of the periodic table.

a) Explain briefly why the elements in the periodic table are arranged in vertical columns.

_____

_____

(1)

Imagine that a new element has been discovered on the Moon. It has been named 'Lunum'. On the Moon it was a silvery colour but rapidly tarnished when brought back to Earth.

Lunum can be cut with a knife and bursts into flame on contact with water, releasing hydrogen gas.

b) Using the periodic table given in Figure 1, give the symbol of one element with similar properties.

_____

(1)

c) Explain why Lunum tarnished on Earth yet was silvery on the Moon.

_____

_____

(2)

d) How would you test Lunum's magnetic properties? What is the likely outcome of the test?

Test _____

_____

Outcome _____

(2)

e) i) Lunum is given the symbol Lm; write the chemical formula for:

   1 Lunum chloride _____

   2 Lunum oxide _____

(3)

   ii) Describe three properties you would expect Lunum chloride to have.
   (3 lines available)

(3)

f) Lunum is unlikely to be found in its pure state on earth. Suggest a reason for this.
(2 lines available)

(2)

(NISEC; 1988)

QUESTION 7

a) Table 1 compares the number of protons and electrons in sodium and chlorine atoms and gives the arrangement of electrons in each atom.

	Sodium Na	*Chlorine Cl*
Number of protons	–	17
Number of electrons	11	–
Arrangement of electrons	2,8,1	2,8,7

Table 1

i) Complete the table above.   *(2)*

ii) Which particles, apart from protons, are found in the nucleus of a sodium or chlorine atom?   *(1)*

iii) In which group of the periodic table are the elements sodium and chlorine placed?

Sodium _____ Chlorine _____

(2)

b) Table 2 compares the number of protons and electrons in sodium and chloride *ions*.

	Sodium Na$^+$	*Chlorine Cl$^-$*
Number of protons	11	17
Number of electrons	10	18
Arrangement of electrons	2,8	2,8,8

Table 2

    i) What change takes place when a sodium ion is formed from a sodium atom?   *(1)*

    ii) What change takes place when a chloride ion is formed from a chlorine atom?

_____

    (1)

c) Figure A below shows the arrangement of sodium and chloride *ions* in a crystal of sodium chloride.

Figure A

    ● Sodium ions
    ○ Chloride ions

    i) State **two** changes which take place in the crystal when melting occurs.

    1 _____

    2 _____

    (2)

    ii) Why does sodium chloride have a high melting point?

_____

    (1)
    (Total marks 10)
    (LEAG; Specimen)

QUESTION 8

Three pieces of information are given below.
    1 Substances can be elements, compounds or mixtures.
    2 Elements can be metals or non-metals.
    3 A group in the periodic table contains elements having similar properties.
Using only this information, say which **one** of the substances in **each** of the following lists is different from the other three.
    For **each** list give the reason for your choice.

a) Carbon, iron, copper, magnesium.

_____

_____

    (1)

b) Neon, hydrogen, argon, helium.

_____

_____

    (1)

c) Sulphur dioxide, zinc oxide, copper (II) sulphate, air.

_____

_____

    (1)
    (WJEC; 1988)

QUESTION 9

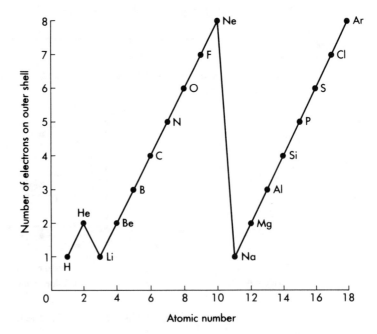

a) The graph shows the relationship between the number of electrons in the outer shell of the first 18 elements in the periodic table and their atomic numbers.
   Use the graph to help you answer the following questions.

i) Name **two metals** having two electrons on their outer shells.

_____

(2)

ii) Name **two non-metals** having seven electrons on their outer shells.

_____

(2)

b) Name the kind of bond formed between elements when

i) the outer electrons are donated and received

_____

ii) the outer electrons are shared

_____

(2)

iii) Considering i) and ii) above, write down the formula of the compounds formed between

    1 aluminium (Al) and chlorine (Cl)   *Al Cl₃* _____

    2 boron (B) and fluorine (F) _____*BF₃*_____

    3 carbon (C) and fluorine (F) ____*CF₄*_____

(3)

iv) What kind of bonds are formed between carbon and fluorine?

_____*Covalent*_____

(1)

(WJEC; Specimen)

QUESTION 10

a) The element astatine has an atomic (proton) number of 85 and a mass number of 210.

i) How many protons are in the nucleus? _____

(1)

ii) How many neutrons are in the nucleus? _____

(2)

iii) How many electrons are orbiting the nucleus? _____

(1)

b) Astatine is at the bottom of the same group of the periodic table as chlorine, bromine and iodine. The table below gives some information about these elements.

i) Use the patterns shown in the table to fill in the spaces for astatine.

	Chlorine	Bromine	Iodine	Astatine
At room temperature	gas	liquid	solid	1
Reaction with iron	very fast	fast	slow	2
Reaction with potassium iodide solution	reacts	reacts	no reaction	3
Effect on indicator paper	bleaches	bleaches	bleaches	4

(4)

ii) Which **two** of these elements have their molecules closest together at room temperature?

1 _____

2 _____

(1)

iii) Which **one** of these elements is most likely to have a smell at room temperature?

_____

(1)

(SEG; 1988)

QUESTION 11

Fluorine (F) is the most reactive element in group VII of the periodic table of elements. Fluorine reacts with all metals and most non-metals. During the last seventy years or so, it has become an important industrial chemical.

a) Suggest **one** reason why we do not study fluorine in school laboratories.

_____

(1)

b) One compound in which fluorine occurs is fluorspar. Fluorspar is heated with concentrated sulphuric acid to make hydrogen fluoride. Hydrogen fluoride is a gas which does not conduct electricity. It reacts with water to produce highly corrosive hydrofluoric acid.

i) Complete this flow chart for the manufacture of hydrofluoric acid by writing in the names of the correct substances in the boxes.

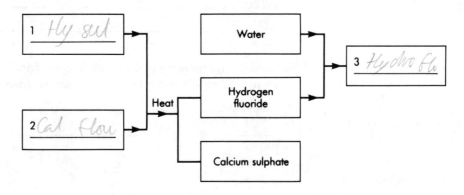

ii) Briefly explain **two** different pollution problems which might result from manufacture of hydrogen fluoride.

Problem 1 _____

_____

_____

(2)

Problem 2 _____

_____

_____

(2)

c) A large chemical company has several chemical plants throughout Europe at which concentrated sulphuric acid is manufactured. However, at only a few of these is hydrogen fluoride also manufactured.

Suggest **two** different reasons why you think hydrogen fluoride is manufactured only at a few of these plants.

Reason 1 _____

_____

(2)

Reason 2 _____

_____

(2)

d) A lot of fluorine is used in the manufacture of fluorocarbons and other compounds.

Tetrafluoroethene (C_2F_4) is polymerised into PTFE, which is used as the non-stick coating on cooking utensils.

Difluorodichloromethane (CF_2Cl_2) is used in aerosols and in the cooling coils of refrigerators.

i) Briefly explain what is meant by the word *polymerised*.

_____

_____

_____

(1)

ii) Suggest **two** properties which PTFE should have if it is to be used as a non-stick coating on cooking utensils.

Property 1 _____

_____

(1)

Property 2 _____

_____

(1)

iii) Suggest **one** property of difluorodichloromethane (CF_2Cl_2) which makes it suitable for use in aerosols **and** in the cooling coils of refrigerators.

Property _____

_____

(2)

(SEG; 1988)

A N S W E R S   T O
E X A M I N A T I O N   Q U E S T I O N S

ANSWER 1

Key A. It indicates hydrogen.

ANSWER 2

Key D. The halogens are group 7 elements, in the last but one column.

ANSWER 3

Key B. The reactive metals are the group 1 alkali metals.

ANSWER 4

Key C, 11. The atomic number is the number of protons. Option A is the number of electrons in the outer shell. Option D is the number of neutrons.

ANSWER 5

Key A, valency of 1. The number of electrons in the outer shell.

ANSWER 6

a) The column number is the number of electrons in the outer shell.
b) Li
c) The oxygen in the atmosphere of the Earth caused a chemical reaction.
d) Hold it near a suspended magnet and see if the magnet moved. I would not expect it to move, as the other metals in the group are not magnetic.
e) i) 1 $LmCl$ 2 Lm_2O
   ii) It would be a solid.
       It would dissolve in water and conduct electricity.
       It would be an ionic compound.
f) It is a very reactive metal and would be found combined with another element.

ANSWER 7

a) i) Sodium has 11 protons. Chlorine has 17 electrons.
    ii) neutrons
    iii) Sodium is in group 1. Chlorine is in group 7.
b) i) An electron is lost from the sodium atom.
    ii) An electron is gained by the chlorine atom.
c) 1) 1 The atoms vibrate more quickly.
        2 The bonds between the sodium ions and chloride ions are broken.
    ii) A lot of energy is needed to break the bonds.

ANSWER 8

a) Carbon is different because it is a non-metal.
b) Hydrogen is different because the others are all non-reactive inert gases.
c) Air is different because it is a mixture of different elements not chemically combined together.

ANSWER 9

a) i) magnesium, beryllium
    ii) fluorine, chlorine
b) i) ionic bonding
    ii) covalent bonding

      iii) 1 $AlCl_3$
          2 BF_3
          3 CF_4
  c) covalent

ANSWER 10

a) i) 85
    ii) 125 (210 − 85)
    iii) 85 (same as proton number)
b) i) 1 solid 2 no reaction/very slow reaction 3 no reaction 4 bleaches
    ii) iodine and astatine
    iii) chlorine

ANSWER 11

a) It is very reactive and possibly too dangerous to use.
b) i) 1 fluorspar 2 concentrated sulphuric acid 3 hydrofluoric acid
    ii) Problem 1 – hydrogen fluoride is a very acidic gas. It can dissolve in water vapour in the atmosphere and cause acid rain, which damages buildings and kills trees and fish.
        Problem 2 – hydrogen fluoride gas can dissolve in water vapour in the atmosphere to form a corrosive acid which will cause metals to go rusty very quickly.
c) Reason 1 – availability of fluorspar
   Reason 2 – adequate amounts produced for present use
d) i) many small identical monomers joined together to form a long chain polymer
    ii) Property 1 – very high melting point
        Property 2 – non-reactive with food
    iii) low boiling point

A STUDENT'S ANSWER WITH EXAMINER'S COMMENTS

100 g of WONDERWHITE toothpaste is made up as follows:

calcium carbonate	50%
glycerol	23%
distilled water	20%
bonding agent	3%
detergent	2%

Peppermint flavouring and the fluorine compounds NaF and Na_2FPO_3 are also present in small quantities.

a) Name the element found in

    i) group 1 of the periodic table   <u>Sodium ✓</u>

    ii) group 7 of the periodic table   <u>Fluorine ✓</u>

                                        (1)

b) i) What is the purpose of the fluoride in toothpaste?
      <u>to stop decay ✓</u>

    ii) What gas is produced when an acid is added to calcium carbonate?
       <u>carbon dioxide ✓</u>

    iii) How does calcium benefit the human body?
       <u>strong bones ✓</u>

                                          ($1\frac{1}{2}$)

"Good. You have used the information given in the question."

"Yes."

"Good."

"And teeth."

c) i) How many different atoms are there in the compound having the formula Na_2FPO_3?

4 different

"Good. Na, F, P, O."

ii) What is the total number of atoms in one molecule of this compound?

7

iii) Calculate the number of grams of distilled water needed to make 250 g of toothpaste.

50 grams

"Well done. 20% of water is needed in 100 g."

(1½)

d) A summary of the properties of some of the elements in group 7 is given below.

Name	*Symbol*	*Colour*	*State at room temperature (20°C)*	*M. pt °C*	*B. pt °C*
Chlorine	Cl	greenish/ yellow	gas	–101	–34
Bromine	Br	dark red	liquid	–7	58
Iodine	I	dark grey		114	183

Study the table and then answer the following questions.

i) What is the state of iodine at room temperature?

solid

"Yes. It doesn't melt until 114°C."

(1)

ii) Astatine (At) is another member of group 7 and comes below iodine in the group.

Considering the patterns shown in the table, **predict**

1 the colour of astatine very dark grey or black

"Good prediction."

2 its state at room temperature solid

(2)

(WJEC; 1988)

CHEMICAL REACTIONS

WRITING CHEMICAL EQUATIONS

IONIC EQUATIONS

PATTERNS OF PARTICLE INTERACTIONS

ENERGY AND REACTIONS

RATE OF REACTION

CATALYSTS

CALCULATIONS IN CHEMICAL REACTIONS

GETTING STARTED

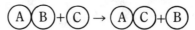

Chemical reactions are described as interactions between particles (atoms molecules or ions) which involve the 'breaking' and 'making' of chemical bonds. They follow a general pattern:

Reactants ⎯⎯⎯⎯⎯⎯⎯⎯⎯⎯⎯⎯⎯⎯⎯⟶ **Products**
(starting materials)   (new materials)

In any chemical reaction **new substances** are always formed. These have different sets of either physical or chemical properties to those of the reactants. However, in any chemical reaction the **mass** always stays the same. That is, the *total mass of the products* is always the same as the *total mass of the reactants*. The reason for this is that chemical reactions only involve the *rearrangement* of the particles involved.

$$\text{(A)(B)} + \text{(C)} \rightarrow \text{(A)(C)} + \text{(B)}$$

This idea is similar to dismantling a lego model of a house, and using the same bricks to build a small factory. This allows us to write equations and to make calculations for particle interactions, such as the mass of reactants needed to produce 1 kg of a certain product, an invaluable ability in the chemical industry.

Not all substances will react with each other, but many do. Some combinations of reactants need a push to get them going – usually in the form of heat. This is referred to as the *activation energy*. Reactions with high activation energies are slow. In the chemical industry *catalysts* are often used to *speed up reactions*, because time is money.

Chemical reactions always involve *energy*. In some reactions, energy is transferred to the surroundings in the form of heat (*heat given out*); these are called *exothermic reactions*. Here the products are *warmer* than the reactants. In other reactions, energy in the form of heat is transferred from the surroundings to the substances (*heat taken in*); these are called *endothermic reactions*. Here the products are *cooler* than the reactants. In the chemical industry ways are often looked for to save energy, because energy costs money.

ESSENTIAL PRINCIPLES

❝ Try and work through this section slowly and logically ❞

A chemical reaction always follows the general pattern:

Reactant(s) → Product(s)

There may be one or more reactants and one or more products, but the mass of the reactants at the beginning will be the *same* as the mass of the products at the end. In an equation representing the reaction, you will have the same number of atoms (represented by their symbols) on the left hand side as you will have on the right hand side. Bear in mind that all that is happening is a *rearrangement* of these atoms.

EXAMPLE 1

Sodium reacts with chlorine to form sodium chloride
Step 1   Write the equation in words.

sodium + chlorine   →   sodium chloride

Step 2   Write each substance as a formula (see page 180).

$Na \;+\; Cl_2 \;\rightarrow\; NaCl$

Remember, sodium is an element, Na; reactive gaseous elements are diatomic, Cl_2; the formula for sodium chloride is NaCl (Na^+Cl^-).

Step 3   Imagine the reaction as particles.

$Na + Cl_2 \;\rightarrow\; NaCl$

$\text{(Na)} + \text{(Cl)(Cl)} \rightarrow \text{(Na)(Cl)}$

Step 4   Balance the equation.

There are 2 Cl on the left, so there must be 2 Cl on the right. The only way to obtain this is to have 2 NaCl on the right, as follows:

2 NaCl   (Na)(Cl)
         (Na)(Cl)

$Na \;+\; Cl_2 \;\rightarrow\; 2NaCl$

$\text{(Na)} + \text{(Cl)(Cl)} \rightarrow \begin{matrix}\text{(Na)(Cl)}\\\text{(Na)(Cl)}\end{matrix}$

Now, to *balance* the equation, we must have 2 Na on the left.

$2Na \;+\; Cl_2 \;\rightarrow\; 2NaCl$

(Na)
      + (Cl)(Cl) →   (Na)(Cl)
(Na)   (Na)(Cl)

4 atoms   4 atoms

Remember, when balancing an equation: **never** change the actual formulae.

EXAMPLE 2

Magnesium reacts with hydrochloric acid to produce magnesium chloride and hydrogen.

Step 1   Write the equation in words.

magnesium + hydrochloric acid → magnesium chloride + hydrogen

Step 2   Write each substance as a formula.

$Mg + HCl \rightarrow MgCl_2 + H_2$

Step 3   Imagine the reaction as particles.

$\text{(Mg)} + \text{(H)(Cl)} \rightarrow \text{(Mg)}\begin{smallmatrix}\text{(Cl)}\\\text{(Cl)}\end{smallmatrix} + \text{(H)(H)}$

Step 4   Balance the equation.

$$Mg + 2HCl \rightarrow MgCl_2 + H_2$$

5 atoms   5 atoms

EXAMPLE 3

Sulphuric acid neutralises sodium hydroxide.

Step 1   Write the equation in words.

sodium hydroxide + sulphuric acid $\rightarrow$ sodium sulphate + water

Step 2   Write each substance as a formula.

$$NaOH + H_2SO_4 \rightarrow Na_2SO_4 + H_2O$$

Step 3   Imagine the reaction as particles.

Step 4   Balance the equation.

$$2NaOH + H_2SO_4 \rightarrow Na_2SO_4 + 2H_2O$$

This example also shows that we can regard some groups of particles as one unit which is not usually changed in a chemical reaction, for example the sulphate ion: SO_4^{2-}. Other such examples are the hydroxide ion (OH^-), the nitrate ion (NO_3^-) and sometimes the carbonate ion (CO_3^{2-}) in displacement reactions.

More unusual examples are the hydrogen carbonate ion (HCO_3^-), the sulphite ion (SO_3^{2-}) and the nitrite ion (NO_2^-).

STATE SYMBOLS

The equations written above tell us which substances react, but they do not tell us the *state* of the reactants or products. This is important, since some reactants will only react if they are in a particular state. For example, they may need to be in a gaseous form, or to be dissolved in water. We can show the state of reactants and products by adding symbols of state:

- (g) represents a state of *gas*;
- (l) represents a state of *liquid*;
- (s) represents a state of *solid*;
- (aq) represents the aqueous state *(dissolved in water)*

For example, in the equation

$$Mg(s) + 2HCl(aq) \rightarrow MgCl_2(aq) + H_2(g)$$

HCl(aq) indicates that *dilute* hydrochloric acid is being used.

2 IONIC EQUATIONS

There is another way of showing reactions involving ions. These are called *ionic equations*. In these equations, ions that are unaffected in a reaction are ignored and only those that are affected in some way are written down. To illustrate this, in Example 3 of the previous sections, the sulphate ion (SO_4^{2-}) and the sodium ion (Na^+) are unaffected, so we can ignore them. We can rewrite the equation in ionic terms as:

$$OH^-(aq) + H^+(aq) \rightarrow H_2O(l)$$

This ionic equation is also the general pattern for all neutralisation reactions.

3 ▷ PATTERNS OF PARTICLE INTERACTIONS

" Look for patterns "

The number of possible particle interactions may seem bewildering at first, but fortunately there are *patterns* that will help us *predict* what will happen for different types of particle interactions.

PATTERNS OF MOLECULE INTERACTIONS

Combustion of fuels

Fuels are substances that give out a lot of energy when they burn; their reactions are strongly *exothermic*. The fuels react with the oxygen in the air. The *fossil fuels* we use (coal, gas and oil) contain carbon and hydrogen and are referred to as *hydrocarbons*. The products of complete combustion are carbon dioxide and water.

Coal is mainly carbon:

carbon + oxygen → carbon dioxide

$$C + O_2 → CO_2$$

Natural gas is methane:

methane + oxygen → carbon dioxide + water

$$CH_4 + 2O_2 → CO_2 + 2H_2O$$

Combustion in action

Natural gas is often considered to be a very suitable fuel for greenhouses since it produces not only heat, but also carbon dioxide, which the plants can use as well as water to keep the atmosphere humid. However, if natural gas is burned in a limited amount of air, then combustion is *incomplete* and carbon monoxide (CO) will also be produced. The gas is poisonous because it combines strongly with haemoglobin in the blood, forming *carboxy-haemoglobin*, preventing it from carrying oxygen around the body. For this reason it is important to keep a room well ventilated when coal or gas is being burned.

Respiration and photosynthesis

Respiration, which takes place in the cells of the body, is very similar to the combustion reactions. The fuel this time is food (carbohydrates and sugars). This process can be written as:

food + oxygen → carbon dioxide + water + energy

If we choose glucose ($C_6H_{12}O_6$), as an example of food, then this can be represented as

$$C_6H_{12}O_6 + 6O_2 → 6CO_2 + 6H_2O + \text{energy}$$

Photosynthesis is in effect the opposite of respiration; the plant combines carbon dioxide from the air, and water taken in through the roots. The energy for this reaction is provided by sunlight:

energy + carbon dioxide + water → sugar + oxygen

$$\text{energy} + 6CO_2 + 6H_2O → C_6H_{12}O_6 + 6O_2$$

Photosynthesis and respiration in action

" Check back to Energy, Chapter 3 here "

Respiration in animals (and in green plants at night) releases carbon dioxide into the air. Most of this carbon dioxide is converted back into sugars and carbohydrates by green plants, which in turn release oxygen into the atmosphere. As a result, the balance of 20% oxygen to <0.5% carbon dioxide is maintained. This balance is being upset by man. For example, by burning fossil fuels (increasing carbon dioxide levels) and by cutting down large areas of rain forest (reducing oxygen levels), man has created a slight increase in the levels of carbon dioxide in the atmosphere recently. This in turn has given rise to concern that the Earth will warm up slightly, owing to the greenhouse effect.

PATTERNS OF ION INTERACTIONS

Redox reactions

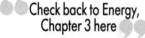

" Learn this difference "

A *redox reaction* is one in which oxidation and reduction take place. *Oxidation* is the addition of oxygen or the removal of hydrogen. It is also the removal of electrons. *Reduction* is the removal of oxygen or the addition of hydrogen. It is also the addition of electrons.

Substances that are good at oxidising substances are called *oxidising agents*, eg oxygen and chlorine. Substances that are good at reducing other substances are called *reducing agents*, eg carbon and hydrogen.

As an example, in the reaction between lead oxide and carbon, lead oxide is the oxidising agent and carbon is the reducing agent:

lead oxide + carbon → lead + carbon dioxide

$2PbO$ + C   → $2Pb$ + CO_2

The lead oxide has been reduced by carbon to lead (the oxygen has been removed), while the carbon has been oxidised to carbon dioxide (oxygen has been added).

Another example is the reaction between iron and chlorine gas:

iron + chlorine → iron (III) chloride

$2Fe$ + $3Cl_2$ → $2FeCl_3$

The iron has been oxidised to iron chloride. Three electrons have been removed from the iron atom. Chlorine has been reduced to the chloride ion, one electron has been added to each of the three chlorine atoms.

Redox reactions in action

Oxidation cannot take place without reduction, so the reactions are called *redox reactions*. Reducing agents are used in the extraction of metals from their ores. Carbon (in the form of coke) can be used to extract lead, iron and zinc. In all these cases the metal ore is being reduced to the metal by the removal of oxygen.

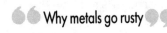 **Why metals go rusty**

An understanding of oxidation is useful when dealing with the corrosion of metals. *Corrosion* is a process which involves the production of metal ions from their atoms (oxidation – the removal of electrons). For example, iron rusts to form iron oxide in the presence of oxygen and water. The reaction could be represented by:

$Fe - 3e^-$ → Fe^{3+}

Displacement reactions

Displacement reactions are examples of redox reactions which involve an element and a salt solution.

- *Metal/salt solutions*: some metals will displace other metal ions from solutions of their salts. The metal's ability to do this is related to its position in the reactivity series (see Chapter 17). If a metal is *above* the metal ion in solution, then one will *displace* the other. For example:

  zinc + copper sulphate → zinc sulphate + copper

  Zn + $CuSO_4$ → $ZnSO_4$ + Cu

  $Zn(s)$ + $Cu^{2+}(aq)$ → $Zn^{2+}(aq)$ + $Cu(s)$

- *Halogen/halide solutions:* a halogen can also displace a halide from a solution of its salt. Its ability to do this depends on its reactivity, ie its position in the periodic table. *Remember* the order of reactivity F>Cl>Br>I of the halogens:

  chlorine + potassium iodide → potassium chloride + iodine

  Cl_2 + $2KI$ → $2KCl$ + I_2

  $Cl_2(g)$ + $2I^-(aq)$ → $2Cl^-(aq)$ + I_2

Chlorine is *more reactive* than iodine, so it has a *greater attraction* for electrons, and so it displaces the iodine.

Precipitation reactions

Some reactions between solutions of metal salts will take place because there is a possibility of a *solid* being formed. This solid is called a *precipitate*.

potassium iodide + lead nitrate → potassium nitrate + lead iodide

$2KI(aq)$ + $Pb(NO_3)_2(aq)$ → $2KNO_3(aq)$ + $PbI_2(s)$

Notice that all that has happened is that the ions have swapped partners. This chemical change occurs because one possible combination, PbI_2, is insoluble in water.

66 Hard water 99

Precipitation in action

Precipitation reactions can be used to remove the hardness from water. Hardness in water is caused by the presence of calcium or magnesium ions. These ions can be *precipitated out* of solution (so removing the hardness) by adding sodium carbonate (washing soda). Calcium carbonate and magnesium carbonate, which are both insoluble, are formed (see page 237).

Neutralisation reactions

66 Check with Chapter 16 99

In these reactions an acid is *neutralised* by a base. A salt and water are formed. The general pattern of the reaction is as follows:

$$acid \; + \; base \; \rightarrow \; salt \; + \; water$$

In ionic terms, this reaction is expressed as

$$H^+(aq) \; + \; OH^-(aq) \; \rightarrow \; H_2O(l)$$

An example is the reaction between hydrocholoric acid and sodium hydroxide:

$$HCl \; + \; NaOH \; \rightarrow \; NaCl \; + \; H_2O$$

PATTERNS FOR REVERSIBLE REACTIONS

Some reactions involving particles are *reversible*, ie they can proceed in both directions even at the same time. An example occurs in the Haber process, where nitrogen and hydrogen are combined to produce ammonia, but ammonia simultaneously decomposes to produce nitrogen and hydrogen.

$$nitrogen \; + \; hydrogen \; \rightleftharpoons \; ammonia$$
$$N_2 \quad + \quad 3H_2 \qquad \rightleftharpoons \qquad 2NH_3$$

The sign $\rightleftharpoons$ indicates that the reaction can go in *both* directions. By changing the conditions, we can determine in which direction the reaction proceeds, and what proportion of ammonia is formed.

- High *pressure* favours the production of ammonia.
- High temperature increases the rate of reaction between nitrogen and hydrogen (production of ammonia).
- However, high *temperature* also favours the decomposition of ammonia (production of nitrogen and hydrogen).

A balance has to be made. Optimum conditions are usually about 400° C.

Another example is the hydration (water content) of copper sulphate crystals. (This can be used as a test for water.)

$$\text{Copper sulphate crystals } (blue) \; \overset{heat}{\rightleftharpoons} \; \text{anhydrous copper sulphate } (white) + water$$

4 > ENERGY AND REACTIONS

ENERGY AND CHEMICAL BONDS

In any chemical change, energy is either given out or absorbed. In any reaction between particles, bonds holding the particles in the reactants together will need to be broken, and new bonds will need to be formed when the particles rearrange themselves to form the products.

- Energy is needed to *break* bonds.
- Energy is released when bonds are *formed*.

66 Understand the difference between these two 99

If the energy that is released when new bonds are formed in the products is *greater than* the energy required to break the bonds in the reactants, then the reaction is *exothermic* (energy is released to the surroundings). If the reverse is true, then the reaction is *endothermic*. The amount of energy that is absorbed or released in a reaction is referred to as the *heat of reaction* and is measured in kJ/mol. A kJ, or a kilojoule, is a unit of energy; a mol, or mole, is a measure of a quantity of particles (see page 202).

The heat of reaction is given the symbol ΔH. If a reaction is exothermic, then ΔH is negative, and energy is given out. If a reaction is endothermic, then ΔH is positive, and energy is absorbed.

The following is an example of an exothermic reaction:

$$HCl(aq) \quad + \quad NaOH(aq) \quad \rightarrow \quad NaCl(aq) \quad +H_2O(l)$$
$$\Delta H = -55.9kJ/mol$$

The amount of energy that is absorbed or released in a reaction can be calculated from *bond energies*. The amount of energy that is required to break different bonds have been calculated. Consider the reaction between hydrogen and chlorine, to produce hydrogen chloride:

$$H_2(g) \quad + \quad Cl_2(g) \quad \rightarrow \quad 2HCl$$

Bonds present H—H   Cl—Cl   →   H—Cl
                                H—Cl

In the case of the *reactants*
  ■ the energy needed to break one H—H bond is +437 kJ/mol;
  ■ the energy needed to break one Cl—Cl bond is +244 kJ/mol.
The total energy required to break all bonds = +437 +244 = +681 kJ/mol.

In the case of the *products*
  ■ the energy released when one H—Cl bond is formed is −433 kJ/mol;
  ■ the total energy released on forming 2 H—Cl bonds = 2×(−433) = −866 kJ/mol.
As a result, the energy *change* for the reaction is

$$\Delta H = +681 - 866 = -185kJ/mol : \text{The reaction is } exothermic.$$

These overall energy changes for a reaction can be represented on an energy level diagram (Figure 15.1).

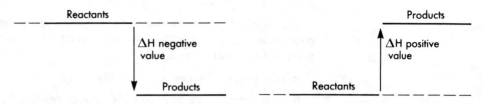

Fig 15.1 Energy level diagrams.   Exothermic reaction   Endothermic reaction

Activation energy

Almost all chemical changes need an amount of energy to get them going. This initial amount of energy can be quite small or sometimes quite large. This initial energy requirement is called the *activation energy* and is often the energy required initially to break bonds to allow a reaction to proceed. Fuels need to be supplied with a source of heat to *start* the combustion reaction, eg from a match. Activation energy must not be confused 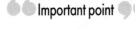 with the energy change in exothermic or endothermic reactions, both of which may require an initial input of energy.

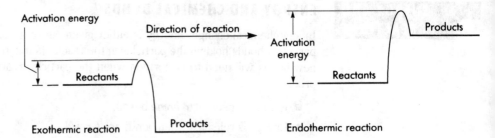

Fig 15.2 Activation energy.   Exothermic reaction   Endothermic reaction

5 ⟩   RATE OF REACTION

The speed at which the reaction takes place can vary and depends on a number of factors:

  ■ the surface area of solid reactants;

  ■ the concentration of reactants (including pressure in the case of gases);

  ■ the temperature;

  ■ the presence of a catalyst.

In order for a chemical reaction to take place, the particles of the reactants must *collide* (bump into each other). The *more often* the particles collide, the more likely they are to react, and so the *faster* the reaction.

INCREASING THE SPEED OF A REACTION

Increasing the surface area of solid reactants

A greater surface area will provide more opportunities for particles to collide. For example, calcium carbonate will react with hydrochloric acid to produce calcium chloride, water and carbon dioxide:

$$CaCO_3 \; + \; 2HCl \; \rightarrow \; CaCl_2 \; + \; H_2O \; + \; CO_2$$

Powdered calcium carbonate will react much faster than lumps of calcium carbonate (marble chips), because the surface area of the powder is much greater. There will be more calcium carbonate in contact with the acid. Stirring the powder in the acid will further increase the speed of reaction for the same reason.

Transporting or storing fine powders which can burn is a problem, since it might only take a spark to cause a very rapid reaction (explosion); eg flour, especially in flour mills when powder is in the atmosphere.

Increasing the concentration of the reactants

This will increase the number of particles present and so increase the chance of any collision. For example, in the reaction above, if the concentration of the hydrochloric acid is increased, then there is more chance of the particles interacting, and so the reaction will proceed at a faster rate.

Increasing the temperature of the reactants

Increasing the temperature of reactants provides the particles with *more kinetic energy*, so they will move faster. This increases the number of collisions per second, and hence increases the rate of the reaction. In the reaction above, increasing the temperature of the acid will increase the speed of the hydrochloric acid particles and so the number of collisions per second.

6 > CATALYSTS

A *catalyst* is a substance that changes the rate of a chemical reaction, but remains unchanged at the end of a reaction and can be re-used. Catalysts are used to speed up reactions. Substances used to slow down reactions are called *inhibitors*.

GAS REACTIONS AND CATALYSTS

One way in which catalysts are thought to work in reactions involving gases is that the surface of the catalyst provides sites where the reacting molecules can meet. The transition metals are often used as catalysts in this way.

Manufacture of ammonia

$$N_2 \; + \; 3H_2 \; \rightleftharpoons \; 2NH_3$$

Iron is used as a catalyst. Nitrogen and hydrogen do not combine in the gas state; when they collide they bounce off each other without reacting. However, they are *adsorbed* on to the catalyst surface, where they come into contact and react.

Manufacture of sulphuric acid

One stage involves the production of sulphur trioxide from sulphur dioxide:

$$2SO_2 \; + \; O_2 \; \rightleftharpoons \; 2SO_3$$

Vanadium (V) oxide is the catalyst and works in a similar way to the iron in the previous example.

Pollution control on cars

Technological application

Petrol engines in cars burn petrol (a hydrocarbon fuel) and produce carbon dioxide and water as waste products. In addition, however, carbon monoxide and some oxides of nitrogen are produced which pollute the atmosphere. The car exhaust systems in California (where the problem of pollution from cars is a serious one) are fitted with a metal catalyst. As the hot exhaust gases pass over the catalyst, the pollutants are converted into carbon dioxide and nitrogen.

Antioxidants

Certain chemicals can be added to foods which slow up the natural oxidation of foods. These chemicals (antioxidants) are acting as catalysts; they are reducing the rate of a chemical reaction which would otherwise result in loss of flavour and decay.

ENZYMES

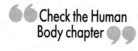
Check the Human
Body chapter

Many chemical reactions take place in living things (often in the cells). These reactions are controlled by biological catalysts called *enzymes*. Enzymes are protein molecules, which consist of long chains that can be folded and coiled into different shapes. Each enzyme has its own special shape; it is this shape which causes the enzyme to act as a catalyst. Figure 15.3 shows how the molecule(s) on which the enzyme acts fits the protein molecule like a key in a lock.

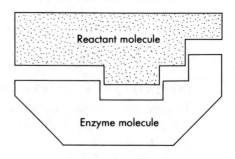

Fig 15.3 Enzyme action: the lock
and key principle.

Enzymes have unique properties:

- They are *specific*: because the way an enzyme works depends on its shape, it will only work for one molecule or reaction.
- They will only work within a small temperature range, eg enzymes in the human body will only work around normal body temperature (37°C).
- They are very sensitive to pH changes and most only work within small pH ranges, eg pH6 → pH7.
- They can help large molecules break into smaller ones, help small molecules join to form larger ones, or help atoms rearrange within a molecule.

Enzymes in action

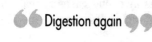
Digestion again

Enzymes take part in every stage of the digestive process, helping to break large molecules into smaller ones. The enzyme in saliva, called *salivary amylase*, breaks down starch into smaller sugar molecules.

Yeasts contain enzymes which help convert sugar into alcohol in the process of brewing.

Enzymes are becoming increasingly important in industry, eg for the manufacture of biodegradable dressings for wounds, biological washing powders, new food sources – mycoprotein.

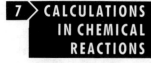
**7 > CALCULATIONS
IN CHEMICAL
REACTIONS**

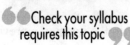
Check your syllabus
requires this topic

As we saw previously, in any chemical change:

- the total mass of the products = the total mass of the reactants;
- the total number of atoms in the products = the total number of atoms in the reactants.

These two facts allow us to make *calculations* involving chemical reactions. In order to do this in a satisfactory way, we need some means of counting the number of particles present; for this purpose a unit called the MOLE was invented. It is a measure of the amount of substance; it is equivalent to

6×10^{23} particles (a very large number)

When large amounts of coins are handed into the bank they do not count them individually but rather they weigh them. In order to convert the weight of the coins to a number, the bank needs to know certain facts – 'How much do 100 1p coins weigh?' or 'How much do 100 2p coins weigh?'

We can apply the same principle to particles, since each atom has its own distinct mass: the *relative atomic mass*. The number we use has to be very much larger than 100, since the mass of each atom is very small. That number is the MOLE. The conversion of numbers to mass is very simple:

MOLES OF ATOMS

The relative atomic mass of an atom in grammes contains one mole (1 mol) of **atoms**.

Atom	Atomic mass	Mass of 1 mol of atoms
hydrogen	1	1g
carbon	12	12g
oxygen	16	16g
chlorine	35.5	35.5g
sodium	23	23g

In other words, in 32g of oxygen we have 2 mol of atoms; in 8g of oxygen we have 0.5 mol of atoms.

Mole is the name; mol is the unit

MOLES OF MOLECULES

The *molecular mass* in grammes contains 1 mol of **molecules**.

Molecule	Molecular Formula	Mass of molecule	Mass of 1 mol of molecules
oxygen	O_2	32	32g
water	H_2O	18	18g
carbon dioxide	CO_2	44	44g
hydrogen	H_2	2	2g

In other words, in 36g of water there are 2 moles; in 9g of water there are 0.5 moles.

MOLES OF IONIC COMPOUNDS AND IONS

The same rules apply for formulae representing *ionic compounds* and for *individual ions*.

Compound or ion	Formula/ion	Formula mass/ mass of ion	Mass of 1 mol
hydrochloric acid	HCl	36.5	36.5g
sodium hydroxide	NaOH	40	40g
sulphuric acid	H_2SO_4	98	98g
sulphate ion	SO_4^{2-}	96	96g
chloride ion	Cl^-	35.5	35.5g

USING THE MOLE IDEA

What mass of magnesium chloride is produced when 12 g of magnesium reacts with excess hydrochloric acid? (Excess means that you have more acid than you need, so the mass of this compound is not a restriction and can be ignored.)

Write down the equation for the reaction:

$$Mg \ + \ 2HCl \ \rightarrow \ MgCl_2 \ + \ H_2$$

This tells us that *one* particle of magnesium produces *one* particle of magnesium chloride. Therefore, *one* mole of magnesium produces *one* mole of magnesium chloride. To answer the question:

Step 1:   Convert masses to moles.

The atomic mass of magnesium is 24, so the mass of 1 mol of magnesium is 24g. The number of moles present in 12 g of Mg = 0.5.

Step 2:   Use the equation.

1 mol of Mg produces 1 mol of $MgCl_2$, so 0.5 mol of Mg produces 0.5 mol of $MgCl_2$.

Step 3:   Convert moles to mass.

1 mol of $MgCl_2$ has a mass of 95 g, so 0.5 mol of $MgCl_2$ has a mass of
0.5 × 95 g = 47.5 g

Answer: 47.5 g of $MgCl_2$ is produced.

MOLAR SOLUTIONS

Often reactions take place in solution, so we need to know concentrations of the reactants
in solutions. Concentrations are given in mol/dm^3.

 **1 cm³ = ¹⁄₁₀₀₀ dm³**

A solution which contains 1 mol/dm^3 contains 1 mol per dm^3 (litre) or, in words, one
mole per cubic decimetre, and this is often expressed as a 1 M solution (1 molar). Thus a
2 M solution contains 2 mol/dm^3.

A 1 M solution of sulphuric acid contains 1 mol of H_2SO_4/dm^3, or in other words, 98 g
of H_2SO_4/dm^3. We can use this information to work out the number of moles present in a
solution. For example, how many moles are present in 25 cm^3 of a 2 mol/dm^3 solution of
NaOH?

$$\text{No. of moles} = \text{concentration} \times \text{volume (in } dm^3) = 2 \times \frac{25}{1000} = 0.05 \text{ mol.}$$

These principles can be used to calculate the concentration of solutions. For example, if
25 cm^3 of a 2 mol/dm^3 solution of sodium hydroxide exactly reacts with 10 cm^3 of sulphuric
acid, what is the concentration of the sulphuric acid?

Use the equation for the reaction:

$$2NaOH + H_2SO_4 \rightarrow Na_2SO_4 + 2H_2O$$

Step 1:   From the question, the number of moles of NaOH used

= concentration × volume
=   2   × 25/1000
= 0.05 mol

Step 2:   From the equation, 2 mol of NaOH reacts with 1 mol of H_2SO_4. Therefore,
0.05 mol of NaOH reacts with 0.025 mol of H_2SO_4.

Step 3:   Since no. of moles = concentration × volume
0.025   = concentration × 10/1000
2.5   = concentration

Therefore, the concentration of $H_2SO_4 = 2.5 \text{ mol/dm}^3$.

EXAMINATION QUESTIONS

MULTIPLE CHOICE

QUESTION 1

Which of the following formulae correctly shows the reaction between sodium and
chlorine?

A Na   + Cl_2 → $NaCl_2$
B Na_2 + Cl_2 → Na_2Cl_2
C Na   +   Cl   →   NaCl
D 2 Na   + Cl_2 →   2 NaCl
E 2 Na   + Cl_2 →   2 $NaCl_2$

QUESTION 2

Which pair of substances are pollutants produced by a petrol-burning engine?
A carbon and sulphur dioxide
B carbon monoxide and lead compounds
C carbon monoxide and steam
D carbon dioxide and steam
E nitrogen dioxide and steam

QUESTION 3

Which one of the following is the main reason for using catalysts in industrial processes?
A to increase the temperature of the reaction mixtures
B to increase the yield of the reaction mixtures
C to increase the rate of formation of the products
D to remove impurities from the reaction mixtures.

(SEG; Specimen)

QUESTION 4

Which of the following reactions is a redox reaction?
A changing lead oxide to lead, using carbon
B neutralising sodium hydroxide
C making carbohydrates during photosynthesis
D releasing energy during respiration

QUESTION 5

A chemical reaction occurs when
A an electric current is passed through a copper wire
B salt solution is heated
C crude oil is distilled
D dilute hydrochloric acid is added to magnesium ribbon
E ice melts to form water

QUESTION 6

What is the mass of oxygen contained in 36g of pure water?
A 16g; B 32g; C 48g; D 64g; E 70g

QUESTION 7

A metal, M, forms a hydroxide, $M(OH)_3$. The mass of one mole of the hydroxide is 78 g.
What is the relative atomic mass of M? (H = 1, O = 16)
A 27; B 30; C 59; D 61; E 78

(LEAG; 1988)

QUESTION 8

What is the concentration in mol/dm^3 (mol/litre) of 250 cm^3 of a solution containing 1.0 g of sodium hydroxide? ($M_r = 40$)
A 0.025; B 0.1; C 0.25; D 1.0; E 2.0

STRUCTURED QUESTIONS

QUESTION 9

In an experiment to find a suitable catalyst for a certain reaction, the following results were obtained.

Temperature of each experiment (°C)	Substance under test as a catalyst	Time for the reaction to be completed (seconds)
20	cobalt chloride	18
20	sodium nitrate	30
20	cobalt nitrate	12
20	sodium chloride	41

a) Use the table to answer the following questions.
    i) Which substance gives the greatest increase in the rate of reaction?

    _____

    ii) Which substance is the least effective as a catalyst?

    _____

iii) Which metal ion is most likely to be the best catalyst?

_____

iv) Which ion is the least effective as a catalyst?

_____

(4)

b) Give two reasons why catalysts are very important to the efficiency of several industrial processes. Give two processes in which catalysts are used.

_____

_____

_____

(4)

(WJEC; Specimen)

QUESTION 10

A student added magnesium ribbon to dilute hydrochloric acid and recorded the volume of hydrogen released every 30 seconds; the results are shown below.

Time(s)	Volume of hydrogen (cm^3)
0	0
30	25
60	50
90	75
100	100

a) What is the relationship between the volume of gas released and the time taken?

_____

_____

(2)

b) How would you present the results so that the relationship might be more easily seen?

_____

_____

(1)

c) If you were doing this experiment, describe two safety precautions you would take.

i) _____

_____

ii) _____

_____

(NISEC; Specimen)

QUESTION 11 (EXTENSION QUESTION)

a) When hydrogen peroxide is left to stand in a clear glass container, it slowly decomposes to produce oxygen and water.

    i) Write a balanced symbolic equation to show how 2 mol of hydrogen peroxide decomposes. $2H_2O_2 \rightarrow 2H_2O + O_2$ *(2)*

    ii) From your equation calculate how many moles of oxygen would be produced if 10 mol of hydrogen peroxide completely decomposed.   *(1)*

    iii) Hydrogen peroxide can be used by hairdressers. Suggest a reason why it is usually stored in brown bottles.   *(1)*

b) Adding manganese (IV) oxide to hydrogen peroxide affects the rate at which oxygen is produced, as shown in the graphs below.

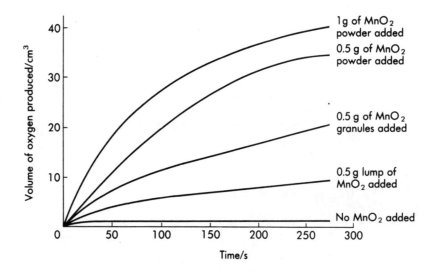

i) What volume of oxygen will be produced after 125 s by adding 1 g of MnO_2 powder?   *(1)*

ii) From the information on the graphs, state **two** factors which affect the rate of oxygen production and the evidence for your answer.   *(4)*

iii) Give **one** other factor, not indicated on the graphs, which might affect the rate of reaction.   *(1)*

c) Devise a simple experiment that would enable you to check whether any of the manganese (IV) dioxide had been used up in the reaction. State clearly which procedures you would take and what measurements you would make. You need not include a diagram.   *(5)*

(MEG; 1988)

ANSWERS TO
EXAMINATION QUESTIONS

MULTIPLE CHOICE

ANSWER 1

Key D; There must be four atoms on each side to balance.

ANSWER 2

Key B; steam is not considered to be a pollutant, so the correct answer is carbon monoxide and lead compounds.

ANSWER 3

Key C; remember catalysts increase the rate of reactions but are not used up by the reactions.

ANSWER 4

Key A; the redox reaction here involves the removal of oxygen from lead oxide and the addition of oxygen to carbon to form carbon dioxide.

ANSWER 5

Key D; the other choices are physical changes.

ANSWER 6

Key B; The mass of one mole of water is 18 g [(2 × 1) + 16 = 18]. There are 2 moles of water which contain 2 mol of oxygen = 2 × 16 = 32 g.

ANSWER 7

Key A; The relative formula mass of the hydroxide OH is 17. There are three hydroxides, so the mass is 3 × 17 = 51. Then, 78 − 51 = 27, the mass of one mole of M.

ANSWER 8

Key B; There is 1 g in 250 cm^3, so there are 4 g in 1 litre. The mass of one mole of NaOH is 40, so 4 ÷ 40 is 0.1.

STRUCTURED QUESTIONS

ANSWER 9

a)   i) cobalt nitrate
     ii) sodium chloride
    iii) cobalt
     iv) sodium

b)   they increase the rate of reaction;
     they lower the amount of energy required to start a reaction;
     manufacture of sulphuric acid;
     manufacture of ammonia.

ANSWER 10

a)   The volume of gas increases as the time increases, every 30 seconds; 25 cm^3 of gas is released until the final 10 seconds.
b)   on a graph
c)   i) wear safety goggles
     ii) make sure no acid is spilt

ANSWER 11 (EXTENSION QUESTION)

a)   i) $2\,H_2O_2 \;\rightarrow\; 2\,H_2O + O_2$
     ii) 5 mol
    iii) to stop light affecting the substance

b)   i) 30 cm^3
     ii) Mass of Mn O_2; 1 g of powder works faster than 0.5 g
         powder is faster than granules as there is more surface area
    iii) temperature

c)   Weigh the dry manganese dioxide, then add to hydrogen peroxide. When reaction stops, dry and weigh again. If the two weights are the same, then no manganese dioxide has been used.

A STUDENT'S ANSWER WITH EXAMINER'S COMMENTS

Our atmosphere is a mixture of gases.

a) Which gas makes up most of this mixture?

nitrogen ✓

66 Good. 99

(1)

b) Energy is released within most organisms by a chemical reaction called *respiration*.

i) Which gas is used up during respiration?

oxygen ✓

(1)

ii) Which natural process replaces the gas used up in respiration?

photosynthesis ✓

(1)

c) Explain how each of the following could change the amount of *carbon dioxide* in our atmosphere.

i) people cutting down large areas of forest.

trees remove carbon dioxide so less trees means not so much ✓ CO_2 removed

66 Good – the level would increase (state the change). Include equation as well. 99

(3)

ii) people burning more fossil fuels.

fossil fuels produce CO_2 so more would be produced

Fuel + oxygen → CO_2 + H_2O

66 Yes. Again state that the level would increase. Good idea to use equation. 99

(3)

d) What effect will cutting down trees **and** burning fossil fuels have on the amount of *oxygen* in our atmosphere?

It will decrease the oxygen as fuel uses up oxygen to burn.

(1)

(SEG; 1988)

CHAPTER

ACIDITY

ACIDS AND WATER

ALKALIS

DETECTING ACIDS AND ALKALIS

FOLLOWING ACID/ ALKALI REACTIONS

MAKING ACIDS AND ALKALIS

PATTERNS OF ACID REACTIONS

ACIDS IN ACTION

SALTS

SALTS IN ACTION

GETTING STARTED

Almost all compounds which contain ions can be classified as either acid, base or salt.

Acids are substances which have a sharp or sour taste. We can recognise this taste in fruits or in vinegar. Acids can also be corrosive; they can dissolve many substances such as metals and some rocks. This can be very useful but can also be a nuisance, as with the corrosion of iron and buildings by acids in the atmosphere, eg acid rain.

Bases are substances which can *neutralise* acids; they react with acids to produce salts. Bases include the oxides, hydroxides and carbonates of metals. Most bases are insoluble in water; those which do dissolve are called *alkalis*.

Salts are substances which are formed when acids are neutralised by bases. These salts are giant ionic structures and often form crystals. The neutralisation of acids by bases can be explained in terms of the interaction between hydrogen ions (H^+) and hydroxide ions (OH^-).

$$H^+ \quad + \quad OH^- \quad \rightarrow \quad H_2O$$

ESSENTIAL PRINCIPLES

An *acid* is a substance which:

- has a sour taste;
- will change the colour of plant dyes (indicators);
- will neutralise bases;
- will react with many metals to form salts;
- produces hydrogen ions when dissolved in water.

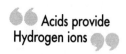

1 > ACIDS AND WATER

ACIDS IN WATER CONTAIN HYDROGEN IONS

Acids only behave as acids when they are dissolved in water. So we only really meet them as solutions in water. The reason for this is that water is a *polar* solvent. In water the acid produces hydrogen ions (H^+). All acids contain hydrogen ions in water. The importance of water can be demonstrated by dissolving some citric acid crystals (the acid from fruits such as oranges and lemons) in water and some citric acid crystals in another solvent, such as ethoxyethane (ether).

When the citric acid crystals are dissolved in *ether* the solution will *not* affect the colour of indicators, nor will it react with bases or metals. However, in *water* the citric acid behaves as an acid, changing the colour of the indicator.

In fact, the acid reacts with the water to produce a hydrated hydrogen ion called a hydroxonium ion (H_3O^+):

$$H^+ \ + \ H_2O \ \rightarrow \ H_3O^+$$

It is really this ion that is responsible for acidity; however, in order to keep things simple we can think of acids as just providing hydrogen ions in water. These symbols can be regarded as representing the same ions:

$$H^+ \qquad H^+(aq) \qquad H_3O^+(aq)$$

66 Acids provide Hydrogen ions 99

STRONG AND WEAK ACIDS

Those acids which give up all their hydrogen ions in water are called *strong* acids whereas those which only provide some of their hydrogen ions are called *weak* acids.

Strong acids	Weak acids
sulphuric acid	citric acid (citrous fruits)
nitric acid	ethanoic (acetic) acid (vinegar)
hydrochloric acid	malic acid (apples)

SOME COMMON ACIDS

Acid	Formula	Ions present		
hydrochloric acid	HCl	H^+	Cl^-	(chloride)
sulphuric acid	H_2SO_4	$2H^+$	SO_4^{2-}	(sulphate)
nitric acid	HNO_3	H^+	NO_3^-	(nitrate)
ethanoic acid	CH_3COOH	H^+	CH_3COO^-	(ethanoate)

Notice the names of acids are taken from the ion present. This ion is referred to as the *acid radical*. Ethanoic acid (acetic acid) is a *weak* acid, because not all of the ethanoic acid molecules in solution split up to provide hydrogen ions, but only a proportion of them.

CONCENTRATION OF ACID SOLUTIONS

Acid solutions can be *concentrated* or *dilute*, depending upon how much water is present. The concentration of a solution can be measured in mol/dm^3 (see page 204). For example, a 1 M (1 molar) solution of sulphuric acid contains 98g H_2SO_4 per dm^3. This is calculated from the formula mass of $H_2SO_4 = (2 \times 1) + 32 + (4 \times 16) = 98$.

Strong acids must not be confused with *concentrated* acids. We can have concentrated solutions of strong *and* weak acids as well as dilute solutions of strong *and* weak acids. The acids that are used in a laboratory are dilute acids of concentrations 2 M, 1 M, 0.1 M etc.

2 ＞ ALKALIS

An *alkali* is a substance which:

- is a soluble base;
- will change the colour of indicators;
- will neutralise acids;
- contains hydroxide ions.

SOME COMMON ALKALIS

Name	Formula	Ions present	
sodium hydroxide	NaOH	Na^+ (sodium)	OH^-
ammonium hydroxide	NH_4OH	NH_4^+ (ammonium)	OH^-
calcium hydroxide	$Ca(OH)_2$	Ca^{2+} (calcium)	$2OH^-$

In the same way as there are strong and weak acids, so there are strong and weak alkalis. Aqueous sodium hydroxide is a strong alkali, whereas aqueous ammonia is a weak alkali.

3 ＞ DETECTING ACIDS AND ALKALIS

There are two main ways of *detecting* acids and alkalis:

1 using *indicators*: substances whose colours are changed by acids and alkalis;
2 using *pH meters*: instruments whose meter reading is affected by the H^+ and OH^- ions in the solution.

INDICATORS

Learn the pH scale

The most commonly used indicator is *universal indicator*, since it not only tells us if something is acid or alkaline but also if the acid (or alkali) is strong or weak. It can be used as a liquid (usually green) or soaked on to a type of blotting paper and used as a paper. The paper, of course, has to be wet in order to work, since acids only behave as acids in solution. The *colour* of the indicator matches a number which indicates the acidity of the solution.

The strength of an acid or alkali is measured on the *pH* scale. The pH scale has a range of 1 to 14 and is a measure of the hydrogen ion concentration (acidity). Notice that low numbers indicate *high* acidity (and high H^+ ion concentration).

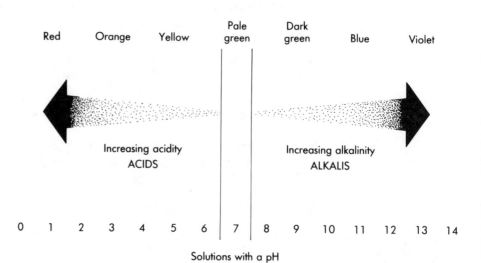

Fig 16.1 The pH scale.

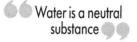
Water is a neutral substance

- If a solution turns the indicator *light green*, then it is *neutral* and has a pH of 7.
- If a solution turns the indicator *yellow* then it is a *weak acid* and has a pH of 6.

Other indicators

The reactions of other, less common, indicators are as follows:

Indicator	in acid	in alkali	in water (neutral)
litmus	red	blue	purple
phenolphthalein	colourless	pink	colourless

4 FOLLOWING ACID/ALKALI REACTIONS

Check in your notes to see if you have done this at school

Indicators can also be used to *follow* the course of a neutralisation reaction between an acid and an alkali. If universal indicator is added to a strong alkaline solution, the indicator will turn *violet*. If a *solution of acid* is added, a small amount at a time, then the indicator will change colour *through blue to green*, at which point the solution is *neutral* (the acid has reacted with all the alkali present). If acid *continues* to be added, the indicator will eventually turn *red*, indicating the solution is now *strongly acidic*. You may have performed an experiment such as this and will have noticed how difficult it is to add just the right amount of acid to produce a neutral solution (green colour with the indicator). If you need to produce a neutral solution, an accurate measuring device (a *burette*) is required and it would also be helpful to use an indicator (like phenolphthalein) which has a more distinct colour change. The process, shown in Figure 16.2, is called *titration*. The acid is titrated into the alkali, using an indicator to show when the exact amount of acid has been added.

An example is the reaction between hydrochloric acid and sodium hydroxide, when a salt (sodium chloride) and water are produced. We can use the titration method to find the exact quantity of hydrochloric acid to neutralise the sodium hydroxide solution exactly.

hydrochloric acid + sodium hydroxide → sodium chloride + water
$HCl(aq)$ + $NaOH(aq)$ → $NaCl(aq)$ + $H_2O(l)$

A measured volume of sodium hydroxide is placed in the flask, together with a few drops of indicator. The hydrochloric acid is then added from the burette, a little at a time, and the liquid is swirled in the flask to make sure the solutions are mixed. When the indicator *just changes colour* then the exact amount of acid has been added to neutralise the alkali. The volume of the acid required can be read off the burette. If the same experiment is repeated with the same volumes of acid and alkali but without the indicator, then a neutral solution can be produced which contains only sodium chloride and water. This can be shown by evaporating the water in the flask, when crystals of sodium chloride will be left.

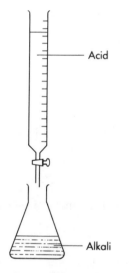
— Acid

— Alkali

Fig 16.2 Titration of acid and alkali.

5 MAKING ACIDS AND ALKALIS

The oxides of non-metals when dissolved in water give acidic solutions. The oxides of metals are bases and those which dissolve in water produce alkaline solutions. Thus acids and alkalis relate to the elements' position in the periodic table (see Figure 16.3).

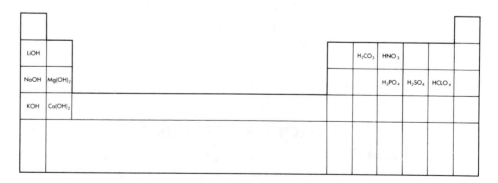

Fig 16.3 The change from alkalis on the left to acids on the right when oxides of elements react with water.

6 PATTERNS OF ACID REACTIONS

Acids are very useful substances, because they react with a large number of other substances in fairly *predictable* ways. They are used extensively in industry in the manufacture of a large variety of materials.

REACTIONS WITH METALS

The reaction follows a general pattern:

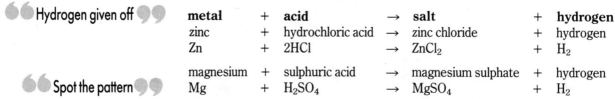

metal	+	acid	→	salt	+	hydrogen
zinc	+	hydrochloric acid	→	zinc chloride	+	hydrogen
Zn	+	2HCl	→	$ZnCl_2$	+	H_2
magnesium	+	sulphuric acid	→	magnesium sulphate	+	hydrogen
Mg	+	H_2SO_4	→	$MgSO_4$	+	H_2

Spot the pattern

The solution that is produced is neutral, and the salt produced depends on the acid.

Check Chapter 14 here

Some metals react with acids faster than others. The metal's reactivity depends on its position in the *reactivity series* (see Chapter 17).

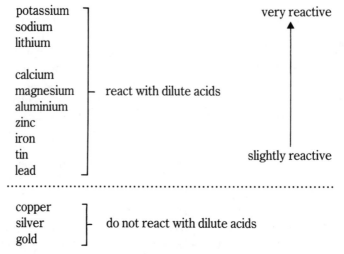

When hydrogen gas is produced it can be tested for by igniting a test tube of hydrogen with a lighted splint; the result is a 'pop'.

Test for H_2

REACTIONS WITH METAL OXIDES

Metal oxides are bases and react with acids to produce salt and water. All metal oxides will react with dilute acids. The reaction follows a general pattern:

metal oxide	+	acid	→	salt	+	water
copper (II) oxide	+	nitric acid	→	copper nitrate	+	water
CuO	+	$2HNO_3$	→	$Cu(NO_3)_2$	+	H_2O
magnesium oxide	+	sulphuric acid	→	magnesium sulphate	+	water
MgO	+	H_2SO_4	→	$MgSO_4$	+	H_2O

REACTIONS WITH METAL HYDROXIDES

Metal hydroxides are bases which will react with acids to produce salt and water. Metal hydroxides which are soluble are called *alkalis*. All metal hydroxides react with acids. The reaction follows a general pattern:

metal hydroxide	+	acid	→	salt	+	water
calcium hydroxide	+	hydrochloric acid	→	calcium chloride	+	water
$Ca(OH)_2$	+	2HCl	→	$CaCl_2$	+	$2H_2O$
potassium hydroxide	+	sulphuric acid	→	potassium sulphate	+	water
2KOH	+	H_2SO_4	→	K_2SO_4	+	$2H_2O$

REACTION WITH CARBONATES

CO_2 given off

Metal carbonates can be thought of as bases; they too will react with acids to produce salt and water, but they also produce carbon dioxide. The reaction follows a general pattern:

acid	+	carbonate	→	salt	+	water	+	carbon dioxide
sodium carbonate	+	nitric acid	→	sodium nitrate	+	water	+	carbon dioxide
Na_2CO_3	+	$2HNO_3$	→	$2NaNO_3$	+	H_2O	+	CO_2

$$\text{calcium carbonate} + \text{hydrochloric acid} \rightarrow \text{calcium chloride} + \text{water} + \text{carbon dioxide}$$

$$CaCO_3 + 2HCl \rightarrow CaCl_2 + H_2O + CO_2$$

Spot the pattern

This is a general pattern for all carbonates, and as some rocks are carbonates it can be used as a test to help identify rocks. For example, limestone, marble and chalk are all mainly calcium carbonate and will therefore react with hydrochloric acid. When a small amount of acid is placed on the surface the rocks fizz and give off carbon dioxide.

There is an exception to this 'rule'; sulphuric acid will not react well with calcium carbonate rock, since during the reaction a layer of calcium sulphate builds up on the surface, preventing any further reaction.

Test for CO₂

The carbon dioxide produced can be tested for by bubbling the gas through limewater, when the limewater turns cloudy.

7 > ACIDS IN ACTION

ACID RAIN

The rain which normally falls is very slightly acidic (pH 5). This is due to a small amount of carbon dioxide from the atmosphere which dissolves in the rain water to produce a weakly acidic solution:

$$H_2O + CO_2 \rightarrow H_2CO_3$$

Check Energy, Chapter 3

Acid rain, however, has a pH of between 5 and about 2.2. The strongest acid rain has an acidity comparable to that of lemon juice. The causes of acid rain are not fully understood, but enough is known to realise that the burning of fossil fuels (hydrocarbons) and the exhaust emission from cars contribute greatly to acid rain.

Fossil fuels like coal and oil contain impurities of sulphur, so that when they burn they produce sulphur dioxide in addition to the normal products of combustion (carbon dioxide and water). Sulphur dioxide is an acidic gas. The exhausts of cars also emit gases other than the normal products of combustion. In the car engine where the petrol (hydrocarbon fuel) is burned, the temperature is so high that nitrogen from the air reacts with oxygen to form oxides of nitrogen which escape through the exhaust, together with unburned hydrocarbons and carbon monoxide.

This mixture of gases (particularly sulphur dioxide and the oxides of nitrogen) react in the atmosphere with water to produce rain which contains sulphuric and nitric acids. It is this that gives the rain its reactivity. Acid rain will obviously be a problem in parts of the world which are industrialised (burn fossil fuels in power stations and factories) and have large numbers of cars, eg Europe, USA, Canada and Japan.

Effects of acid rain

Acid rain will corrode metals and will react with some building materials (limestone and marble), gradually eating them away. Perhaps the largest worry, however, is the effect it has, either directly or indirectly, on living things.

When acid rain falls on to the soil it progressively dissolves away many of the minerals (salts) in the soil. Metal ions are leached (dissolved) out of the soil and washed into rivers and lakes, which become increasingly acidic and increasingly concentrated in metal ions. The first metal ions to be removed from the soil are magnesium (Mg^{2+}) and calcium (Ca^{2+}), because they dissolve most easily. These are needed by plants to ensure healthy growth, so are no longer available.

The next metal ions to be leached out of the soil are aluminium (Al^{3+}) and the heavier metal ions of lead (Pb^{2+}), and copper (Cu^{2+}). These ions are particularly troublesome, since they are poisonous. Dissolved aluminium in the water prevents the gills of fish working, as well as being poisonous to other organisms, including ourselves. (*Note*: it is not the acid water that kills the fish, but the dissolved metal ions.)

The areas that are affected more than others are those with thin soil covering and granite rock, such as Scotland, Dartmoor, the Black Forest in Germany, and Scandinavia. Areas which are lucky enough to have deep soil covering limestone rock are not so badly affected, since the limestone rock and its soil can neutralise the effects of the acid rain. The degree to which an area is affected also depends on its position, since the acidic gases are carried on prevailing winds.

Combating acid rain

1 Some lakes which are very acidic have large amounts of lime (calcium hydroxide) added to them to neutralise the acidity. This is only a temporary measure, however, since it has to be frequently repeated and costs a large amount of money.

2 Power stations which burn coal and oil can be fitted with equipment which will remove the sulphur dioxide from the gases before they are released into the atmosphere.

3 Car exhausts can be fitted with catalytic converters which can convert the harmful gases into harmless ones. These cannot be fitted to the majority of cars in this country, however, since most cars run on leaded petrol. The lead in the petrol will prevent the catalyst from working.

ACIDS AND FOOD PRESERVATION

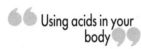

The pickling of foods such as onions and eggs and the making of chutneys helps preserve the food. The acid that is used is found in vinegar. This acid is called ethanoic acid (acetic acid is its more common name). The reason it works is that any bacteria which enter the food are killed by dehydration due to osmosis (see Chapter 13). It also means that the pH is too low for enzymes (biological catalysts) to work, and this prevents the natural deterioration of food.

ACIDS AND DIGESTION

The human digestive system contains many different enzymes whose job it is to help the large food molecules of carbohydrates and proteins to be broken down into smaller molecules. The carbohydrates end up as simple sugars and the proteins as amino acids. These much smaller molecules are able to pass through the wall of the gut and so to be passed around the body. The enzymes which are responsible for this breakdown only work within limited pH ranges, so the acidity at various parts of the digestive system is important.

Saliva in the mouth contains the enzyme *salivary amylase*, which converts starch into sugar. It works best at body temperature and at a pH of between 6 and 7 (about neutral).

The stomach lining produces gastric juice. This contains hydrochloric acid (about pH 2), which kills most of the microorganisms in the food. Gastric juice also contains the enzyme *pepsin*, which starts to break down large protein molecules. Pepsin obviously works best at a much lower pH than salivary amylase. In the small intestine more enzymes act on the food. Also bile, an alkaline liquid produced by the liver, is released into the small intestine. Bile helps to emulsify fats; this means it helps break large fat droplets into much smaller ones (this is a property of all alkalis). The bile also helps neutralise the hydrochloric acid from the stomach, enabling other enzymes which require higher pH values to work on the food molecules.

Indigestion is often caused by too much acid in the stomach and can be relieved by taking 'antacid' tablets. These contain bases which neutralise the excess acid in the stomach. Examples are Settlers and Rennies, which both contain calcium carbonate and magnesium hydroxide.

ACIDITY AND THE SOIL

Most plants prefer to grow in a soil which is slightly acidic, about pH 6–7. There are even some plants which prefer more acidic soils (pH 4.5–6) such as azaleas, rhododendrons and heathers. No plants will grow in strongly alkaline soils, however, although some plants will grow in weakly alkaline soils (up to pH 8). When there is a change from growing one type of plant to another, the acidity of the soil has sometimes to be changed to get the best results. In addition the soil acidity itself may well change over a period of time because of the plants themselves. Needing to reduce the acidity of the soil is a common problem to farmers; they do this by adding lime to the soil. Lime is calcium oxide, but calcium hydroxide (slaked lime) or calcium carbonate (limestone or chalk) is often used:

$$CaO + 2H^+ \rightarrow Ca^{2+} + H_2O$$
(lime or quicklime)
$$Ca(OH)_2 + 2H^+ \rightarrow Ca^{2+} + 2H_2O$$
(slaked lime)
$$CaCO_3 + 2H^+ \rightarrow Ca^{2+} + H_2O + CO_2$$
(limestone)

ACIDS IN INDUSTRY

Sulphuric acid is one of the most important acids in industry and is produced in very large quantities each year. It has a wide variety of uses in the manufacture of other substances. Sulphuric acid is manufactured by the contact process. Sulphur is the starting point:

$$S \quad \rightarrow \quad SO_2 \quad \rightarrow \quad SO_3 \quad \rightarrow \quad H_2SO_4$$

| | heated in air | reacts with more oxygen over catalyst | reacts with water | |

Sulphuric acid is needed for the manufacture of agricultural chemicals (fertilisers), plastics, paints and pigments, detergents and soaps, fibres, dyestuffs, oil and petrol, as well as other chemicals (including other acids).

Nitric acid is another important industrial chemical, and is manufactured in quantity for use mainly in the manufacture of fertilisers and explosives.

8 ▷ SALTS

These are ionic substances which are formed in reactions between acids and bases or between acids and metals. If solutions of these salts are allowed to evaporate, then crystals (giant ionic structures) are formed. Solutions of these salts will conduct electricity, showing that they contain ions.

NAMING SALTS

The name of the salt depends on the ions present. Each salt contains a positive ion, or *cation*, that is derived from the metal, eg Na^+, Mg^{2+}. In addition, each salt contains a negative ion, or *anion* that is derived, from the acid, eg SO_4^{2-} (sulphate), or CO_3^{2-} (carbonate).

The name of the salt comes from a combination of both ions, eg magnesium sulphate ($Mg^{2+} SO_4^{2-}$). The charge on the metal ion depends on its group in the periodic table (see page 176 and Figure 16.4). Some metals (those from the transition metal block in the periodic table) can have ions with different charges. An example is iron, where the charge on the ion is indicated by roman numerals in the name:

iron (II) sulphate $FeSO_4$ Fe^{2+} ion present
iron (III) sulphate $Fe_2(SO_4)_3$ Fe^{3+} ion present

Li⁺														O²⁻	F⁻	
Na⁺	Mg²⁺									Al³⁺			S²⁻	Cl⁻		
K⁺	Ca²⁺	Transition metal ions can have ions with different charges but in common salts are often 1+, 2+ or 3+							Sn²⁺ or Sn⁴⁺						
									Pb²⁺ or Pb⁴⁺						

Fig 16.4 The charge on the ion depends on its group in the periodic table.

PATTERNS FOR SALTS

Solubility

In the case of cations, all salts containing sodium, potassium or ammonium ions are soluble. Although the ammonium ion (NH_4^+) is not a metal ion, it may be regarded as such in salts.

In the case of anions, all *nitrates* (NO_3^-) are soluble; all *chlorides* (Cl^-) are soluble (except silver and lead); all *sulphates* (SO_4^{2-}) are soluble (except barium, calcium and lead); but all *carbonates* (CO_3^{2-}) are *insoluble* (except Na^+, K^+, NH_4^+).

The solubility of a salt often increases with temperature, although there are a few exceptions. The reason for this is that in order for the water to dissolve the salt it has to break down the ionic lattice (Figure 16.5). The higher the temperature, the greater the kinetic energy of the particles (water molecules and ions). *Remember*: water is able to dissolve ionic substances because it is a polar molecule (see Chapter 14).

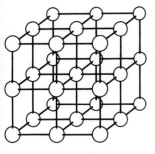

Fig 16.5 Ionic lattice of a salt.

COLOUR OF SALTS

The colour of salts is often due to the metal ion present.

Ion	Colour	Ion	Colour
Na^+	colourless	Fe^{2+}	green
K^+	colourless	Fe^{3+}	red
Cu^{2+}	blue/green		

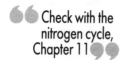

9 ▷ SALTS IN ACTION

Check with the nitrogen cycle, Chapter 11

Salts are present in the sea and in the soil and provide plants with the elements they need. For example, nitrogen as *nitrates* (NO_3^-) in the soil provides the plant with vital materials to manufacture amino acids. Phosphorus, as *phosphates* (PO_4^{3-}) is essential for energy transfer within the plant cell. In addition, potassium (K^+) makes many enzymes active, while calcium (Ca^{2+}) provides a raw material for cell walls. Magnesium (Mg^{2+}) is a vital component of chlorophyll, and sulphur, as sulphates (SO_4^{2-}), is a component of some amino acids. Because each of these elements is needed by plants, their salts are manufactured as fertilisers. Examples are ammonium nitrate, ammonium phosphate and potassium chloride. Fertilisers containing these three salts are called N, P, K fertilisers because they provide nitrogen (N), phosphorus (P) and potassium (K).

As well as in agriculture, salts are used in other, industrial or medical, applications. Calcium sulphate (gypsum) is used as wall plaster and plaster of Paris. Silver chloride is used as photographic film emulsion. Iron (II) sulphate is used in iron tablets to treat anaemia.

EXAMINATION QUESTIONS

MULTIPLE CHOICE

Questions 1–3 below refer to the following pH numbers.
A pH 1; B pH 4; C pH 7; D pH 10; E pH 14

QUESTION 1

What is the pH of a strongly alkaline solution?

QUESTION 2

What is the pH of a neutral solution?

QUESTION 3

What is the pH of a weakly acidic solution?

QUESTION 4

How many grams of sulphuric acid H_2SO_4, are present in a 2 M solution of sulphuric acid? (H = 1, S = 32, O = 16)
A 49 g; B 50 g; C 98 g; D 194 g; E 196 g

QUESTION 5

What gas is released when zinc reacts with hydrochloric acid?
A carbon dioxide   D nitrogen
B chlorine   E oxygen
C hydrogen

QUESTION 6

What new substance, apart from magnesium sulphate, is formed when magnesium oxide
reacts with sulphuric acid?

A carbon dioxide   D a salt
B hydrogen   E water
C oxygen

QUESTION 7

How would you correctly identify the gas produced when an acid reacts with a carbonate?

A use a glowing splint   D use limewater
B use a lighted splint   E pass the gas through an acid
C carefully smell the gas

STRUCTURED QUESTIONS

QUESTION 8

a) A list of pH values is given below:

   pH 1   pH 4   pH 7   pH 9   pH 14

   Select from this list the pH value of each of the following substances. Each value may
   be used once, more than once or not at all.

   i) distilled water_____

   (1)

   ii) toothpaste_____

   (1)

   iii) vinegar_____

   (1)

b) A householder bought a bottle of the stain remover called ATAKA shown alongside.

   i) Which piece of laboratory apparatus would you use to confirm that the bottle
       contains 250 cm³?

       _____

       (1)

   ii) A little of the liquid is accidentally dropped on the carpet. Suggest a household
       substance which could be used to prevent damage, and explain your choice.

       name _____

       explanation _____

       _____

       (3)

       (NISEC; Specimen)

ATAKA

Contains Formic Acid

Keep out of reach
of children

Do not breathe in vapour

Wash off skin immediately

CORROSIVE POISON

CAUSES BURNS

NOT TO BE TAKEN

Contents 250cm³

QUESTION 9

In a chemist's shop, two brands of indigestion tablets are on sale, Burney and Rumbley.
Sarah did an experiment to try to find out which one would be better.

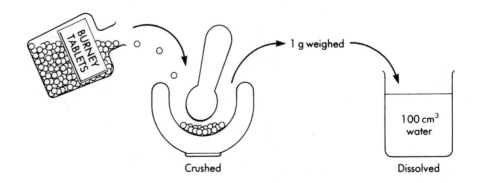

Crushed   Dissolved

She crushed the tablets and dissolved 1 g of each kind of tablet in 100 cm³ of distilled water. Then she did an experiment to find out what volume of the same acid solution was needed to neutralise each tablet solution.

a) What is the chemical in the stomach that can cause indigestion?

_____

(1)

b) i) What is meant by a *neutral* solution?

_____

_____

(1)

ii) Give **two** reasons why Sarah crushed the tablets rather than using whole tablets.

1 _____

2 _____

(2)

The apparatus she used is shown below.

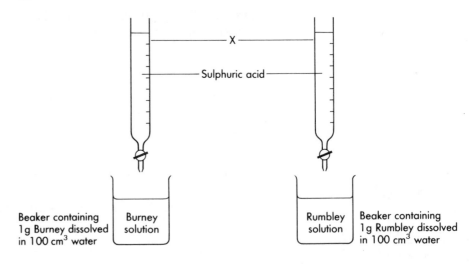

c) i) What is the name of the apparatus **X** that she used?

_____

(1)

ii) What indicator might Sarah use to show when neutralisation has taken place?

_____

(1)

iii) What colour change would have taken place at neutralisation?

Colour in tablet solution	Colour at neutralisation

(2)

iv) Name **one** chemical which you might find in an indigestion tablet.

_____

(1)

v) Write a word equation for the reaction of sulphuric acid with this chemical.

_____

(2)

d)   The results of the experiment were as follows:

| Volume of sulphuric acid needed to neutralise Burney tablet solution = 25 cm^3 |
| Volume of sulphuric acid needed to neutralise Rumbley tablet solution = 20 cm^3 |

  i) Which of the tablets would be better to cure indigestion?

_____

  ii) Give a reason for your answer.

_____

_____

(2)

e)   State and explain **two** safety measures (precautions) that Sarah should take whilst doing this experiment.

Safety measure	*Reason*
1 _____ _____ _____	_____ _____ _____ _____
2 _____ _____ _____	_____ _____ _____ _____

(2)
(Total marks 15)
(LEAG; 1988)

QUESTION 10

a)   The components of washing powders Soapso and Sudso are listed below.

Washing powder	*Soapso*	*Sudso*
Sodium sulphate %	29	35
Sodium carbonate %	20	0
Sodium silicate %	20	26
Sodium soap %	0	6
Detergent %	15	13

Dilute nitric acid was added to each powder in turn. Only one of the powders fizzed. The gas turned limewater milky.

  i) Which powder fizzed?   _____

(1)

  ii) Which sodium compound was reacting with the acid?   _____

(1)

  iii) Name the gas given off.   _____

(1)

   iv) In the space below draw and label apparatus which you would use to add the acid to the soap powder. Your diagram should show how you would pass the gas through limewater.

   v) Why is it sensible to wear gloves when using nitric acid?

_____

_____

_____

(1)

b)

i) From the items above select **one** which is *not* acidic. _____

(1)

ii) Name **one** which would have a pH value below 7. _____

(1)

Soothers

NEW IMPROVED SOOTHERS BRING
30% MORE ACID NEUTRALISING POWER

EACH TABLET CONTAINS: Calcium Carbonate B.P. 534mg.
Magnesium Hydroxide B.P. 160mg.
KEEP OUT OF REACH OF CHILDREN.

**'MILK OF MAGNESIA'
LIQUID**

Shake bottle well before using. Please use
'Milk of Magnesia' within six months
of opening. Each 5ml contains 415mg
MAGNESIUM HYDROXIDE B.P.

BENNIES

Each tablet contains: Calcium Carbonate 680mg.
Light Magnesium Carbonate Ph. Fur. 80mg.
If symptoms persist, consult your doctor.

iii) Soothers, Bennies and Milk of Magnesia all claim to neutralise acid indigestion.

What is meant by 'neutralise'? _____

_____

(1)

iv) Name the **two** substances produced when Milk of Magnesia reacts with hydrochloric acid.

A_____   B_____

(2)

v) Where in the body might this reaction occur? _____

(1)

vi) If each packet of Soothers contains 12 tablets, what is the total mass of magnesium hydroxide in the packet?

_____

(1)

vii) Imagine some powdered Bennies were accidentally mixed with washing soda. Using your knowledge of the chemical properties of the contents of each, describe how you would separate them.

_____

_____

_____

_____

(4)

c) Study the graph below, which shows the variation of pH in the mouth of a child who only eats at meal times.

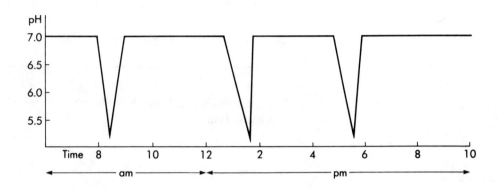

i) At what time in the morning does the child start eating?

_____

(1)

ii) Explain what causes the increase in acidity. _____

_____

_____

(2)

iii) What effect will the acid have on the teeth? _____

_____

(1)

iv) For how long after starting each meal does the child's mouth remain acid?

_____

(1)

v) Draw on the graph what would happen if the child ate sweets at 10 a.m.   *(1)*

vi) What would be the effect on the acidity in the mouth of continuously eating sweets throughout the day?

_____

(1)

(NISEC; 1988)

QUESTION 11

The manufacture of sulphuric acid can be represented by the following flowchart:

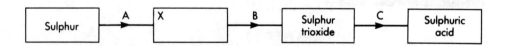

a) Stage A involves the burning of sulphur.

i) Write in the box labelled **X** the name of the main substance formed.   *(1)*

ii) Write a chemical equation for this reaction.

_____

(1)

b) Vanadium (V) oxide is a catalyst for the reaction.

   i) What effect does vanadium (V) oxide have on the reaction?

   _____

                                                                              (1)

   ii) State **one** other general property of a catalyst.

   _____

                                                                              (1)

   iii) Sulphur trioxide is not dissolved directly in water at stage C. Describe how stage
        C is carried out.

   _____

   _____

   _____

                                                                              (3)

c) i) Sulphur dioxide is produced in most power stations in Britain as part of the waste
       gases. Explain what effect this gas may have on

       1 living organisms _____

       _____

       _____

       2 buildings _____

       _____

       _____

       _____

                                                                              (5)

    ii) Suggest a method of removing sulphur dioxide from the waste gases.

    _____

    _____

    _____

                                                                              (2)
                                                               (LEAG; Specimen)

ANSWERS TO
EXAMINATION QUESTIONS

MULTIPLE CHOICE

ANSWER 1

Key E, pH 14.

ANSWER 2

Key C, pH 7.

ANSWER 3

Key B, pH 4.

ANSWER 4

Key E, 196 g. The solution is 2 M, so it's $2 \times [2+32+(16\times4)] = 196$.

ANSWER 5

Key C, hydrogen. Option A, carbon dioxide, is released when acids react with carbonates.

ANSWER 6

Key E, water. Option B, hydrogen, is released when acids react with metals, not metal oxides.

ANSWER 7

Key D, limewater. The gas released by acids and carbonates is carbon dioxide, which turns limewater milky. Option A is the test for oxygen, and option B is the test for hydrogen.

STRUCTURED
QUESTIONS

ANSWER 8

a)   i) pH 7; ii) pH 9; iii) pH 4
b)   i) a measuring cylinder or graduated beaker
      ii) Most household cleaners are alkaline and would neutralise the acidic Ataka.

ANSWER 9

a) hydrochloric acid
b)   i) a solution that is neither acidic nor alkaline
     ii) 1 to increase the surface area
        2 to increase the rate of reaction
c)   i) a burette
     ii) universal indicator
     iii) purple or blue in solution, green at neutralisation
     iv) calcium carbonate
     v) calcium carbonate + sulphuric acid = calcium sulphate + carbon dioxide + water
d)   i) Burney tablets
     ii) They are a stronger tablet, as more acid is needed to neutralise them.
e)   1 to wear safety goggles – to stop any acid entering the eyes
     2 to wear plastic gloves – to stop acid getting on the skin.

ANSWER 10

a)   i) Soapso
      ii) Sodium carbonate
      iii) carbon dioxide
      iv)

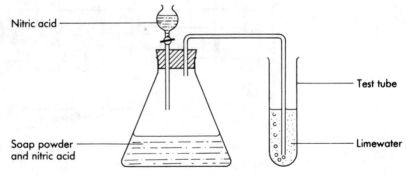

      v) Nitric acid is corrosive and can burn your skin.

b)   i) bicarbonate of soda (or Milk of Magnesia)
      ii) lemonade (or vinegar)
      iii) to remove the acidity
      iv) A, magnesium chloride; B, water
      v) in the stomach
      vi) 1,920 mg
      vii) Calcium carbonate and magnesium carbonate are insoluble, so you could mix with
           water. The washing soda dissolves but the Bennies contains insoluble substances,
           so filter and evaporate to dryness.

c)   i) 8 am
     ii) drinking an acidic drink, eg orange juice
     iii) attacks the enamel
     iv) about 1 hour
     v) The line should dip to pH 5.5 after 10 a.m., and then rise to pH 7.0 by 11 a.m.
     vi) The pH would be about 5.5, slightly acidic all day.

ANSWER 11

a)   i) **X** is sulphur dioxide
     ii) $S + O_2 \rightarrow SO_2$

b)   i) increases the rate of reaction
     ii) is not used up in the reaction
     iii) Sulphur trioxide is dissolved in 98% sulphuric acid, and water is then added.

c)   i) 1 can kill leaves on trees, so trees die; can cause breathing problems for humans
        2 causes damages to limestone buildings, as it corrodes the limestone and causes
           the buildings to crumble.
     ii) to pass the waste gases through an alkali to neutralise the sulphur dioxide.

A STUDENT'S ANSWER WITH
EXAMINER'S COMMENTS

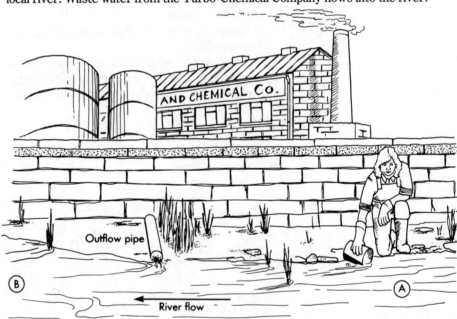

Judith Harris is an Environmental Health Officer. She took samples of water from the local river. Waste water from the Turbo-Chemical Company flows into the river.

Judith then measured the pH of the water. She found that water from point A had a pH of 7.0 while that at point B had a pH of 2.0.

a)   iii) What can you state about the river water at A and at B?

66 State water at A is neutral. 99

> The water at B is acidic.

_____

                                                                              (2)

     ii) What is likely to have changed the pH value of the water in travelling from A to B?

66 Yes, but it is the waste water from the pipe which is important. 99

> The outflow pipe.

_____

                                                                              (1)

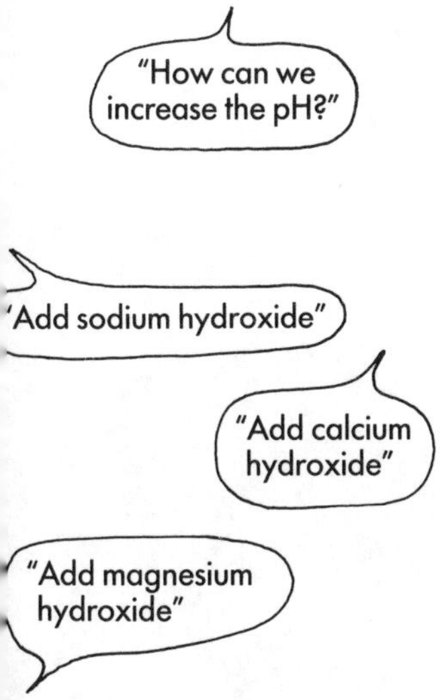

"How can we increase the pH?"

"Add sodium hydroxide"

"Add calcium hydroxide"

"Add magnesium hydroxide"

Figure 1

66 Yes, and state pH 14.0 for the second mark 99

66 Good. 99

66 Yes and it has the highest pH. 99

66 State: take pH of waste water; use measured volume of waste water eg 1 litre; add *measured* amount of sodium hydroxide; stir to dissolve; record result each time; continue until pH 7. 99

b)   The local Environmental Health Regulations state that waste water from factories must have a pH between 7.5 and 9.5. The pH can be increased by adding alkaline substances. Mr Harminder Singh, the works chemist, talked to three of his laboratory technicians about possible substances to be added to the waste water (Figure 1). Some facts about these substances are shown in Table 1.

Alkaline substance	Solubility at 10°C (g/100 g of water)	pH of saturated solution
Calcium hydroxide	0.125	12.0
Magnesium hydroxide	0.070	9.3
Sodium hydroxide	102	14.0

Table 1

i)   Which is the most soluble of these alkaline substances, and what is the pH of its saturated solution?

sodium hydroxide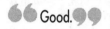

(2)

ii)   What would be the effect of adding too much calcium hydroxide?

The waste water would be too alkaline.

(1)

iii)   Which saturated solution has the lowest pH?

Magnesium hydroxide

(1)

iv)   Which substance should Mr Singh choose? Why should he choose it?

Sodium hydroxide
It is very soluble

(3)

v)   You are provided with several litres of the waste water and the following apparatus and chemicals:
        beakers with a 1 litre mark
        balance
        universal indicator paper
        glass stirring rods
        suitable containers for weighing the chosen substance
        spatula
        chosen substance

Describe how you would find out how much of the chosen substance has to be added to the waste water to increase its pH to about 8.0.

Add some of the substance to the waste water, stir and take the pH. Add some more until the pH is neutral.

(8)

(Total marks 18)
(LEAG; 1988)

METALS AND POLYMERS

GETTING STARTED

We make use of materials according to their properties, which in turn are determined by the way in which their atoms are bonded together. Two very useful groups of materials are *metals* and *polymers* (a type of macromolecule). Understanding the *structure* of these helps the scientist to manufacture materials for specific purposes, as well as to have a better understanding of their properties.

All *metals* are elements (an individual metal contains only one type of atom). Metals exist as compounds in rocks; those rocks which contain large enough quantities of metals to be mined are called ores. Metals can be extracted from ores by techniques such as smelting (reduction using carbon) or electrolysis. Metals have a number of useful properties:

- conductors of heat and electricity;
- solids (except mercury);
- strong, malleable and ductile;
- high melting points and densities;
- shiny.

There are exceptions to these general properties, and different metals do exhibit these properties to varying degrees, eg copper is used for electrical wiring because it is a better conductor than many. It is important to realise, however, that the choice of a metal for a particular job not only depends on its properties but also on its cost. (Gold is a better conductor than copper but is not used in electrical wiring though it is used for electrical contacts in microchips in computers!)

Many *macromolecules* (large molecules) are based on carbon and its ability to form long chains. Macromolecules have a number of useful properties; they are found in living things, eg as wool (a protein), or as starch (a carbohydrate). They can also be man-made from carbon-based compounds, eg detergents and polymers. Scientists can *synthesise* (make) macromolecules such as polymers to have specific properties, eg polythene is a long carbon chain which has attached to it hydrogen atoms. By replacing the hydrogen atoms with fluorine atoms, a different polymer can be made (PTFE) which is used on non-stick frying pans. The properties of these compounds are determined by the way the carbon atoms are *joined* in the chain (single bonds or double bonds, etc.) and the type of atoms *attached* to the chain.

ESSENTIAL PRINCIPLES

1 ▶ METALS AS ELEMENTS

❝❝ Check with Chapter 14 ❞❞

All metals are *elements* and are grouped on the left-hand side of the periodic table. The common everyday metals are found in the block referred to as the *transition metals*. Metals are giant structures in which the metal atoms exist as positive ions in a sea of electrons (see page 179). This gives rise to their characteristic physical properties of strength, hardness and the ability to conduct electricity.

							1 **H** Hydrogen 1										4 **He** Helium 2
7 **Li** Lithium 3	9 **Be** Beryllium 4											11 **B** Boron 5	12 **C** Carbon 6	14 **N** Nitrogen 7	16 **O** Oxygen 8	19 **F** Fluorine 9	20 **Ne** Neon 10
23 **Na** Sodium 11	24 **Mg** Magnesium 12											27 **Al** Aluminium 13	28 **Si** Silicon 14	31 **P** Phosphorus 15	32 **S** Sulphur 16	35.5 **Cl** Chlorine 17	40 **Ar** Argon 18
39 **K** Potassium 19	40 **Ca** Calcium 20	45 **Sc** Scandium 21	48 **Ti** Titanium 22	51 **V** Vanadium 23	52 **Cr** Chromium 24	55 **Mn** Manganese 25	56 **Fe** Iron 26	59 **Co** Cobalt 27	59 **Ni** Nickel 28	64 **Cu** Copper 29	65 **Zn** Zinc 30	70 **Ga** Gallium 31	73 **Ge** Germanium 32	75 **As** Arsenic 33	79 **Se** Selenium 34	80 **Br** Bromine 35	84 **Kr** Krypton 36
85 **Rb** Rubidium 37	88 **Sr** Strontium 38	89 **Y** Yttrium 39	91 **Zr** Zirconium 40	93 **Nb** Niobium 41	96 **Mo** Molybdenum 42	**Tc** Technetium 43	101 **Ru** Ruthenium 44	103 **Rh** Rhodium 45	106 **Pd** Palladium 46	108 **Ag** Silver 47	112 **Cd** Cadmium 48	115 **In** Indium 49	119 **Sn** Tin 50	122 **Sb** Antimony 51	128 **Te** Tellurium 52	127 **I** Iodine 53	131 **Xe** Xenon 54
133 **Cs** Caesium 55	137 **Ba** Barium 56	139 **La** Lanthanum 57 ·	178 **Hf** Hafnium 72	181 **Ta** Tantalum 73	184 **W** Tungsten 74	186 **Re** Rhenium 75	190 **Os** Osmium 76	192 **Ir** Iridium 77	195 **Pt** Platinum 78	197 **Au** Gold 79	201 **Hg** Mercury 80	204 **Tl** Thallium 81	207 **Pb** Lead 82	209 **Bi** Bismuth 83	**Po** Polonium	**At** Astatine 85	**Rn** Radon 86
Fr Francium 87	226 **Ra** Radium 88	227 **Ac** Actinium 89 †															

◄——————— Metals ————————————————————————————————————► ◄ Non-Metals ►

Fig 17.1 The position of metals in the periodic table.

In the majority of their reactions, metal atoms react to form *positive ions*. The charge on the ion depends on the *position* in the periodic table.

Group	Charge on ion	Example
1	1+	Na
2	2+	Ca
3	3+	Al

The transition metals can form ions with *different* charges; they are said to have *variable valency*. In compounds, the charge on the metal ion is indicated by roman numerals. Transition metal compounds are often coloured.

Compound	Colour	Formula	Metal ion
Copper (II) sulphate	blue	$CuSO_4$	Cu^{2+}
Iron (II) sulphate	green	$FeSO_4$	Fe^{2+}
Iron (III) oxide	red	Fe_2O_3	Fe^{3+}
Copper (I) oxide	red	Cu_2O	Cu^{+}
Copper (II) oxide	black	CuO	Cu^{2+}

2 ▶ PROPERTIES AND USES OF METALS

❝❝ Some uses of metals ❞❞

The general physical properties of metals, which provide them with a variety of uses, are shown in Figure 17.2.

Some metals have individual properties which gives them particular uses. *Iron*, for example, can be easily magnetised, so is used to make magnets and electromagnets; *mercury* is a liquid which expands well on heating, so is used in the manufacture of thermometers. *Gold* is a metal which is rare and never corrodes, so can be used as a money standard and for making jewellery.

Metal	Property	Use
Iron	toughness	equipment and machinery that will be knocked about in use – steel
Aluminium, silver	metallic sheen	mirrors, reflectors
Aluminium, gold	reflecting heat and light	coating of firemen's protective clothing; space 'shuttle' heat shield of gold foil
Zinc, copper	malleability	easy shaping of metal structures by presses, also 'hand beating' of metals into shape – brass
Copper, aluminium, gold	ductility	wide variety of wires – electrical and ornamental
Iron, aluminium, tungsten	high melting point	wires for electric fires, metals for boilers, cookers, pans, electric light filaments (tungsten m.p. about 3500°C)
Aluminium, iron, copper	good heat conductor	radiators in central heating systems, copper for cooking pans
Copper, aluminium	electrical conductivity	electrical wiring
Lead, aluminium, iron, zinc	corrosion resistance	roofing, flashings, foil and food containers – soft drink and beer cans, zinc coating - 'galvanised' steel
Aluminium, magnesium	low density	aircraft construction, lightweight vehicles and wheels

Fig. 17.2 Some typical metals and their uses

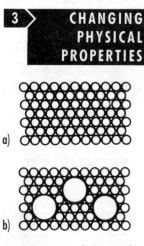

Fig 17.3 Atoms in a) pure metal and b) an alloy

3 CHANGING PHYSICAL PROPERTIES

MAKING ALLOYS

Alloys are solid mixtures of metals and are formed by melting together two or more different metals. The properties of the alloy that is formed are *not* simply an average of the properties of the original metals. The properties also depend on the proportion of each metal present, eg solder is an alloy of lead (67%) and zinc (33%) and has a lower melting point. This is not to say, however, that the properties of new alloys are simply a hit or miss affair. The properties of alloys are determined partly by the *metal atoms present*, but more importantly by how these atoms can *pack together* in the structure (see Figure 17.3). With information such as this, scientists can produce alloys with specific properties.

One very important group of alloys is *steels*. Steel is an alloy of the metal iron mixed with a small quantity of carbon (a non-metal). The introduction of a small quantity of carbon increases the strength of the iron enormously, because the carbon atoms fit into the giant structure of iron atoms, preventing the iron atoms moving so freely when the material is hammered, twisted or stretched.

Different steels can be produced with different properties, depending on the amount of carbon present. In addition, other metals can be added, such as chromium and tungsten, to change the properties still further.

HEAT TREATMENT AND WORK HARDENING

Heating a metal such as steel and then allowing it to cool down quickly or slowly can change its properties, eg hot metal that is cooled quickly by quenching (plunging into cold water) will often make the metal more brittle.

Metal that is continually being worked (hammered or bent into shape) will gradually become harder; this is called *work hardening*. This can be removed by heating and by allowing the metal to cool down slowly; this is called *annealing*.

Examples of common alloys

Alloy	Use	Constituents	Important Properties
spring steel	suspension springs	iron; 0.3%–0.6% carbon	Contains sufficient carbon that will produce a spring metal
stainless steel	surgical instruments cutlery	iron; <1% carbon; 18% chromium	resistant to corrosion
chromium–vanadium steel	axles and wrenches	iron; chromium; vanadium; carbon	very strong, great resistance to strain
high speed tungsten steels	cutting metals; drills, etc.	iron with up to 20% tungsten	maintains sharp edge at high temperatures
brass	screws; taps; ornaments	copper/zinc. The more zinc there is the stronger the alloy (up to 34% zinc)	strong; does not easily corrode
bronze	castings of intricate shapes statues, etc.	copper; up to 12% tin	easily cast; resists corrosion
an aluminium alloy	aircraft framework	aluminium; copper magnesium	very strong for its weight; aluminium is a light metal but is not very strong so is alloyed with other metals to increase strength

Learn one or two examples

These are just some examples of some useful alloys. Exam questions involving alloys often require you to match the properties of an alloy which may be given to a particular use.

4 > **THE CHEMICAL PROPERTIES OF METALS**

Check with Chapter 14, Periodic Table

THE REACTIVITY SERIES

When metals react they do so to form positive ions. Some metals are more reactive than others; this means the atoms form ions more easily. The metals can be placed in order of their reactivity, which depends on the ease with which they can form positive ions. This is referred to as the *reactivity series* for metals. This order of reactivity tends to be about the same no matter with what the metals are reacting.

Reactivity series

Spot the pattern

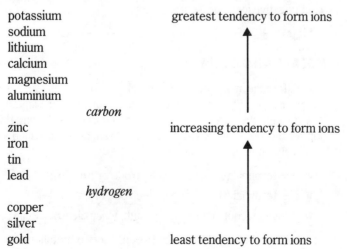

potassium	greatest tendency to form ions
sodium	
lithium	
calcium	
magnesium	
aluminium	
carbon	
zinc	increasing tendency to form ions
iron	
tin	
lead	
hydrogen	
copper	
silver	
gold	least tendency to form ions

The reactivity series can help us understand:

- why some metals corrode and not others;
- how we can prevent corrosion;
- why some metals react with dilute acids and not others;
- why some metals are extracted from their ores by reduction with carbon and why some can only be extracted by electrolysis;
- why metals were discovered in the order they were.

REACTIONS OF METALS

Metal and oxygen

"There's a pattern here"

When heated in air, metals are *oxidised* to form metal oxides which are bases. The more reactive metals will burn in air. Gold and silver are metals which are not oxidised by heating in air. For example,

$$2Mg(s) + O_2(g) \rightarrow 2MgO(s)$$

Metals and water

The more reactive metals react with water to produce hydrogen. Potassium, sodium, lithium and calcium will react with cold water, to produce hydroxides:

$$2Na(s) + 2H_2O(l) \rightarrow 2NaOH(aq) + H_2(g)$$

On the other hand, magnesium, zinc and iron will only react with steam, to form oxides:

"And a pattern here"

$$Zn(s) + H_2O(g) \rightarrow ZnO(s) + H_2(g)$$

Metals and acids

All the metals in the reactivity series above copper will form hydrogen by reacting with hydrochloric acid. For example,

$$Mg(s) + 2HCl(aq) \rightarrow MgCl_2(aq) + H_2(g)$$

"Metals plus acids produce hydrogen"

Dilute nitric acid, however, does not give hydrogen. The lower in the reactivity series the metal, the slower the reaction.

Metals and metal salt solutions

"Identify the pattern"

If a metal is placed in a solution of the salt of another metal, a reaction may or may not take place. We can predict whether a reaction *will* occur if we know the position of the metals in the reactivity series. A metal high in the reactivity series, which has the greater tendency to form ions, will *displace* a metal low in the reactivity series from solution. For example,

$$Mg(s) + CuSO_4(aq) \rightarrow MgSO_4(aq) + Cu(s)$$

Mg is above Cu in the reactivity series, so electrons are transferred from the magnesium atom to the copper ion. This can be shown as an *ionic* equation, since it does not matter what negative ion is present:

$$Mg(s) + Cu^{2+}(aq) \rightarrow Mg^{2+}(aq) + Cu(s)$$

METALS AND CELLS

The difference in tendency of metals to form ions can be very useful. If two different metals are placed in a solution containing ions and are linked by a wire, then electrons will flow through the wire. This means that a current is flowing through the wire, and there is a voltage between the two metals. This arrangement is called a *simple cell* (see Figure 17.4).

All cells contain three things:

- a + terminal (the positive electrode or **anode**);
- a − terminal (the negative electrode or **cathode**);
- a solution containing ions through which electricity can pass – the **electrolyte**.

The voltage that is produced between the two metals generally depends on their relative positions in the reactivity series. If the metals are far apart in the reactivity series then a large voltage is produced, whereas if the two metals in the pair are close together then a small voltage is produced. Let's refer back to the reactivity series:

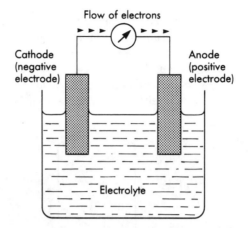

Fig 17.4 A simple cell.

Metal pair	Voltage produced
magnesium/copper	large voltage
iron/zinc	small voltage

Dry cells (batteries) that you can buy essentially consist of metal pairs in an electrolyte, except that one of the metals is replaced by carbon (in the form of graphite). In normal dry cells the electrolyte is a weak acid; alkaline batteries have electrolytes which are alkalis.

METALS AND CORROSION

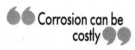
Corrosion can be costly

Corrosion is a chemical reaction. Corrosion of a metal will only take place if the metal is in contact with a solution containing ions. When the metal corrodes it loses electrons to form positive ions:

Metal atom − **electron(s)** → **metal ion**
M(s) − e⁻ → M⁺

Metals corrode at different rates, depending on their position in the reactivity series. Magnesium will corrode more quickly than copper, because it is higher in the reactivity series and has a greater tendency to form ions. As an example, iron will corrode (rust) when it is in contact with water and air. The water acts as a weak electrolyte (a solution containing ions) because it contains dissolved substances. Iron will corrode much more quickly when in contact with sea water, because this is a much stronger electrolyte (it contains a larger amount of dissolved salts). This is a real problem for ships; also cars that are kept near the sea (in seaside towns) tend to corrode more quickly than their counterparts inland. The reaction occurring in the corrosion of iron is as follows:

Fe(s) − 3e⁻ → Fe³⁺(aq)

Corrosion can be a greater problem with structures built of more than one metal, eg if the steel plates of a ship's hull are riveted together with brass rivets, then the steel will corrode much more quickly than if the rivets were also made of steel. The sea water is acting as the electrolyte, so that a simple cell is set up between the iron (steel) and the copper (in the brass). The iron has a greater tendency to form ions than the copper, so will corrode much more rapidly.

The *rate of corrosion* of a metal therefore depends on:

- the position of the metal in the reactivity series;
- the concentration of the electrolyte with which the metal is in contact;
- the nature of any other metal with which it is in contact;
- the temperature of the metal (this is why car exhausts corrode quickly) – a higher temperature speeds up chemical reactions.

Preventing corrosion

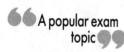
A popular exam topic

1 **Surface coating**: the simplest method of preventing metals from corroding is either to paint the metal or to cover it with a polymer layer which is bonded to the surface. Some oil rigs in the North Sea are protected in this way.

2 **Sacrificial protection**: in this process one metal is 'sacrificed' to protect another. In *galvanising*, iron is coated with a thin layer of zinc. Since the zinc is higher in the reactivity series, it will corrode, leaving the iron metal intact. A similar method is used to protect ships and oil rig platforms in the North Sea. This time, large blocks of zinc are welded to the ship's hull or the legs of the oil rig. These corrode away, protecting the legs, and can be easily replaced with new ones.

Technological application

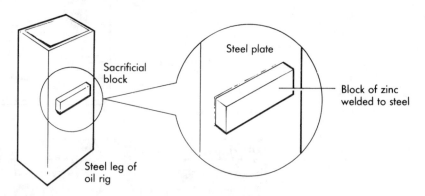

Fig 17.5 Sacrificial corrosion.

3 **Electroplating**: another method of preventing corrosion is to cover the surface of the metal with a thin layer of another metal which does not corrode. This is done by placing the metal to be protected in an electrolysis cell connected as the cathode (see page 177). Examples of electroplating are tin cans (steel coated with a thin layer of tin), and chromium-plated bumpers on cars.

5 THE HISTORY OF METALS

The most abundant metal in the Earth's crust is aluminium, yet it was one of the last to be discovered. Why should this be so? Yet again, reference to the reactivity series can help us answer this question.

Metal	Approximate date of first use
Gold, silver, copper	5000 BC
Tin	2500 BC
Iron	1200 BC
Zinc	BC/AD
Aluminium	AD 1825

If we compare this list with the reactivity series, we can see that it shows the *reverse* pattern. In other words, the metals that were *discovered first* were those that showed the *least* tendency to form ions. In fact the metals gold and silver and small amounts of copper can be found on the ground in their *native state*, ie as the metals themselves. The other metals however only exist in the Earth's crust as compounds, ie the metals are present as metal ions chemically locked with other substances. The *more reactive* a metal (the higher in the reactivity series), the *more stable* it becomes as a *compound*. This means that it will be difficult to extract it from its ore (to change the ion into an atom).

6 THE EXTRACTION OF METALS

Many metals exist in the Earth's crust as metal ores. Some of the most common are shown in the table below.

Metal ore	Compound	Formula	Metal
Limestone	calcium carbonate	$CaCO_3$	calcium
Bauxite	aluminium oxide	Al_2O_3	aluminium
Haematite	iron oxide	Fe_2O_3	iron
Pyrites	iron sulphide	FeS_2	iron
Galena	lead sulphide	PbS	lead
Chalcopyrite	copper iron sulphide	$CuFeS_2$	copper

There are two basic techniques for extracting the metal from the ore; either **reduction**, using heat energy and carbon as the reducing agent, or **electrolysis**, using electrical energy. In either case the problem is the same – to reduce the metal *ion* to a metal *atom*. The technique that is chosen depends on cost and the reactivity of the metal.

REDUCTION BY CARBON

Carbon is a suitable reducing agent for obtaining many metals from their oxides. For example,

lead oxide	+	carbon	→	lead	+	carbon dioxide
$2PbO$	+	C	→	$2Pb$	+	CO_2

Coke is a relatively cheap and abundant source of carbon which is capable of reducing oxides of all the metals below aluminium in the reactivity series. Coke is therefore suitable for large-scale metal extraction.

Iron extraction

Iron is extracted from its ore *haematite* (which contains iron oxide) by smelting in a *blast furnace*. Once the furnace is started it operates as a continuous process, the raw materials being added at the top and the molten iron and molten waste being run off at the bottom.

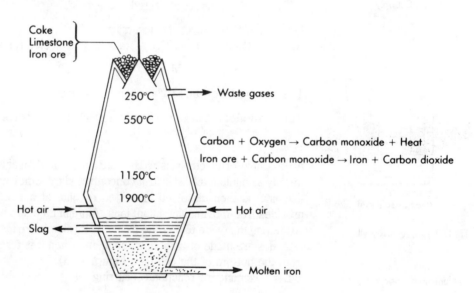

Fig 17.6 The blast furnace used to extract iron from iron ore.

The raw materials include *iron oxide ore*, which will be reduced to iron; *coke*, which provides the reducing agent; and *limestone*, which is added to remove the waste material from the iron ore.

During the process, at the *bottom* of the furnace a *blast* of hot air is forced up into the hot, raw materials. The air provides oxygen, which reacts with the carbon to produce carbon monoxide:

$$2C(s) \ + \ O_2(g) \ \rightarrow \ 2CO(g)$$

Carbon monoxide is a powerful reducing agent, and reduces the iron oxide to iron, which is molten at the temperature of the furnace:

carbon monoxide	+	iron oxide	→	iron	+	carbon dioxide
$3CO(g)$	+	$Fe_2O_3(s)$	→	$2Fe(l)$	+	$3CO_2(g)$

Iron ore contains a lot of rocky material as impurity (mainly silica). This would soon clog the furnace and have to be removed, requiring the furnace to be shut down and allowed to cool – a very costly process. The limestone (calcium carbonate) reacts with the silica at high temperature to produce a molten glassy material (calcium silicate). This is less dense than the molten iron and floats to the top of the molten iron; where it is tapped off as *slag*.

The molten iron is very dense and travels down through the furnace. It is tapped off at the bottom hole into large moulds called pigs. The iron that is produced is called *pig iron*.

The hot waste gases (including carbon monoxide and carbon dioxide) are removed through the top of the furnace.

Other metals, such as lead, zinc and copper, can also be extracted in this way. Sulphide ores (eg galena, PbS) first have to be roasted in air to convert the compound to a metal oxide:

lead sulphide   +   oxygen   →   lead oxide   +   sulphur dioxide
$2PbS(s)$ + $3O_2(g)$ → $2PbO(s)$ + $SO_2(g)$

ELECTROLYSIS

Another method of reducing a metal ore to the metal is by the process of **electrolysis**. Metals are present in metal ores as *positive ions*. If electricity is passed into a solution of the ore, or into the molten ore (both states where the ions are free to move), then the positive metal ions will be attracted to the negative electrodes. All the metals can be extracted from their ores by electrolysis.

An electrolysis cell always contains a positive electrode (*anode*), a negative electrode (*cathode*) and an electrolyte – a liquid containing ions (an aqueous solution of an ionic substance or a molten ionic substance).

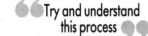

The anode and cathode are connected to an electrical power source. The electricity is conducted through the liquid electrolyte by the ions themselves moving.

> The *positive* metal ions are attracted to the *cathode*.
> The *negative* ions are attracted to the *anode*.

Let's examine the reactions occurring.
At the cathode: the positive metal ions gain an electron and become **atoms**:

$$M^+ + e^{-1} \rightarrow M$$

The metal is deposited as a layer on the cathode.

At the anode: the negative ions lose electrons and become **atoms**:

$$X^- - e^{-1} \rightarrow X$$

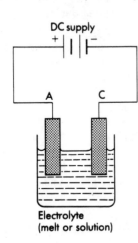

Fig 17.7 An electrolysis cell.

An example of electrolysis is the extraction of aluminium from its ore. The ore bauxite (mainly aluminium oxide) is first concentrated by removing the impurities. The concentrate (alumina) is then dissolved in molten cryolite at about 1000°C to give a solution which provides free-moving aluminium ions. Aluminium oxide has a melting point above 2000°C, so melting the oxide to provide free moving aluminium ions is not practical. The anodes and cathodes are made of carbon. Aluminium, when it is formed, is molten, so it is tapped off from the bottom of the cell (see Figure 17.8).

Let's examine the reactions occurring.

At the cathode: $Al^{3+} + 3e^{-1} \rightarrow Al$
At the anode: $2O^{2-} - 4e^{-1} \rightarrow O_2$

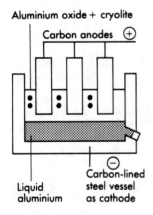

Fig 17.8 The electrolysis of alumina to extract aluminium.

All metals above aluminium in the reactivity series are normally extracted by electrolysis, because they are too reactive to be reduced by carbon. Sometimes metals lower down, such as zinc, are extracted by electrolysis.

THE CHOICE OF EXTRACTION METHOD

Metals exist in ores in an oxidised state. In order to extract the metal, the ores all have to be reduced; this requires adding electrons to the metal ion and so requires energy:

metal ion   +   electrons $\overset{\text{reduction}}{\rightarrow}$ metal atom

The choice of the extraction method for a metal depends largely on two things:

1 the activity of the metal;
2 the cost of energy to perform the reduction.

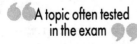

Carbon can act as a reducing agent for all the less reactive metals (those below aluminium in the series). Carbon in the form of coke is plentiful and its combustion provides a relatively cheap form of energy (in the form of heat). Electrolysis is normally much more expensive, so is used if there is no alternative. However, an electrolysis metal extraction plant is often sited to take advantage of cheap electrical power, eg hydro-electric power. There is also an advantage in a metal extraction plant being sited near the mine, since the transport of crude ore would cost more than the transport of the metal.

7 > MACRO-MOLECULES

Macromolecules are large molecules which can have very useful properties. Some macromolecules are very large, consisting of long chains of smaller molecules linked together, forming a repeating pattern. These are called *polymers*; the smaller molecules which form the pattern are called *monomers*.

DETERGENTS

"Check if your syllabus requires this topic"

The job of a detergent is to help water clean materials by washing away grease and dirt. Water is a good solvent, particularly for ionic substances, but it is not good at dissolving greasy substances. The detergent molecules help by breaking up the grease into smaller globules which can be carried away by the water.

How detergents work

Detergent molecules consist of long carbon chains which have two different parts. One part of the molecule is water-loving (*hydrophilic*) because it carries an electric charge (ionic). The other part of the molecule is water-hating (*hydrophobic*) because of the long covalently bonded chain. To help explain the process we can represent these molecules as pin shapes (see Figure 17.9).

The water-hating (or grease-loving) part of the molecule buries itself in the grease while the water-loving part stays in the water. During agitation the water can get between the grease and the surface to be cleaned. The grease forms globules that are kept apart by the charges on the detergent ('like' charges repel). The detergent and grease form an emulsion in the water.

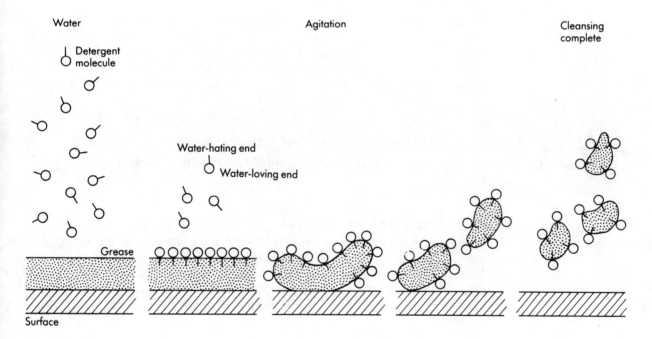

Fig 17.9 How detergents work.

Detergents in action

There are two types of detergents. *Soap detergents* are made from animal or vegetable fats and alkalis. Sodium stearate (see Figure 17.10) is a typical soap. In water, the sodium ion floats free, leaving one end of the molecule negatively charged.

Soapless detergents are made using chemicals from oil and acids. A typical soapless detergent is shown in Figure 17.11. Again in water, the sodium ion is separated from the molecule, leaving one end negatively charged.

HARD AND SOFT WATER

Tap water often contains dissolved salts, depending on what type of rock the rain water has washed through. Water in different parts of the country will contain different salts, and in different amounts. The types of water are known as *hard* or *soft*.

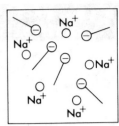

A soap molecule

Soap molecules
in water

Fig 17.10 A typical soap (sodium stearate).

A detergent molecule

Detergent molecules
in water

Fig 17.11 A typical soapless detergent.

Hard water contains either magnesium or calcium salts (ie Mg^{2+} or Ca^{2+} ions).
Soft water contains none, or only very few, dissolved magnesium or calcium salts, although it may contain other dissolved salts.

The problem with hard water is that the calcium ions or magnesium ions in it will react with soaps. They attach themselves to soap molecules, forming an insoluble 'scum' on the surface of the water. The soap can no longer emulsify grease, so more soap has to be added to hard water than to soft water to do the same job. Soapless detergents do *not* behave in this way. No scum is formed with hard water, and hence no detergent is wasted.

sodium stearate   +   calcium ions   →   calcium stearate   +   sodium ions

$$2NaSt(aq)\quad +\quad Ca^{2+}(aq)\quad →\quad CaSt_2(s)\quad +\quad 2Na^+(aq)$$

Fig. 17.12 The reaction between soap and ions in hard water

Note: St represents the stearate part of the molecule ($C_{17}H_{35}COO^-$)

Removing hardness in water

Hard water can cause more serious problems than wasting soap, so it is important to be able to remove the hardness. The common salts which cause hardness are calcium hydrogen carbonate, calcium sulphate, magnesium hydrogencarbonate and magnesium sulphate. When hard water is heated, a chemical reaction occurs, producing insoluble carbonates. This is the *fur* or limescale that appears inside hot water pipes and kettles.

$$\text{heat}$$
$$Ca(HCO_3)_2(aq)\quad →\quad CaCO_3(s)\quad +\quad H_2O(l)\quad +\quad CO_2(g)$$

This furring up of pipes can cause damage and reduces the efficiency of hot water heating systems. The hardness of water can be removed by boiling, but this is expensive and not always convenient, so alternative methods have been developed. *Water softeners* are chemicals that can be added to water to remove calcium ions from solution by precipitating them out. Sodium carbonate is an example. *Ion exchange resins* are the active components in water softener units that are built into many dishwashing machines. The ion exchange resins work by replacing calcium ions with sodium ions, so they need to be regularly topped up with salt (sodium chloride).

8 ▶ **NATURAL AND SYNTHETIC POLYMERS**

Polymer molecules are very long chains consisting of repeating *monomer* units. There can be between 1000 and 50 000 monomers in a chain.

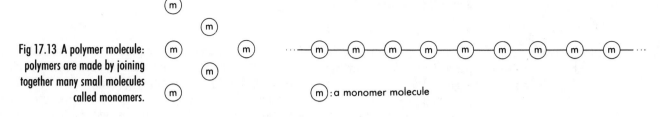

Fig 17.13 A polymer molecule:
polymers are made by joining
together many small molecules
called monomers.

NATURAL POLYMERS

Starch

Starch is a natural polymer, which is made by green plants. It consists of long chains of *glucose* molecules (the monomer) joined together. Starch is a carbohydrate (contains carbon, hydrogen and oxygen atoms only) and as a food is a useful source of energy. The starch molecule is too large, however, to pass through the gut wall into the blood system and must be converted into smaller units in the digestive system.

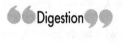

Starch can be broken down by reaction with water into smaller units; the process is called hydrolysis. *Salivary amylase* (the enzyme in saliva) catalyses the hydrolysis of starch into a sugar called maltose (which is effectively a double glucose molecule). *Acids* can also catalyse the hydrolysis, but this time the product is glucose. In the stomach, hydrochloric acid breaks down any unconverted starch or maltose molecules into glucose molecules, which are small enough to pass through the gut wall.

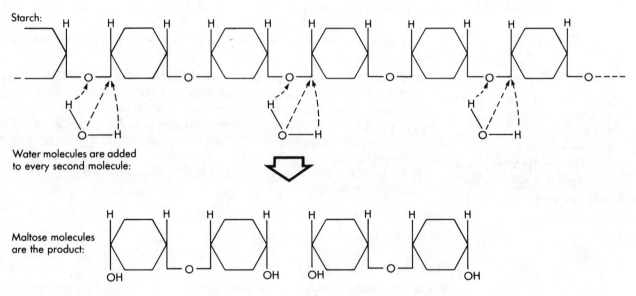

Fig 17.14 Salivary amylase
catalyses the breakdown of starch by
hydrolysis (adding water).

Proteins

These are polymers which are made up of different combinations of monomer units called *amino acids*. There are twenty different naturally occurring amino acids. Each amino acid contains a nitrogen atom. Amino acids are essential for cell growth and repair. Proteins are also broken down in the digestive system to the monomer units (amino acids) by the action of enzymes.

Other natural polymers include wool, cotton, cellulose and rubber.

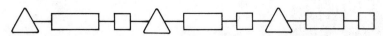

Fig 17.15 Proteins are polymers,
the monomer units are amino acids.

SYNTHETIC POLYMERS

Plastics

Plastics form a group of synthetic polymers which have a wide range of mouldability, particularly at high temperatures. In plastics the polymers do not all have the same chain lengths. Polymers are manufactured with the object of building up compounds which have predicted properties (they can be tailor-made to suit a purpose). Since the properties depend on the degree of polymerisation (length of the chain) it is necessary to stop the polymerisation when desired. This may be done in various ways, eg by varying the concentration of the catalyst. These plastics are supplied by a manufacturer in a variety of forms, eg powder, granules or sticky liquids. These are then converted into the final product, often by heating and moulding in some way.

There are *two main types* of plastics:

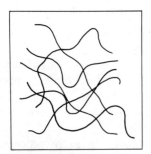

Fig 17.16 Structure of thermosoftening plastics.

■ *Thermosoftening plastics*: these are plastics which can be softened when heated and harden again when they cool down. This can be repeated many times. *Nylon*, for example, can be melted and extruded through tiny holes to produce a fibre, or moulded to produce an object of any desired shape. The molecules in thermosoftening plastics are separate from each other and are held together by weak intermolecular forces. Heating provides the molecules with more energy, so they slip past each other more easily. On cooling, they lose this extra energy, and the weak forces of attraction take over again, so the plastic becomes rigid.

Some of these plastics can have different densities, eg *high*- or *low*-density polythene. The molecules in high-density polythene are much closer together, and lie almost parallel to each other. This type of polythene stands up to more wear and tear and softens at a higher temperature.

Examples of thermosoftening plastics are nylon, polythene, polypropylene, PVC and polystyrene.

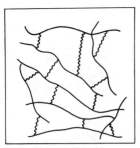

Fig 17.17 Structure of themosetting plastics.

■ *Thermosetting plastics*: these are plastics which can be heated and moulded only once, since when they cool and harden they cannot be remoulded by heating. They are manufactured in two stages. In stage 1, a resin is produced of long chains, which is heated and moulded. In stage 2, cross links between the molecules are formed. The cross links are strong chemical bonds which hold the shape rigid, and are not broken down by reheating.

Examples of thermosetting plastics are bakelite, epoxy resin and melamine-formaldehyde.

The uses of plastics are shown in Figure 17.18.

Advantages of plastics

■ They are cheap and easy to mould into shapes.

■ They are not corroded and can resist chemical attack.

■ They are waterproof.

■ They can easily be coloured.

■ They are lightweight.

Disadvantages of plastics

■ Their manufacture uses raw material derived from oil (a non-renewable resource).

■ They are flammable and give off toxic fumes when they burn.

■ They cannot easily be disposed of; plastics waste in land fill sites will not break down in the soil.

> Try to understand the basic ideas about polymers

> The properties of polymers affect the way they are used

Thermosoftening plastics

Plastic	Uses
Polyethene (Polythene)	bags, films for packaging toys, household goods, insulation for electrical wiring
Polypropylene	tableware, chair seats, toilet seats, heels for shoes, filaments for brushes
PVC	water pipes, drain pipes, packaging gramophone records, coating fabrics, rainwear, floor tiles
Polystyrene	household containers, toys, expanded foam insulating material, packaging
Polyester	clothes, sheets, ropes, tents, sails, safety belts

Thermosetting plastics

Plastic	Uses
Bakelite	electrical switch and plug covers, bottle and container tops, door handles, ash trays
Urea-formaldehyde resins	adhesives, surface coatings of metal, laminating timbers
Melamine-formaldehyde resin	moulding, laminated sheet, table ware
Polyester resin	reinforced with glass fibres used in boat and car body production, crash helmets, varnish and paint
Polyurethanes	in foam form for sponges, cushions, buoyancy in boat hulls

Fig. 17.18 Uses of plastics

E X A M I N A T I O N   Q U E S T I O N S

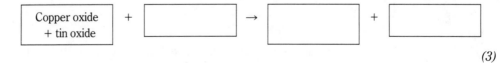

STRUCTURED QUESTIONS

QUESTION 1

The first humans used stones to make their tools. Our history has been influenced by metals and their discovery. The dates are shown in Table 1 below.

Table 1

Metals	Dates of Discovery
Gold	Before 6500 BC
Bronze	6500 BC
Iron	1750 BC
Aluminium	
Sodium	After AD 1800
Magnesium	

a)   Gold was discovered very early. Why was this? (4 lines available)   *(1)*

b)   Bronze, a mixture of copper and tin, was used early in human history. The copper and tin were extracted by heating their ores (oxides) with carbon.

Complete the word equation for the extraction of copper and tin (bronze)

Copper oxide + tin oxide	+		→		+	

(3)

c)   The next metal to be extracted from its ore (oxide) by heating with carbon was iron. Figure 1 overleaf shows the furnace that is now used.

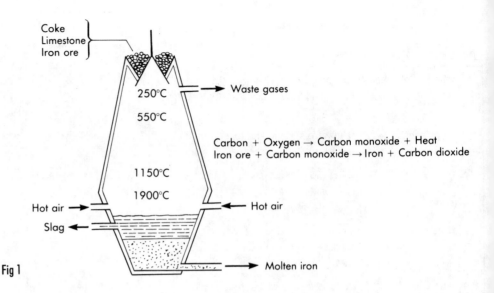

Fig 1

Use the diagram to find **two** reasons why this discovery took place so long after the discovery of bronze.

Reason 1 (3 lines available)

Reason 2 (3 lines available)

(4)

d) Aluminium, sodium and magnesium could only be extracted from their ores after we began to use electricity. Why was this? (4 lines available)   *(2)*

(10 marks total)

(LEAG; 1988)

QUESTION 2

There are more atoms of aluminium in the Earth's crust than of any other metal. Until about 100 years ago it was rare and expensive, but now it has many uses. It is the lightest of the common metals and is easily shaped.

a)   i) Aluminium can be made easily from bauxite (aluminium oxide) by heating it with a more reactive metal. Give **one** example of a metal which might be used.

_____

(1)

ii) Suggest **one** reason why this method is not widely used.

_____

_____

(1)

iii) Bauxite is found in the Earth's crust. What name do we give to compounds such as this?

_____

(1)

Aluminium is usually extracted by passing electricity through a cell containing molten *alumina* mixed with molten *cryolite*. The diagram on page 243 shows the main parts of the cell used.

b) What is the name of this type of extraction process?

_____

(1)

c) The temperature in the cell stays at about 1000 degrees Celsius (°C) but it is not heated from outside at all.

Suggest how this temperature is maintained. (3 lines available)   *(2)*

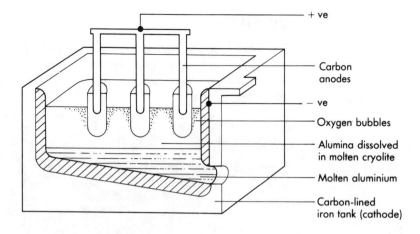

d) Suggest and explain why aluminium was so expensive one hundred years ago.

Suggestion _____

(1)

Explanation _____

_____

(1)

e) Aluminium appears to be unreactive. This is because a coating of aluminium oxide quickly forms on the outside of the metal. Without its oxide layer, aluminium is reactive and burns easily.

Aluminium has replaced other metals in a number of uses. It is used for overhead power cables instead of copper, and because it is a good reflector of heat it can be used to trap heat inside an area or keep it out.

 i) Suggest **one** property which aluminium **must** have if it is used for overhead power cables.

_____

(1)

 ii) Suggest and explain **one** reason, apart from cost, for the use of aluminium instead of copper for these cables.

Reason _____

(1)

Explanation _____

_____

(1)

 iii) Tiny babies are sometimes wrapped in a blanket made from polyester fabric coated with a thin film of aluminium. Suggest and explain **one** reason why this is done.

Reason _____

(1)

Explanation _____

_____

(1)

 iv) Many cars are now partly made of aluminium, but the main frame is still made of steel. Apart from cost, suggest why they are made this way. (4 lines available) *(3)*

(SEG; 1988)

QUESTION 3

When iron rusts, it combines with the oxygen of the air to form iron dioxide. The rusting of seven identical nails was investigated by treating each nail as shown in the table below. All seven nails were left exposed to the atmosphere for a few months. (One of the results in the table is incorrect.)

Nail	Treatment given to each nail	Cost of Treatment	Mass of the nail and coating before exposure	Mass of the nail and coating after exposure
A	waxed	cheap	5.0 g	5.3 g
B	oiled	cheap	5.0 g	4.1 g
C	chromium plated	expensive	5.0 g	5.0 g
D	painted	cheap	5.0 g	5.4 g
E	galvanised	fairly expensive	5.0 g	5.1 g
F	dipped in salt	cheap	5.0 g	6.7 g
G	untreated	NIL	4.9 g	6.1 g

a) By reference to the table, say which nail has received

   i) the coating which gives the best protection

   _____

   (1)

   ii) a treatment that could be used to protect steel car bumpers from rusting

   _____

   (1)

   iii) a treatment which would be the most practical to use to protect iron railings from rusting

   _____

   (1)

   iv) in which case is there an obvious mistake in the mass of the nail and coating after the experiment

   _____

   (1)

b) Give the name of another naturally occurring substance that with oxygen will cause iron to rust.

   _____

   (1)

c) Give the name of the process that takes place when any metal reacts with oxygen to form an oxide.

   _____

   (1)
   (WJEC; Specimen)

QUESTION 4

Table A below shows the action of heat on six metal oxides.

Metal oxide	Appearance of oxide	Change on heating	Change on cooling after heating
Copper (II) oxide CuO	black powder	none	none
Mercury (II) oxide HgO	red powder	turns black oxygen evolved	silver droplets of mercury formed
Zinc oxide ZnO	white powder	yellow powder	white powder
Lead (IV) oxide PbO₂	chocolate brown powder	melts oxygen evolved	yellow powder
Calcium oxide CaO	white powder	none	none
Lead (II) oxide PbO	yellow powder	melts, no oxygen	yellow powder

Table A

a)   Which element is present in all of the metal oxides in the table?

_____

(1)

b)   Using the table, name

    i) **two** metal oxides chemically unchanged by heating.

_____ and _____

(2)

    ii) **one** metal oxide which changes on heating but changes back on cooling.

_____

(1)

    iii) **two** metal oxides that decompose on heating

_____ and _____

(2)

c)   How would you test whether oxygen was produced when the oxides were heated?

_____

_____

(1)

d)   Five common gases are carbon dioxide, chlorine, nitrogen, hydrogen and oxygen.

    i) Which one of these gases is

       (1) a compound_____

       (2) coloured?_____

(2)

    ii) Name **two** of these gases which extinguish a lighted splint without burning.

_____

_____

(2)

e)   A scientist wished to test a mineral. When dilute hydrochloric acid was added to the mineral, a colourless gas was produced which extinguished a lighted splint and turned limewater cloudy.

When the mineral was heated, carbon dioxide was produced and the solid remaining was yellow in colour when hot and white when it cooled down.

    i) Use the table of metal oxides (Table A) to identify the solid formed when the mineral was heated.

    The solid formed was _____

(1)

    ii) Which chemical compound does the mineral mainly consist of?

_____

(2)
(Total marks 14)
(LEAG; Specimen)

QUESTION 5 (EXTENSION QUESTION)

a)   Starch molecules consist of long chains of smaller glucose molecules.

    i) Suggest **two** ways by which starch molecules can be broken down.   *(2)*

    ii) What is the name of this process?   *(1)*

    iii) Name another product of this reaction.   *(1)*

b) In industrial brewing processes yeast is added to glucose solution and left to ferment at 25°C.

    i) What does the yeast do to the glucose molecules?   *(1)*

    ii) What are the products of fermentation?   *(3)*

    iii) What will be the effect of raising the temperature to 35°C?   *(1)*

    iv) Explain why boiling the yeast/glucose mixture stops the reaction.   *(2)*

c) Describe how animals obtain and use glucose.   *(4)*

(MEG; 1988)

QUESTION 6 (EXTENSION QUESTION)

The diagrams below show a range of everyday objects which can be made from polymers.

a) Describe what you understand by the term 'polymer'.   *(3)*

b) Draw a diagram to show the general structure of polymers.   *(2)*

A student tested three types of polymers and made the following observations.

Type	Observations
A	hard and rigid, did not melt at low temperatures
B	stretchy, returns to original shape
C	melts on heating, easily moulded

c) Suggest which **one** of these types is a thermosetting plastic, and state your reasoning. *(2)*

d) Suggest what property of elastomers distinguishes them from thermoplastic and thermosetting polymers. *(1)*

e) For **each** of the following jobs, explain why a particular plastic has been used:

    i) covering electric cables – polyvinyl chloride;   *(2)*

    ii) making shirts and blouses – nylon;   *(2)*

    iii) packaging for TV sets – polystyrene.   *(2)*

f) Some metal frying pans are coated with an unusual thermoplastic called PTFE (polytetrafluorethylene), commonly known as teflon.

    i) Suggest why PTFE is an unusual example of a thermoplastic.   *(2)*

    ii) Suggest **two** advantages of using PTFE to coat metal frying pans.   *(2)*

(MEG; 1988)

ANSWERS TO
EXAMINATION QUESTIONS

ANSWER 1

a)   Gold is not combined with other elements in the Earth's surface.

b)   copper oxide   +   carbon   =   copper   +   carbon dioxide
     +   tin oxide   + tin

c)   Reason 1 – very high temperatures are required to extract the iron from iron ore.
     Reason 2 – a way of making carbon monoxide had to be found which would remove the oxygen from the iron ore.

d)   Very large amounts of energy are required to separate the metals from their ores.

ANSWER 2

a)   i)   magnesium (or sodium)
     ii) magnesium is very reactive and expensive
     iii) ores

b)   electrolysis

c)   heat generated by electric current passing through the cell during electrolysis, which balances heat loss to surroundings.

d)   Because the method of extraction was being developed and large amounts of electricity were required.

e)   i)   conduct electricity
     ii) Reason – they are much lighter.
          Explanation – the metal is less dense.
     iii) Reason – babies lose a lot of body heat.
          Explanation – aluminium reflects heat.
     iv) Aluminium is very lightweight but may dent easily. Steel is used for the main body of the car, as it is stronger.

ANSWER 3

a)   i)   C
     ii) C
     iii) D
     iv) B

b)   water

c)   oxidation

ANSWER 4

a)   oxygen

b)   i)   copper oxide and calcium oxide
     ii) zinc oxide
     iii) mercury oxide and lead oxide

c)   Hold a glowing splint near the test tube. The splint should relight if oxygen is evolved.

d)   i)   1 carbon dioxide
             2 chlorine
     ii) carbon dioxide and nitrogen

e)   i)   zinc oxide
     ii) zinc carbonate

ANSWER 5

a)   i) By boiling in acid; by mixing with amylase
     ii) hydrolysis
     iii) maltose

b)   i) They break it down to release energy.
     ii) carbon dioxide + alcohol + energy
     iii) to increase the rate of the reaction
     iv) Enzymes which are proteins are destroyed by boiling.

c)   Animals eat other animals or plants, and digest food into small molecules, which are transported to cells of body via blood stream. Cells release energy from glucose during respiration.

ANSWER 6

a)   long chains of repeating small units

b)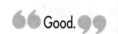

c)   type A, because it did not melt at low temperatures

d)   They return to their original shape after stretching.

e)   i) very flexible; non-conductor
     ii) can be made into threads and woven into fabric very hard-wearing
     iii) can be made into foam which contains air to absorb shocks on impact

f)   i) It has a very high melting point.
     ii) Food does not stick to the pan; it protects the pan from chipping and going rusty.

A STUDENT'S ANSWER WITH EXAMINER'S COMMENTS

a)   Which **two** of the following substances are needed for iron to corrode (rust) at room temperature?
         A   carbon dioxide
         B   nitrogen
         C   oxygen
         D   sodium chloride (salt)
         E   water

"Good."

         C oxygen   E water

                                                                                                    (2)

b)   The rate at which iron corrodes depends upon the climate and the location. Table 3 gives information about the climate and location of cities, and the amount of corrosion that occurs.

City	Temperature	Amount of moisture in the atmosphere	Location	Rate of corrosion
Birmingham	moderate	moderate	inland	moderate
Bogota	high	high	inland	high
Nairobi	high	low	inland	low
Seattle	moderate	moderate	coastal	high
Singapore	high	high	coastal	very high
Sydney	moderate	high	coastal	high
Vladivostok	low	moderate	coastal	moderate

Table 3

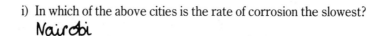

❝ Good. You have used the information and selected 'low'. ❞

❝ But in a) you state water is necessary; so a better answer is that sea coastal air holds more moisture. ❞

i) In which of the above cities is the rate of corrosion the slowest?

Nairobi

(1)

ii) Explain why corrosion is faster at coastal places than inland.

More salt in the air.

(2)

c) Figure 1 gives some information about different ways of preventing iron corroding.

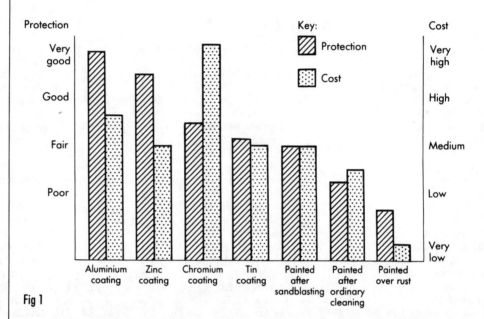

Fig 1

Suggest the most suitable method for protecting an iron bridge in the following cities. Give reasons for your choices.

i) Singapore: aluminium coating as Singapore has a very high rate of corrosion and this method gives the best protection although expensive.

ii) Birmingham: tin coating. there is only a moderate rate of corrosion and tin coating is quite good enough.

(6)
(Total marks 11)
(LEAG; 1988)

❝ Good. You have made 3 points for 3 marks. ❞

❝ Yes. Include medium cost as well for 3rd mark. ❞

INDEX